Race and Sex in Latin America

Anthropology, Culture and Society

Series Editors:
Professor Vered Amit, Concordia University
and
Dr Jon P. Mitchell, University of Sussex

Published titles include:

Home Spaces, Street Styles:
Contesting Power and Identity
in a South African City
LESLIE J. BANK

On the Game:
Women and Sex Work
SOPHIE DAY

Slave of Allah:
Zacarias Moussaoui vs the USA
KATHERINE C. DONAHUE

A History of Anthropology
THOMAS HYLLAND ERIKSEN
AND FINN SIVERT NIELSEN

Ethnicity and Nationalism:
Anthropological Perspectives
Second Edition
THOMAS HYLLAND ERIKSEN

Globalisation:
Studies in Anthropology
Edited by THOMAS HYLLAND ERIKSEN

Small Places, Large Issues:
An Introduction to Social and Cultural
Anthropology
Second Edition
THOMAS HYLLAND ERIKSEN

What is Anthropology?
THOMAS HYLLAND ERIKSEN

Anthropology, Development and the
Post-Modern Challenge
KATY GARDNER AND DAVID LEWIS

Corruption:
Anthropological Perspectives
Edited by DIETER HALLER
AND CRIS SHORE

Culture and Well-Being:
Anthropological Approaches to
Freedom and Political Ethics
Edited by ALBERTO CORSÍN JIMÉNEZ

Cultures of Fear:
A Critical Reader
Edited by ULI LINKE AND
DANIELLE TAANA SMITH

Fair Trade and a Global Commodity:
Coffee in Costa Rica
PETER LUETCHFORD

The Will of the Many:
How the Alterglobalisation Movement
is Changing the Face of Democracy
MARIANNE MAECKELBERGH

The Aid Effect:
Giving and Governing in International
Development
Edited by DAVID MOSSE
AND DAVID LEWIS

Cultivating Development:
An Ethnography of
Aid Policy and Practice
DAVID MOSSE

Anthropology, Art and
Cultural Production
MARUŠKA SVAŠEK

Anthropology at the Dawn
of the Cold War:
The Influence of Foundations,
McCarthyism and the CIA
Edited by DUSTIN M. WAX

Learning Politics from Sivaram:
The Life and Death of a Revolutionary
Tamil Journalist in Sri Lanka
MARK P. WHITAKER

Race and Sex in Latin America

PETER WADE

PLUTO PRESS

First published 2009 by Pluto Press
345 Archway Road, London N6 5AA and
175 Fifth Avenue, New York, NY 10010

www.plutobooks.com

British Library Cataloguing in Publication Data
A catalogue record for this book is available from the British Library

ISBN   978 0 7453 2950 5   Hardback
ISBN   978 0 7453 2949 9   Paperback

Library of Congress Cataloging in Publication Data applied for

10   9   8   7   6   5   4   3   2   1

Designed and produced for Pluto Press by
Chase Publishing Services Ltd, 33 Livonia Road, Sidmouth, EX10 9JB, England
Typeset from disk by Stanford DTP Services, Northampton, England
Printed and bound by CPI Group (UK) Ltd, Croydon, CR0 4YY

CONTENTS

FIGURES

SERIES PREFACE

Anthropology is a discipline based upon in-depth ethnographic works that deal with wider theoretical issues in the context of particular, local conditions – to paraphrase an important volume from the series: *large issues* explored in *small places*. The series has a particular mission: to publish work that moves away from old-style descriptive ethnography – that is strongly area-studies oriented – and offer genuine theoretical arguments that are of interest to a much wider readership but which are nevertheless located and grounded in solid ethnographic research. If anthropology is to argue itself a place in the contemporary intellectual world then it must surely be through such research.

We start from the question: 'what can this ethnographic material tell us about the bigger theoretical issues that concern the social sciences'; rather than 'what can these theoretical ideas tell us about the ethnographic context'. Put this way round, such work becomes *about* large issues, *set in* a (relatively) small place, rather than detailed description of a small place for its own sake. As Clifford Geertz once said: 'anthropologists don't study villages; they study *in* villages'.

By place we mean not only geographical locale, but also other types of 'place' – within political, economic, religious or other social systems. We therefore publish work based on ethnography within political and religious movements, occupational or class groups, youth, development agencies, nationalists; but also work that is more thematically based – on kinship, landscape, the state, violence, corruption, the self. The series publishes four kinds of volume – ethnographic monographs; comparative texts; edited collections; and shorter, polemic essays.

We publish work from all traditions of anthropology, and all parts of the world, which combines theoretical debate with empirical evidence to demonstrate anthropology's unique position in contemporary scholarship and the contemporary world.

Professor Vered Amit
Dr Jon P. Mitchell

ACKNOWLEDGEMENTS

The roots of this book lie in my first in-depth studies of racial identities and relations in Colombia: it was clear from the start that sexual and gender relations were an important aspect of what was going on. I discussed some elements of sex and gender in my book *Blackness and Race Mixture* (1993a) and, later, in the short overview I wrote of *Race and Ethnicity in Latin America* (1997).

The real impetus for the current book, however, was a collaborative project with Colombian, Brazilian and British colleagues which involved a series of interdisciplinary seminars on Race and Sexuality in Latin America, which took place in Britain and Colombia in 2006–7. I am grateful to the British Academy for funding this project as part of their UK–Latin America/Caribbean Link Programme. I would like to thank all the participants in those seminars for their insights, and especially Fernando Urrea and Mara Viveros, who helped organise the events. The seminars resulted in the publication of an edited volume, *Raza, etnicidad y sexualidades: ciudadanía y multiculturalismo en América latina* (eds, Peter Wade, Fernando Urrea Giraldo and Mara Viveros Vigoya, Bogotá, Centro de Estudios Sociales (CES), Universidad Nacional de Colombia, 2008) and a good number of the chapters in that book have proved very useful in the present text.

I would also like to thank Andrew Canessa and Mónica Moreno, who not only participated in the seminar series, but with whom I have exchanged ideas and readings on several occasions. Mónica was also good enough to read the Conclusion and make some helpful suggestions. Joanne Rappaport, Sarah Radcliffe, Fernando Urrea, Ochy Curiel and my doctoral student, Pablo Jaramillo, were also kind enough to respond to emailed enquiries about attitudes to homosexuality within indigenous and Afrodescendant movements. I am obliged to the ESRC Centre for Research for Socio-Cultural Change at the University of Manchester for funding to cover part of the period of research leave during which I wrote this book.

It is a pleasure to publish once more with Pluto Press and my thanks are due to the Series Editors, Vered Amit and Jon Mitchell, and the two anonymous readers, as well as to David Castle, the commissioning editor at Pluto, and Robert Webb and Melanie Patrick on the production side.

Finally, I owe a huge debt of gratitude to Sue, Megan and Ben who allowed me time and space to write, when they had hoped that my being 'on leave' might mean I would do something other than stare at a computer screen all day long.

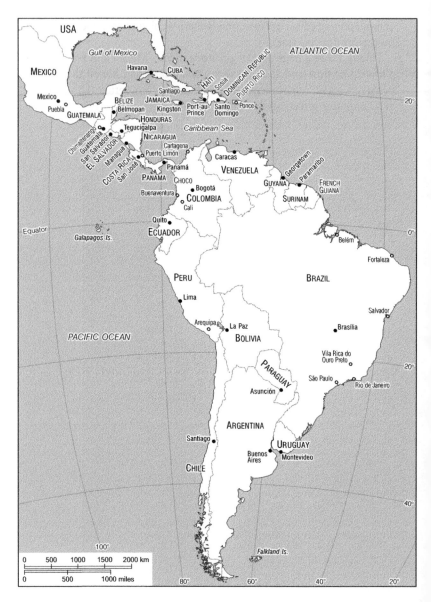

Map of Latin America

1
INTRODUCTION:
DEFINING RACE AND SEX

After working on 'race' in Brazil and France in the 1950s, the French sociologist Roger Bastide wrote an article in which he posed the question of why, during his research, 'the question race always provoked the answer sex' (Bastide 1961). The French sociologist Etienne Balibar put it a little differently when he stated that 'racism always presupposes sexism' (1991: 49), while the US sociologist Joane Nagel thinks that 'sex is the whispered subtext in spoken racial discourse', and more generally that 'ethnic boundaries are also sexual boundaries' (2003: 2, 1). In his study of British colonialism, the historian Ronald Hyam concluded that 'sex is at the very heart of racism' (1990: 203), while the Martinican psychiatrist and revolutionary writer Frantz Fanon, writing from the point of view of the colonised, said: 'If one wants to understand the racial situation psychoanalytically ... considerable importance must be given to sexual phenomena. In the case of the Jew, one thinks of money and its cognates. In the case of the Negro, one thinks of sex' (1986 [1952]: 160). And just in case one might conclude that the racist image of 'the Jew' plays only on the theme of money, Gilman shows that sexual imaginings and theories were key to the nineteenth-century racial category of 'Jew' and played an important role in the way Freud constructed his theories of femininity (1993: ch. 1).

From a variety of perspectives and over a long period, analysts have noted that situations that involve 'race' also often involve 'sex'. The opposite may not necessarily be the case; that is, it is less often averred that when people think about sex they automatically think about race or that racism is 'at the very heart' of sexism, but various scholars do argue that sexual and gender categories have been historically formed in relation to racial ones. Bederman (1995), for example, contends that notions of (white, 'civilised') manliness in the nineteenth- and early twentieth-century United States were shaped in relation to the image of ('uncivilised') black and native American men; and McClintock (1995) argues that notions about gender and sex in imperial Britain were inextricably linked to ideas about race and empire – women might be seen as 'primitives', for example, and analogous to the 'primitives races' in the colonies.

In this book, I explore why these two domains are so closely related. I look at how they 'intersect', as the current terminology often has it, or, to put it in a slightly different way, how they 'mutually constitute' each other; that is, how they come into being in relation to and through each other, thus avoiding the assumption that each domain already exists fully formed and then 'intersects' with the other (not to mention 'intersections' with other domains or vectors, such as class and age). I am also interested in why racially hierarchical social orders, which are rooted in the control and exploitation of (racially identified) peoples and places, including associated lands and resources, also generate complex dynamics of hate and love, fear and fascination, contempt and admiration – in a word, ambivalence, an ambivalence that seems to have a specifically sexual dimension.

My focus in all this is principally on Latin America, mainly because this region's history offers a particular social order in which race and sex relate to each other in interesting ways. Many areas in Latin America experienced intensive processes of 'race mixture' – sexual and cultural interactions between Europeans, indigenous peoples and Africans. Not only was this mixture arguably more pervasive and frequent than in most other areas colonised by Europeans, but from the nineteenth century it also became – albeit unevenly – a symbol for national identities in the region in the shape of a recognition and sometimes a glorification of *mestizaje* (Spanish) or *mestiçagem* (Portuguese), both words deriving from the colonial terms *mestizo* (and *mestiço*), meaning a person born to parents of, for example, European and African or European and indigenous American origins.[1] Countries such as Brazil and Mexico vaunted their mixed origins as the distinctive feature of their national populations and cultures; other countries might recognise their mixed roots without necessarily glorifying them; yet others might play down their African and indigenous roots in favour of a more European image (Appelbaum et al. 2003; Graham 1990; Miller 2004; Wade 1997). In this way, sexual relations between people perceived as being of a different racial origin became a 'foundational fiction' for nations in much of the region (Sommer 1991). Recognising and even glorifying mixture, often located in the past, did not by any means translate into respecting or valuing current indigenous and black peoples: racism could easily coexist with *mestizaje* (Hale 1996; Telles 2004; Wade 1993a, 1997). From the 1960s, indigenous and black rights movements burgeoned and, in the 1990s, many countries enacted constitutional reforms and legal measures designed to create or recognise multicultural nations: this created a changed context for thinking about *mestizaje*: do race and sex relate in new ways in an officially multicultural nation? Despite this fascinating history and contemporary conjuncture, the question of race and sex in Latin America remains relatively understudied, although there is a growing literature on the theme.[2]

Definitions

Given that the terms race, sex and gender are, in the context of current social theory, contested and not clear-cut, it makes sense to give a brief outline of how I understand and use them in this book, which does not mean to say I shall give neat and watertight definitions of each concept.

Race

'Race' is a difficult concept, the definition of which I have written on at some length elsewhere (Wade 1993b, 1997: 6–15; 2002b: 1–16). The key problem centres on balancing change and continuity. The element of change derives from the fact that the term emerged in European languages between the thirteenth and sixteenth centuries to refer to different lineages of people and human diversity (Stolcke 1994: 276). It underwent successive transformations until it reached what many regard as its apogee in the mid-nineteenth century, when the concept became central to thinking about human and social diversity within the framework of social theory and the natural and medical sciences; 'race' was, then, a natural human fact which explained a huge amount about why and how human diversity existed and legitimated a hierarchy in which white Europeans dominated. Then, from the early to mid-twentieth century, the concept declined in importance as a perceived physical 'fact' and became mainly, but not exclusively, understood as an idea, a 'social construct', with no basis in biology, but which has enduring social power in its ability to generate racism, a set of practices and attitudes which discriminate against certain categories of people, not necessarily now defined in terms of their physical natures, but often in terms of their cultures: hence the term 'cultural racism'. With all this historical variation, there is inevitably debate about when 'race' properly speaking emerged: some people date it from the sixteenth century (or even earlier), others prefer to focus on the seventeenth, eighteenth or even nineteenth century as being the true era for the origins of 'race'.

The element of continuity perceived to exist in 'race' derives from the fact that, through all these changes – or perhaps only through some of them – we are faced with varied phenomena that, if not the same, at least seem to bear a 'family resemblance', to use Wittgenstein's term. Race always seems to refer to human difference understood as 'natural' (bearing in mind that concepts of nature have also been historically very varied) and as often related in one way or another to certain aspects of physical appearance, to traits that are transmitted, albeit unevenly and often unpredictably, from one generation to another by sexual reproduction and the transmission of a substance or essence, often glossed as 'blood'. Because of this, the concept of race is often defined in terms of a combination of references to biology, physical appearance (skin colour, etc.), nature, heredity or an internal natural essence of some kind. In this respect, a distinction is often made between race and 'ethnicity', with the latter understood in the social sciences as referring to culture, history and origins of a non-biological, non-natural kind.

A different basis for continuity or common ground is the fact that racial distinctions are often said to emerge with the European discovery and domination through colonialism of other areas of the world. Racial distinctions emerge from the attempt by Europeans to classify and control non-Europeans, albeit these distinctions built on some of those developed by the ancient Greeks and current in Europe before colonialism. 'Race' is thus tied to a specific history of the world, rather than simply being specified by the type of naturalising discourse it uses. The key racial categories have somehow remained remarkably similar, albeit with changing terminologies, subcategories and overlaps: black (originating in Africa), white (originating in Europe), 'Indian' (i.e. native American), Asian/Oriental and Aboriginal Australasian. People from Oceania (roughly Melanesia, Micronesia, Polynesia) are sometimes fitted into the Asian category and other times the Australasian one.[3] Perhaps not surprisingly, these categories correspond roughly to the classificatory system for the continents of the world – Africa, Europe, the Americas, Asia and Australia (and Antarctica) – a system also developed by Europeans.

I prefer an historically inclusive approach that recognises the historical continuities that underlie the variations. It seems to me vital to recognise the role of European domination that operated through classifications which, although they varied greatly in their character and theoretical underpinnings, consistently targeted the same categories of people and used similar types of rationales, and invoked some notion of 'nature' (itself a varying concept) that could be deployed to explain internal, invisible traits (e.g. moral qualities, intelligence, behaviour) and link them to external, visible traits (e.g. skin colour, skull form). I agree, broadly speaking, with the idea that race is a naturalising discourse, but I think it is essential to emphasise that 'naturalisation' is a practice, the effects of which vary according to the way 'nature' is understood.[4] I also think it is important to understand that 'race' does not stand in a relation of opposition to 'ethnicity' (often seen as analogous to the supposedly clear-cut opposition of 'biology' to 'culture'): race works by linking human nature, which may be thought of during specific historical periods as 'biology', to culture. Ethnicity may also carry strongly naturalising connotations, in relation not only to heritage and genealogy, but also to how land, territory and landscape shape people and their cultures (Alonso 1994; Stolcke 1993; Wade 2007a).

Race, as I use it in this book, then, refers to all the practices and ideas that surround racial classifications and distinctions, as outlined above. I shall also employ the widely used term racialisation to refer to the way social phenomena and processes take on racial meanings and functions.

Sex, Sexuality and Gender

If one starts with dictionary definitions of these terms, 'sex' is simply the quality of being male or female. According to the *Oxford English Dictionary*, the focus on genital anatomy to create this bipartite division is 'recent', although Fausto-Sterling (2000) and Laqueur (1990) both suggest that, in the West, it was from the eighteenth century that anatomy became the vital domain in which to attempt the division of human beings into two mutually exclusive and exhaustive classes. 'Sex' can also mean the act of sexual intercourse (a twentieth-century meaning, as in 'to have sex'). 'Sexual', in the *OED*, means anything relating to sex, as defined above, or anything related to sex 'as concerned in generation [i.e. sexual reproduction] or in the processes connected with this'; it is also anything 'relative to the physical intercourse between the sexes or the gratification of sexual appetites'. 'Sexuality' dates, according to the *OED*, from the early eighteenth century as an isolated technical, scientific term referring to the simple presence of sexual reproduction in a species; by the later eighteenth century it comes to mean more broadly the quality of being sexual (as defined above) or having sexual feelings. In the twentieth century – mainly the latter half – it also comes to mean sexual identity based on the object of a person's sexual attractions or desires. Thus emerges the plural 'sexualities', recognising that heterosexual desires are only one set in a very varied range of sexual desires. 'Gender', for the *OED*, is 'a euphemism' for sex, but it is acknowledged that in twentieth-century feminist usage, it refers to cultural distinctions between the sexes.[5]

The dictionary gives us the basis for a very open definition of 'sex' as anything pertaining to the fact of being sexed or having a sex and anything pertaining to the relationships between the sexes. Of course, the *OED* simply summarises Western usage and conceptions and tends to reproduce Western assumptions, so one would need to reject the definition of sex as being only *either* male *or* female, in order to cope with the phenomena of intersexuality (a term encompassing various ways of being biologically both male and female, without human intervention), transsexuality (which can be used to mean physically both male and female as a result of human intervention) and transgenderism (a more open term, which refers to a person who is not unambiguously assignable to either the male or the female gender). One would also have to be careful to avoid the *OED*'s blatantly heteronormative implication that 'sexual' things only occur between men and women, as this would exclude homosexuality or relegate it to a deviation from 'normal' heterosexual behaviour, a normative standard that gay, lesbian and queer theorists and activists have been struggling against for some decades. One can be 'sexual' without doing things directly related to sexual reproduction; indeed, it may well be the case that most sexual activity is not, and is not even intended to be, reproductive.

An openness of definition is, in one sense, useful. One might be tempted to go with a more hierarchical set of definitions (e.g. Karras 2005: 6), in which sex means biological (mainly but not only anatomical) difference; sexuality means emotions, feelings and especially erotic desires that emanate from the fact of having a sex and engaging in acts of sexual intercourse (in the broadest sense); and gender means the various cultural roles, attitudes, practices and meanings associated with a given biological sex. However, such a neat hierarchy will not work. Feminists in the 1960s and 1970s worked hard to emphasise the sex/gender distinction, in which sex was simply the biological differences between men and women. The point was to minimise the role of biology and highlight the role of society and culture in shaping 'men' and 'women', so showing how the same basic biological infrastructure of sex could give rise to very varied cultural super-structures of gender – 'men' and 'women' were very different things in different cultures, not to mention the existence of 'third' sexes and genders, which were not easily placed as either male/man or female/woman (Herdt 1994). But from the mid-1980s, feminists began to question this distinction and point out how 'sex' itself is also shaped by culture and history: the very idea of the biological differences between men and women is wrapped up in the historical developments of medicine and science; the Western notion of a species divided into two opposed, exhaustive and mutually exclusive categories called males and females is not universal and is an historical notion even in the West (Butler 1990, 1993; Fausto-Sterling 1985, 2000; Laqueur 1990; Moore 1994). If sex itself is a cultural construct, then all the more so would be sexual emotions and desires, which cannot be seen as arising automatically from the mere fact of being female or male – as being determined by sex hormones, for example. The rise of LGBT (lesbian, gay, bisexual and transgender/sexual) activism in the 1980s and the emergence of queer theory in the 1990s added to this sense of sexuality as open, flexible and indeterminate.[6]

The view of sexuality as cultural construction was supported by the work of Michel Foucault, who saw sexuality (or, in his terminology, simply 'sex', as he uses the two terms more or less interchangeably) as a domain of knowledge that emerged as a major focus of concern, comment and especially scientific intervention from the eighteenth century and above all in the nineteenth and twentieth centuries (Foucault 1998 [1979]). Prior to this, the Church in particular had been concerned with sex and its regulation, but not in the same way as the medicalised and scientific discourse that now arose and that focused on sex as a way to regulate and administer the life-force of society as a whole. This view implied that, far from sexuality being a natural, universal force, the up-welling of which was subject to repressive control by Victorian society, the European bourgeoisie developed a science of sexuality in which experts and scientists delved into sex, now understood as the key that could unlock the workings of people and society and a realm in which control, regulation and intervention were necessary: women's sexuality was linked to pathological hysteria; children's sexuality was seen as abnormal; masturbation undermined health. The Catholic practice of confession increasingly focused on sex, not just the act, but thoughts about it too, and psychoanalysis – a kind of secular confession – became an important technique for exploring, but also according to Foucault actually creating, sexuality as a key to personal identity. This kind of confessional practice became evident, beyond the psychoanalyst's couch, in the pervasive practice of people talking about their sexuality, although, as Giddens points out, there is a vast difference between the late nineteenth and the late twentieth centuries in terms of the openness and pervasiveness of talk about sexuality. This needs to be explained by institutional changes in society, which Foucault does not really consider, such as the separation of sex from reproduction which contraception permitted; the increasing autonomy of women; the diffusion of notions of romantic love as a key personal goal; and the development of selfhood as a kind of open-ended life project, in which sexuality is a key element (Giddens 1992: ch. 2).

If both sex and sexuality are cultural constructs and not simply natural phenomena, then they are both in the same boat as gender, and we cannot see sex or sexuality as a biological substratum overlain by the cultural elaboration of gender. Yet are they all the same thing? Some feminist thinkers in the 1980s seemed to think so and used sex/sexuality as an overarching concept which subsumed gender (Stanton 1995).[7] Clearly sex, sexuality and gender are closely connected; for example, the sexuality of men and women is often said to be tied to their sexual biology (genitalia, sex hormones, etc.) and male homosexuality has even been linked by some to a supposed 'gay gene'. In turn, gender roles and meanings attached to the categories of male and female are often closely linked to their sexuality. The idea that women are, or should be, domestic creatures, taking primary if not sole responsibility for childrearing and running the domestic realm, is part and parcel of ideas about the protection of feminine 'honour' and sexual reputation. This 'cult of domesticity', as McClintock (1995) calls it, has played a major role in shaping women's role in the labour market, politics and the public realm generally in Western (and many other) societies. As the feminist slogan has it, 'The personal is political': what happens within the confines of the personal realm (the private, domestic sphere, including the bedroom) is also a political matter, which shapes aspects of public life. Similarly, when a man has sex with other men, what he does 'in the bedroom', if knowledge of it goes beyond the bedroom, historically has had a crucial influence on how he is perceived in the public realm.

However, there is still a case for maintaining a distinction of some kind between sex/sexuality and gender. After all, Foucault has been accused of writing a history of sexuality that was not attentive enough to gender – that is, how sexuality differed for men and women, or how discourses on sexuality helped produce gender distinctions (Hunt 1995; Stoler 1995: 93) – so it is clearly possible, if hazardous, to focus on one rather than the other. Moore (1994: 20) observes that while the concepts of sexual difference and gender difference 'collide ... and cannot usefully be separated', it is still the case that they 'cannot become identical'. From the 1990s, queer theory has also tended to drive sexuality and gender apart, wanting to retain a distinction between sexuality and gender, emphasising that the particularity of non-heterosexualities cannot be reduced to gender differences (Campbell 2000: 179). Elizabeth Weed states: 'queer theory ... has been consistent about one aspect of its project: consideration of sex and sexuality cannot be contained by the category of gender'. However, she goes on to say: 'The problem ... is that in this formulation gender becomes the property of feminist enquiry, while the proper study of sex and sexuality is located elsewhere', which, Weed argues, does an injustice to feminist theory (Weed 1997: viii).

The relationship between sex and gender is obviously problematic, but it is not quite the same to write a book about how race relates to gender as it is to write about how race relates to sexuality. The former project might look, for example, at research on racial and gender discrimination in the Brazilian labour market, research which generally does not include any mention of sexuality in terms of ideas, emotions and practices related to being male or female in the sexual sense (e.g. Lovell 1994). The latter project would focus on how race relates to being male or female in the sexual sense. As we have seen, however, it is difficult to give a watertight definition of what the 'sexual sense' is, and we are not helped here by scholars, who often use the terms sexual and sexuality without defining them.[8] As with the concept of race, sexuality is historically variable and therefore inherently impossible to define completely, yet it is assumed that related sets of phenomena are being dealt with and this is demonstrated precisely by the way scholars can use the term without defining it: 'we'/they already 'know' what they are talking about. Implicitly, then, sexuality is grounded on a common-sense activity called 'having sex' and the myriad related activities, feelings and ideas surrounding it.[9] This is the way I shall use the concept, even if it admittedly still begs the question of exactly what constitutes 'having sex' (a question which is more consequential than the easily solved puzzle of whether Bill Clinton's relations with Monica Lewinsky fell into that category). The point is that, as Moore (1994: 27) suggests, we are better off 'working backwards towards sex, gender, sexual difference and the body, rather than taking them as a set of starting points': what 'having sex' means has to be discovered for particular contexts, rather than assumed in the first place.

Sexuality is thus gendered, in the sense that it is imbued with ideas about maleness and femaleness (even if does not take place between men and women) and gender includes sexuality, in the sense that ideas about men and women (and transgendered people) usually involve ideas about sexuality; but sexuality and gender are not identical and their relationships are one focus of analysis. In a reading of *Gone With the Wind*, Eve Sedgwick argues that sexuality, gender and power domination all 'line up in a perfect chain of echoic meaning' for white women, who are, or are taken as, 'ladies' (1985: 8–9). The 'black mammy' figure, however, while a woman and subject to power domination, has, in effect, no sexuality. The relationship between sexuality and gender is different for each woman, and generally 'the shapes of sexuality, and what *counts* as sexuality, both depend on and affect historical power relationships' (1985: 2). Interestingly, this example shows how racial hierarchy shapes sexuality. In this book, then, my principal focus will be on sex/sexuality and I shall use the terms interchangeably, as Foucault does, but this will clearly entail a gendered perspective as well.

Conclusion

The problem which drives this book is, in simple terms, why 'the question race always provoked the answer sex', to use Bastide's phrase, or more generally, why race and sex/gender seem to have what I have termed an 'elective affinity' for each other in systems of domination and hierarchy. In the chapters that follow, I attempt to answer that question, in both theoretical and empirical terms.

In Chapter 2, I examine a number of theoretical perspectives that address that problem. My aim is to bring together three elements: an attention to racist and sexist oppression; an awareness of the productive nature of power, which builds a moral order in the process of dominating certain categories of people; and sensitivity to the formation of a desiring self in an ambivalent relation of love/hate with the other.

Chapter 3 looks at historical aspects of race and sex (including homosexuality) in the colonial period. A central theme is sex as an instrument of racialised conquest, building on Europeans' sexualised images of the African and native American other. I then look at the building of a moral order in the colonies, looking first at the work of the Inquisition on sexual and religious transgression, which targeted black and indigenous subjects. I then analyse how patriarchal and racial domination relate to each other, especially through the interweaving of ideas of purity of blood with ideas about the sexual purity and honour of (white) women and the sexual impurity and dishonour of (non-white) women. This introduces the important role of *mestizaje* as a colonial practice which produced racially intermediate *mestizos* through sexual interactions. Finally, the powerful ambivalence that existed around black and indigenous sexual and magical powers is explored.

Chapter 4 examines the period from independence and into the early twentieth century, when science and nation were key transnational frameworks of ideas and practice. The theme of *mestizaje* continues in this chapter, but now as both a social practice and an ideology of nationhood. Honour continued to work as a key mechanism of racial and sexual domination, but within the project of constructing a nation as a moral and social order: eugenics, social hygiene, masculinity and homosexuality are important here. In this context, I examine in detail how race and sex articulate with each other. Finally, I look at the sexualised primitivism of the early twentieth century, which emerges very clearly in the nationalisation of 'black' music, in which the ambivalence of racialised desire and fear can be seen.

Chapter 5 takes the political economy of sex/race as its theme and addresses the relationship between race, money and sex (e.g. using wealth and status to 'buy' racially hypergamous unions, or using 'blackness' to 'seduce' wealthy partners, in what is often seen as a marketplace of racial, class and gender values). I examine the commodification of racialised sexuality, focusing on three areas: interracial sex and *mestizaje*, beauty and eroticism, and sex tourism and sex worker migration. I argue that race relations in Latin America depend on a balance of racism and racial democracy and that this balance depends to a great extent on the way race and sex articulate to create a mixed society in which both oppression and racial ambiguity and tolerance coexist.

Chapter 6 explores the management of sexuality by the state and NGOs, looking at how medical and welfare interventions and policies are connected to the regulation of sexuality, fertility, disease and family life, among other things. I examine how issues of sexuality (and related issues of gender) articulate with racialised processes of political-cultural activism and multicultural governance, both centred on questions of citizenship. I start by looking at the regulation of reproductive and sexual health, tracing how a multiculturalist recognition of difference, alongside a denial of hierarchy, is underlain by tacit reaffirmations of racial hierarchy, as in *mestizaje*. I then examine sexuality in ethnic-racial social movements, exploring the apparently persistent connection of masculinism and power, which implicitly reinforces some of the basic tenets of male dominance in ideologies of *mestizaje*. In the last sections, I examine sex and race among Latinos in the US, looking first at sexualised images of Latinos and how these are deployed in the construction of the racialised 'Latino' category; and then at how *mestizaje* – the process of interracial sex – is both challenged by and challenges the US racial landscape.

2

EXPLAINING THE ARTICULATION OF RACE AND SEX

My objective in this chapter is to look at ideas about why and how race and sex relate to each other and why they seem to have what Max Weber might have described as an 'elective affinity' for each other, that is, why race so often seems to connote sex, and vice versa. In the first main section, I look at a number of approaches that focus on power and domination as the key to this affinity. I start with a perspective that takes racial domination itself as its main concern, moving to frameworks that combine racism and sexism as they articulate and intersect with each other. These frameworks overlap with Foucauldian theories that start with the productive nature of power and the regulation of sex as a way to exert power but also build a moral order.

In the second main section, I argue that, while power and domination are clearly central and any approach must include them, in order to encompass the very obvious ambivalence that is at the heart of the race/sex conjunction – the coexistence of love and loathing, fear and fascination – we need to address the internal processes in which concepts of self and other are formed and in which desire and fear themselves take shape. I look at perspectives, often of a more psychoanalytic bent, which explore these processes in depth. I then note the critiques that psychoanalytic perspectives have been subject to (especially from the social sciences, but also from philosophy) and look at some examples that suggest a workable balance of social and psychic processes.

Explaining Race and Sex 1:
Power, Domination and Governance

A very common approach in tackling the relationship between race and sex is to view them both through the lens of power, domination and inequality. Indeed, it is fair to say that any and all approaches must look through this lens: to understand race and sex, we must understand racism and sexism as systems of oppression. But there is also the vital question of exactly how we understand the operation of power and oppression and what analytical role we assign to different aspects of these multiple processes. Some analysts focus very centrally on what one might call the sociology or political economy of oppression, on domination as the direct exercise of power on subordinate people.

Race, Sex and Oppression

An early example of this approach is Roger Bastide's essay on 'Dusky Venus' and 'Black Apollo' (1961), which set out to explain why in Brazil there existed (and still exists) a cult of eroticism around the figure of the *mulata*, the dusky Venus, the mixed-race, brown-skinned, but not very black, woman. In contrast, in France, there was a glorification, in some circles at least, of the image of the beautiful and hypersexual black man, the black Apollo. For Bastide, the cult of the *mulata* stems from the relations of dominance between whites and non-whites that existed under slavery (abolished in Brazil in 1888) and continued in post-abolition society. Upper-class white men felt themselves to be in a position where they could (ab)use slave women in particular and lower-class women in general (who were often dark-skinned) without suffering any consequences. The children they fathered did not have to be socially recognised as filial kin (although, in practice, they might be) and the men's extramarital relations were ignored, or seen as normal, in a society in which men were dominant figures. This accessibility of non-white women to white men was enough, in Bastide's view, to convert them into highly sexualised objects of erotic desire. Bastide explains that the fact that it was the *mulata* and not the black woman who became the object of a cult is in terms of the former's greater proximity to a European aesthetic norm of physical beauty. In France, black immigrant men from Africa had become fetishised into sex objects because, Bastide argues, they felt a need to avenge themselves on white Europeans for the humiliations they had suffered at their hands during colonialism – which included the sexual (ab)use of black women by white men – and continued to suffer through racism. One way to exact this vengeance was to conquer as many white women as possible: hence the image of the hypersexual black male.

It is not hard to see weaknesses and omissions in Bastide's argument. He does not address the sexualisation of black men in Brazil and of black (and brown) women in Europe, while, for France, he ignores the longer history of the sexualisation of black men, stretching back to the early encounters of Europeans with Africans – a history which might, in fact, support his argument (Jordan 1977; Nagel 2003: 91–7). More importantly, there are easy assumptions made about how the presumed accessibility of black women in slavery (which would anyway only have been true for a minority of white men) translated into the same accessibility of black and brown women outside slavery and also about the way this historical accessibility might explain the cult of the *mulata* in 1950s Brazil. Women's desires are left out of the picture entirely – why would black men's need for revenge through sexual conquest translate into desire for them by some white women – not to mention some white men, a matter that Bastide does not broach at all)? And (white) men's desires are seen as automatic: if a woman is accessible for sex, a man will want sex with her and sexualise her as a result. But this raises the question of why some dominated women (and men) are more sexualised than others. Jordan argues that for North America 'the entire interracial sexual complex did not pertain to the Indian' (1977: 163). Although there is evidence that native American women – and to a lesser extent men – were sexualised in varying ways in the north and south of the continent, I think it is right to suggest that this was less intense and pervasive than for black men and women.[1]

Yet some of the basics of Bastide's argument have proved enduring: the idea that the power to get sexual access and dominate sexually creates sexual desire for, and thus sexualises, the target of that domination is a common one. The idea that black, or colonised, men feel humiliated and then either want revenge or are fearfully assumed to want revenge, which they will exact through sexual conquest, is also quite common. In the US case, it is often argued that the 'myth of the black rapist', which emerged with force in the late nineteenth-century Southern states, was a tool of political control which relied on the image of a sexually predatory black male seeking revenge (Di Leonardo 1997; Hall 1984; Hernton 1970; Hodes 1993, 1997). The 'myth' argument avoids the imputation that black men will automatically want sexual revenge, but black men's actual desires are left obscure, as in Bastide's argument.

In her pioneering overview of the intersections of race, ethnicity and sexuality, Nagel explores sex and race mainly through the history of the US and follows a similar line to Bastide's. She explains the sexualisation of black women and men in the US in terms of processes of domination (Nagel 2003: ch. 4). This is more than just a question of easy access to dominated women, but the basic approach is similar to Bastide's. Whites made Africans and blacks into sexual Others – seen as radically different, apart from whites, inferior and morally reprehensible in their sexual excesses and lack of control – for three reasons: to justify brutal treatment and especially sexual violation itself; to make black female slaves more saleable (as potential sexual objects); and to justify slave breeding programmes. For black men, the image of the dangerous, hypersexualised predator is linked by Nagel to white fears of vengeance and strategies of political control of slaves and, especially, post-abolition free blacks. (The sexualisation of native Americans is explained in similar terms [2003: 97].) Other aspects of the relationship between race and sex in the US follow from this: the reassertion of an autonomous and powerful black male sexuality in the black civil rights and black power movement is linked to the denial of black male sexual autonomy and freedom under slavery and post-abolition segregation (and seen as a reworking for different political purposes of the image of the sexually potent black man); this black masculinity, along with images of black female sexuality, then caused problems for black women in the civil rights and black identity movements and especially black feminists; the difficult place of homosexuality – sometimes expressed in strong homophobia – among many African Americans, particularly among activists, is also linked to these sexual politics.

Race, Sex and Gender: Intersections and Articulations

Nagel's approach is certainly valid and resonates with that of others, who also emphasise the role of domination and power. Yet Nagel pays surprisingly little direct attention to patriarchy and sexism – in short, to gender relations. In contrast, many authors highlight the fact that power and domination in a racialised system are always gendered: it is usually white men – and heterosexual men at that – who are the most powerful category of people, while the experience and mechanisms of being dominated are different for men and women in important respects, even if they are similar in others.

A pioneering example of this attention to gender is Verena Stolcke's work on nineteenth-century Cuba (Martinez-Alier [Stolcke] 1989 [1974]). She shows how white men secured their dominant position partly by controlling the sexuality of white women, so that family property and inheritance could be controlled and their reputation upheld. 'Honour' was a fundamental concern, and white men took it upon themselves to protect white women's honour and moral reputation by controlling their sexuality and sexual reputation. Only children born within the properly and honourably constituted family were granted full social recognition as offspring. A woman's honour could be endangered by acts of, or rumours about, 'improper' conduct, such as liaisons with inappropriate men, which would almost by definition include men of a lower social status (and thus darker skin) than themselves.

White men, however, could have informal (often extramarital) sexual relations with darker-skinned women of the lower classes without this tarnishing their honour. Children conceived in such relationships were illegitimate and did not receive full social recognition. For black and brown women, however, bearing such a child opened a possible avenue for social mobility, as they might expect to receive some material benefits for themselves and/or their children (even though they were illegitimate) as a result of their relationships with wealthier men. Young white women could also evade control eloping with a man considered inappropriate, thus forcing their parents' hand.

bell hooks follows this lead, arguing that 'racism and sexism are interlocking systems of domination which uphold and sustain one another' and, further, that 'sexuality has always provided gendered metaphors for colonisation' (hooks 1991: 59, 57). hooks, for example, looks at how US black politics was in large part about black men asserting their masculinity and asserts that 'sexism has always been a political stance mediating racial domination, enabling white men and black men to share a common sensibility about sex roles and the importance of male domination' (1991: 59).[2] hooks's work is part of a reaction by feminists of colour, from the 1980s, to the perceived tendency of feminism as formulated by white, Euro-American women to ignore questions of race and racism in their work (Amos and Parmar 1984; Davis 1981). It is these non-white feminists who pioneered the attempt to see race and gender (and sex) in a single analytic frame, a perspective that rapidly took hold (see Zinn and Dill 2005). Moore, for example, recognised the importance of the 'mutual imbrication of race and gender' such that 'one form of difference can be made to stand for another and/or that differences invoked in one context can be used to reformulate differences relevant to another': thus 'men in many oppressed populations are portrayed as both hypermasculine and feminised' (1994: 61) – a paradox which, however, she does not explain.

Anne McClintock also combines race and gender in an integral fashion. She looks at Western imperialism and the associated 'transmission of white, male power through control of colonised women' which is part of 'a hidden order underlying industrial modernity: the conquest of the sexual and labour power of colonised women' (McClintock 1995: 2–3). Her theoretical approach relies on the idea that 'race, class and gender are not distinct realms of experience, existing in splendid isolation from each other; nor can they simply be yoked together retrospectively like armatures of Lego. Rather they come into existence *in and through* relation to each other – if in contradictory and conflictual ways. In this sense, gender, race and class can be called articulated categories' (1995: 5, emphasis in original). Thus, 'gender dynamics were from the outset, fundamental to the securing and maintenance of the imperial enterprise' (ibid.: 7): in the creation of an 'elaborate analogy between race and gender' (ibid.), for example, colonised lands were feminised in a way that legitimated their conquest by men. Or, in a more complex analysis, McClintock argues that the imperial order in the metropolis depended in part on a patriarchal gender system in which there was a 'cult of domesticity' which confined women to the domestic sphere. However, society also depended on the labour of working-class women, especially as servants. One way of handling – without ever resolving – the contradiction between the norm of women as domestic beings and the reality of their paid labour outside their homes was to racialise working women and project onto them images of 'primitives' that derived from the colonies and were applied not only to women but to the working classes in general (1995: ch. 3). It is notable that a good deal of McClintock's analysis shows how imperial, racial ideas served the interests of metropolitan class and gender hierarchies, rather than showing how gender dynamics operated in the imperial control of racialised others.

Patricia Hill Collins (2000), another key figure in black feminism, takes a similar approach to Nagel's, but like McClintock gives a lot more space to sexism and gender relations. Her basic approach focuses on domination and Othering, mainly in the context of the US. Whites oppress black women through economic exploitation, political marginalisation and ideological manipulation. Black women are placed at the intersection of several overlapping and mutually reinforcing modern Western binaries – between white and black (with blacks cast as animal and natural against white humanity and civilisation); between men and women (with women cast as natural); and between civilisation and nature (with nature cast as an object open to exploitation by men). A series of images of black women – as mammies, matriarchs, whores – are deployed to facilitate oppression. Collins argues that 'attempts to control black women's sexuality lie at the heart of black women's oppression' (2000: 81) and that the various images all transmit 'distinctive messages about the proper links among female sexuality, desired levels of fertility for working-class and middle-class black women and US black women's placement in social class and citizenship hierarchies'; the images 'represent elite white male interests in defining black women's sexuality and fertility' (ibid.: 84).

Collins explores different theoretical approaches to understanding the relationship between sex and power and how race – specifically black women – fit in to that relationship (ibid.: 128–48). Importantly, she gives much greater prominence than does Nagel (and, even more so, than Bastide) to questions of gender oppression (i.e. sexism and patriarchy) and to questions about the regulation and control of sexualised, reproductive bodies. A first approach starts with heterosexism – the domination of heterosexuality as the norm – as a system of oppression similar to race, class and gender. Although Collins does not mention it, it is clear that this approach has affinities with queer theory, with its emphasis on analysing the construction and effects of dominant heterosexual categories (see e.g. Ferguson 2003). Black sexuality is defined as deviant because it is seen as hypersexual and pathological, just as homosexuality is defined as deviant because it is non-heterosexual. This gives a key to why and how black men and women are oppressed: their sexualities are the target of discrimination, punishment, control and regulation. According to Collins, this approach allows us to see how black male and female sexualities are similar, but also different, how different categories of black women (e.g. young and old, lesbian and straight) vary in their placement in the heterosexist system and also how white and black sexualities are defined in relation to each other (as normal and abnormal). The problem with the approach, in my view, is that it does not manage to specify how heterosexism links up with other systems of oppression: race, class, gender. Collins (2000: 129) states that such a link is necessary, but does not say how it works. We are left wondering what explains the 'elective affinity' of race and sex.

The second approach she outlines attempts to address this issue and looks at how sexuality figures within separate systems of class, race, nation and gender (i.e. rather than taking heterosexism as a system of oppression in its own right, parallel to these others). Collins illustrates this by showing how the image of the black Jezebel operates in oppressions of race (as a factor in maintaining racial segregation and inequality), of class (as a factor in facilitating the commodification of black female sexuality) and of gender (as a factor in defining white womanhood as pure and normal and underwriting patriarchal notions of gender relations). Collins does not criticise this approach in relation to others, but the evident problem is that the various systems of oppression are separated out: similar images of sexuality may occur in each, but we do not get a coherent account of how they fit together.

This relates to a problem that Collins (2000: 18) mentions elsewhere but does not raise in this context, which is that this approach – like the first approach – ends up with an 'additive' model of oppression: working-class black women suffer specifically because they have racial, gender and class oppression all added on top of one another – a triple burden (see e.g. Cock 1980). Working-class black homosexual women (and men) also suffer multiple burdens: of race and class, plus the various heterosexist discriminations that are entailed in sexist gender relations. This captures a real aspect of what is going on and what is experienced by people who are doubly or triply stigmatised, but what such an additive approach fails to capture is how each system relies on the other, for example, how class oppression works through racial oppression and vice versa, so that class oppression combined with racial oppression is different from class oppression without it. In the end, then, this approach does not explain very well why race and sex seem to 'go together' so frequently and easily.

The third approach described by Collins is the one she evidently favours; it is closest to McClintock's perspective too and relies in part on the concept of 'intersection'. Intersectionality is a term used by Kimberlé Crenshaw to capture the fact that 'the intersection of racism and sexism factors into Black women's lives in ways that cannot be captured wholly by looking at the race or gender dimensions of those experiences separately' (1991: 1244): specifically she argues that experiences of violence – rape, domestic abuse – were qualitatively different for black and white women, because, for example, black women had multiple burdens that prevented them seeking support. Meanwhile both feminism and anti-racism marginalised violence against black women. Nash cautions that 'intersectional projects often replicate precisely the [additive] approaches that they critique' (2008: 6): it is important, then, to show how race and gender mutually shape each other.

This is something that Collins manages, at least in part, in her use of the approach. She looks at how different systems of oppression 'intersect' in varying ways to form a 'matrix of domination' which is historically specific. She states: 'This conceptualisa-tion views sexuality as conceptual glue that binds intersecting oppressions together. Stated differently, intersecting oppressions share certain core features. Manipulating and regulating the sexualities of diverse groups constitutes one such shared feature or site of intersectionality'; and 'intersecting oppressions rely on sexuality to mutually construct one another' (2000: 135). This is an original approach insofar as sexuality is not seen as one more vector that intersects with others, but rather as a means through which or a site at which other vectors can intersect. But Collins does not elaborate much on this and instead proceeds to give a series of examples of 'sites of intersection', such as pornography, prostitution and rape, where one can analyse how sexuality acts as the 'glue' by means of which race, class and gender operate and constitute each other. Her analysis of prostitution, however, reads as very similar to the analysis of the image of the black Jezebel in the second approach, above: Collins shows how the images and practices around (black) prostitution serve the varied interests of class exploitation, racial oppression and sexist gender divisions.

Nevertheless, the theoretical point is that race, class and gender are able to work together and shape each other *because* they can all operate through images and practices around sexuality. And one can see how, as in Stolcke's work on Cuba, Collins is indicating how a sex/gender hierarchy is maintained through racial hierarchy, and vice versa. Images of sexual propriety and immorality constitute whiteness and blackness and provide a mechanism whereby both racial hierarchy (white over black) and sex/gender hierarchy (men over women, hetero over homo) are enacted. The emphasis on the regulation of sexuality also gives a good basis on which to encompass non-hetero sexualities. Rather than non-hetero sexualities being seen as just another form of oppression (in Collins' first approach), or an additional element in a sexist gender system (in her second), they can be analysed in terms of their 'deviance', with this now defined in terms of their perceived outcomes for the moral and biological reproduction of society at large.

This conceptual position is allied to that adopted by Judith Butler who – along with others who have grappled with queer theory (e.g. Hammonds 1994) – has argued that analysis must avoid setting up 'racism and homophobia and misogyny as parallel or analogical relations' (i.e. the additive model). Instead, 'what has to be thought through, is the ways in which these vectors of power require and deploy each other for the purpose of their own articulation' (Butler 1993: 18). Rejecting both an approach that privileges sex/gender difference as more fundamental than other differences and one that juxtaposes distinct spheres of power or adduces a 'list of attributes separated by those proverbial commas (gender, sexuality, race, class)', Butler tries to see how, for race and sexuality, 'one cannot be constituted save through the other'. She suggests, for example, that the hierarchical ordering of humans into 'male' and 'female' does not only take place in relation to a taboo on homosexuality, but also 'through a complex set of racial injunctions which operate in part through the taboo on miscegenation' (1993: 167–8). Racial and gender norms are 'articulated through one another' (ibid.: 182).

What Butler means by articulation is not made very explicit, but a good way of explaining it is to say that, in a simple analogy, one bone (or 'vector') added to another bone gives twice as much bone, but doesn't make a limb; but articulate the bones together and you get a new functional entity, with different effects and powers: the whole is more than the sum of its parts. That 'articulation' also means expression captures the idea that the functional entity in question is also a discursive one, and this usefully unsettles the overly mechanical nature of the bone image: articulated elements do not have an inherent connection but can – through ideological and material labour – be rearticulated into other formations.[3] As Clifford (2001: 478) says, 'When you understand a social or cultural formation as an articulated ensemble it does not allow you to prefigure it on an organic model, as a living, persistent, "growing" body, continuous and developing through time. An articulated ensemble is more like a political coalition or, in its ability to conjoin disparate elements, a cyborg.' Yet the mechanical image of the anatomical joint can capture the emergent potential generated by articulation, as well as the possibility that particular elements – such as race and sex – may articulate together in related, if changing, ways over time.

The concepts of intersection and articulation are not necessarily identical: the image of intersection seems to imply a static point or space delineated by intersecting vectors; the image of (re-)articulation is more dynamic and flexible – and to my mind preferable – yet both capture the fact that the way race and sex (and other vectors) work together is more than just additive. If we think of the ideological–material complex of 'black male sexuality' – for argument's sake, in the US – this is more than just racial oppression (white over black) plus elements of gender/sexuality (men over women): it is a whole distinct 'space' or functional articulation which operates in myriad ways in the context of racial domination (e.g. lynching), gender oppression (the protection of white womanhood), heterosexism (the difficulties of being black and gay), and so on. Like a traffic intersection, it is a crossroads around which grows up a distinctive set of features that would not emerge around each single road alone; like an articulated limb, it brings new potentialities to the individual vectors that make it up.

Collins, however, adds to this picture by specifying sexuality as a common terrain for intersecting vectors of oppression: each vector already implies a concern with sexuality and this allows them to work together. Collins refers very little to Foucault in her book, but his view of sexuality as a key domain for the operation of different forms of power in Western society since the late eighteenth century is clearly relevant here. This implies that the role of sexuality as what Collins calls a 'glue' is not coincidental (as it is in the second approach Collins outlines, where sexuality just happens to appear in each system of oppression), but derives from the central place sexuality has in modern Western society. A further implication is that sexuality's role may be historically specific: sexuality might not have played exactly this role in, say, early colonial Latin America (although, as we shall see, sexuality *was* a key part of racial domination in that context and this indicates that one might want to retain a central role for sexuality in *any* hierarchical system, linked to the role sexual reproduction plays in the maintenance of social inequality). These two implications constitute an important reminder: without them, Collins runs the risk of seeing sexuality as self-evidently implied, always and everywhere, in race, class and gender – which begs the main question of why these vectors get entangled with sexuality at all.

Race, Sex and Regulation

Collins' attention to the regulation of sexuality brings us to a slightly different theoretical vantage point from the one I started with, which emphasises domination and the way this allows white men privileged access to subordinate, racialised women. I might say that while the domination-oriented vantage point attends to the *sexualisation of race*, the sexual regulation vantage point begins with the *racialisation of sex*. Obviously, these are two sides of the same coin, not opposed viewpoints – they both depend on an analysis of power and domination. But the first starts with the fact of racial hierarchy and tries to explain its sexualisation in terms of what that hierarchy allowed racially dominant men to do; while the second starts with the fact of sexuality and its entanglement in systems of power and inequality, and then arrives at the way race gets involved.

Many of the approaches already discussed would be unhappy with this division: McClintock, Moore, Collins, Butler and others want to address the 'mutual constitution' of race and sex/gender (and class) – I believe rightly – and this means not 'starting' analytically with either race or sex/gender, but instead grasping how they 'come into existence *in and through* relation to each other', to use McClintock's phrase. But the distinction serves as a useful device for the current purposes of exposition, because it focuses on the process of sexual reproduction in any social system and especially ones based on hierarchy. If privilege and resources are to be limited to certain classes or categories, then the issue of how property and status are transmitted across generations is vital, entailing questions about who has children with whom and with what consequences – in short, questions about systems of kinship, family, filiation and gendered sexual reproduction. The distinction is also temporarily useful because it brings into sharper focus a Foucauldian perspective (already apparent in the work of such as Moore and Butler), which emphasises that power is *productive* as well as oppressive: these systems of racism and sexism act to oppress certain categories of people, but they also seek to build a certain moral order and shape subjects within that order. A principal means of doing this is through the regulation of sexuality. As we shall see, however, using sex/gender as a starting point, in Foucauldian style, can lead to a neglect of race. Including race as a key analytic concern in effect brings us back to intersections and articulations of race and sex/gender, but now with a greater appreciation of the productive side of power.

The importance of the regulation of sexuality is evident in work on the relationship between nationalism, gender and sexuality, much of which stresses how women – and, more generally, 'proper' heterosexuality – are placed as key objects in the building, reproduction and bounding of the nation (Gopinath 2003; McClintock 1993; Mosse 1985; Nagel 2003: ch. 5; Parker et al. 1992b; Radcliffe 1999; Radcliffe and Westwood 1996; Weinbaum 2004; Yuval-Davis and Anthias 1989; Yuval-Davis and Werbner 1999). Yuval-Davis and Anthias (1989: 7) list the various ways in which women figure in nationalist discourse, including as biological reproducers of national bodies, as cultural nurturers of national citizens, as symbols of nationhood and as participants in national struggles. Women are often seen as guardians and civilisers, although they may also be seen as a threat, especially through their sexuality, if it is channelled into 'improper' directions, such as prostitution (Guy 1991). Likewise, although nationalism vaunts a homosocial brotherhood of men, it avoids the implication of a 'deviant' homosexuality (Gill 1997; Mosse 1985; see also Sedgwick 1985): sexuality must be of the 'proper' kind, conducive to the good of the nation.

The regulation of sexuality also brings us, as I have mentioned, to Foucault and his contention that the history of Western society shows a shift from a 'symbolics of blood' to an 'analytics of sexuality' (Foucault 1998 [1979]). In the former system, there was an emphasis on juridical power held by a sovereign monarch, who exercised direct control over society and people's bodies; issues of kinship, sex and genealogy were important, but depended on what Foucault called the deployment of alliance, in which matrimony and sex were controlled by legal and religious codes in the service of maintaining society and its moral order in a state of homeostasis. In the analytics of sexuality, power becomes 'bio-power' in which the life-force of society, embodied in the sexuality of its citizens, becomes the focus for a whole system of management and administration aimed at increasing and optimising that force in the productive project of building and shaping individual subjects, the national population and ultimately the species. Rather than homeostasis, the aim is now expansion and the ever-increasing regulation of individual bodies. 'Sex is the means of access both to the life of the body and the life of the species' (Foucault 1998 [1979]: 146). This is what gives it such a central position, making it the subject of discursive elaborations about the secrets of life and society, to be controlled by sets of rules about 'normal' and 'deviant' sexualities that apply to whole populations or categories of populations (women, children), rather than just the conjugal couple. Ann Stoler notes that to speak of a straight shift from one system to the other in Foucault's work is too simple:

> The deployment of sexuality is 'superimposed', it does not 'supplant' the deployment of alliance, but is constructed out of the latter, imbuing it with a new tactic of power. The family is the site of this convergence, not a structure of alliance that constrains sexuality, as the conventional account would have it, but that which provides its most crucial support. (Stoler 1995: 38)

As Foucault himself puts it, 'the preoccupation with blood and the law has for nearly two centuries haunted the administration of sexuality' (1998 [1979]: 149).

Stoler (1995: 19–94) explains how race figures in Foucault's account. He identified racism as an ideology that emerged in seventeenth-century Europe, linked to ideas about internal enemies threatening society and the aristocracy defending itself against an emergent bourgeoisie: notions of purity of blood operated in family and noble genealogies. In the nineteenth century, this developed – through a process of the continuous re-inscriptions of meanings that makes it hard to say when race as an ideology really 'began' – into a statist biological racism that worked to define which categories of people and bodies were to be regulated in which ways and worked as much in terms of class divisions as it did in terms of 'internal enemies' (the Jews, the Irish) and external colonial populations (although Foucault only mentions the latter for the late nineteenth century). Some categories of people, including the working classes (and, as McClintock argues, women), were in danger of racial degeneration and threatened society and it moral order with racial contamination. In the defence and productive construction of society, seventeenth-century notions of purity of blood were collectivised and moved from the family to the population and category levels, becoming part of the discourse on sexuality seen in terms of bodily purity, hygiene and vigour.

Stoler contends that Foucault neglects to take account of the role of colonialism (and, indeed, gender) in the way race and sexuality worked together: his approach is altogether too Eurocentric (1995: 91–3). Using her research on Dutch and French colonies in south-east Asia, she argues that a concern with regulating the sexuality of racialised categories of people prefigured the concern with sexuality in Europe itself and that what was happening in the colonies was intimately linked to what was happening in Europe. She also emphasises the coexistence of the symbolics of blood with the analytics of sexuality in the colonial context, arguing that they were entwined from an early date (from the sixteenth century in the Spanish and Portuguese colonies), despite an overall shift towards the regulation of sexuality through science and medicine in the nineteenth century. It is worth noting that JanMohamed also argues that, in the US southern states under slavery and Jim Crow segregation, racialised sexuality had more in common with Foucault's regime of alliance and juridical power than with an analytics of sexuality; for example, in the deployment of ideologies about kinship and the impossibility of a kinship link between whites and blacks (JanMohamed 1990).

Stoler argues that 'discourses of sexuality, racial thinking and rhetorics of nationalism have several things in common' (1995: 133): they all seek to link internal moral essences to external visible markers in strategies of inclusion and exclusion, which are linked to the defence of the social body against degeneration and abnormality. In the Dutch and French colonies of south-east Asia, there was intense administrative concern with the conduct, upbringing and morality, including sexual morality, of colonial populations – not only, indeed not even principally, the native peoples, but rather the white working-class colonials, the local-born white colonials and the mixed-race offspring of Europeans and native people. As Young (1995) has argued, racial thinking often concentrates on the question of mixture and hybridity. Colonial authorities feared that white people in the colonies could easily be contaminated by the climate and by the natives themselves; the proper, controlled sexuality and morality that was thought appropriate to Europeans, whether in Europe or in the colonies, was in danger in the tropics. People's very nature could become degenerate in this environment where Asian natives were seen as sexually uncontrolled and promiscuous. Particularly vulnerable were women, whose honour was to be protected, and children, especially because the latter were often being brought up – even breastfed – by native servants who, it was feared, exercised a corrupting influence.

From a Foucauldian perspective, then, if the question of race provokes the answer sex, it is because sexuality is a privileged site for thinking about moral value and exclusion/inclusion in the context of producing and regulating society, nation and persons. Racial thinking gets drawn into this matrix because it too deals with these issues. The logic of the relationship between race and sexuality in a Foucauldian argument is basically that sexuality is central because it is about the reproduction of society, especially in contexts of hierarchy (and this would be the case, albeit in different ways, under a regime governed by the symbolics of blood or an analytics of sexuality). If society is hierarchical in racialised ways, then sexuality inevitably intertwines with racial thinking – and all the more so in a regime in which sexuality becomes an absolutely central focus of power. The difference between Foucault and Stoler is that the latter shows that 'the cultivations of bourgeois sensibilities [about morality and sexuality] were inextricable from the nationalist and racial underpinnings of them' (1995: 135). Foucault underestimates these links and thus underestimates the constitutive role of race and empire in the construction of notions of sexuality.

The approach which focuses on the regulation of sexuality is an immensely powerful way of understanding how race and sex relate to each other, but there are some potential pitfalls with a Foucauldian approach that need attention. First, Stoler's work shows us that we need to be open-minded about what constitutes 'sexual reproduction'. Her late nineteenth-century subjects believed that white people in the tropics could be shaped or 'contaminated' by the environment and the native people and that this could change their very natures in ways that might be reflected in their offspring. This derived from the widespread Lamarckian belief in the possibility that characteristics acquired in one's lifetime could be passed, through sexual reproduction, to one's children (Wade 2002: 23, 63–5). This alerts us to the need to guard against the assumption that we automatically know what is involved in 'sexual reproduction' in any given context (cf. Weinbaum 2004: 2). An articulation between race and sex in this context would include contamination of white people by the native milieu, which appears to a modern Western observer to be non-sexual.

Second, some care needs to be taken with the notion of sexual and social reproduction. If people in stratified societies are concerned with social reproduction and therefore with sexuality, then it is also the case that social reproduction is not confined to sexual reproduction, but occurs through the many mechanisms which ensure continuity to social orders and institutions, even if sexual reproduction is an underlying necessity for this continuity. Of course, a concern with sexual reproduction can extend well beyond actual reproductive sexual relations between men and women (as Foucault himself shows in detail), such that homosexuality, masturbation and women's sexuality as a female pathology all became key issues in nineteenth-century European ideas about sexuality. But there is also a sense in which an overriding concern with sexuality – seeing it as the vital key to understanding modern Western society – may run the risk of reducing other factors, such as race, to a secondary, derivative status. Thus McClintock argues that 'By privileging sexuality … as the invented principle of social unity, Foucault forgets how an elaborate analogy *between* race and gender became … an organising trope for other social forms' (1995: 7; emphasis in original). And McClintock contends that colonised peoples and lands were feminised, just as women were primitivised. This not only draws our attention to gender – 'feminists have long questioned how Foucault could write a history of sexuality without gender or for that matter without women' (Stoler 1995: 93) – but also to race as a project that, especially in colonialism, had its own dynamic of control and regulation. As we have seen, Stoler's project is to reinstate the context of colonialism and racial hierarchy into Foucault's history of sexuality, so we can see how colonial concerns with the governance of colonised peoples and lands, and the deployment of ideas about race in that context, worked on and through ideas about sexuality.

A slightly different but useful example of an approach that owes much to Foucault in its focus on the regulation of sexuality, but that also enquires into how this relates to race, is the work of Elizabeth Povinelli. Like Collins, she outlines existing approaches that 'add' gender and sexuality to other phenomena such as race or indigeneity (to give race *and* sexuality), or that see race as 'transformed' by sex/gender (to give gendered racial subjects) and she sees these as useful but insufficient (Povinelli 2006: 11–13). Povinelli's own approach and its difference from the existing ones are not stated with such clarity, but she sees it as 'not so different from the biopolitical project that Michel Foucault outlined' in her concern with how 'love, intimacy and sexuality are not about desire, pleasure or sex per se, but about things like geography, history, culpability and obligation; the extraction of wealth and the distribution of life and death; and the seemingly self-evident fact and value of freedom' (ibid.: 9–10). Povinelli's project is to uncover the relationships between forms of love and intimacy and forms of liberal governance and, in an echo of Stoler, she argues that 'If you want to locate the hegemonic home of liberal logics and aspirations, look to love in the settler colonies', such as Australia and the US (ibid.: 17). Like Foucault, she in interested in how liberal governance constructs and uses notions of sexuality (and love and intimacy), but like Stoler, Povinelli gives greater emphasis to empire, and thus race, in this process.

A concrete example is her analysis of laws that regulate Australian Aboriginal land claims. These laws use a notion of 'traditional owners' – those who make the claim under law and thereafter own the land collectively – defined according to Western heterosexist genealogical norms, which assume that legitimate and authentic kinship links are established by heterosexual reproduction. These links serve to delimit a set of kin who are the 'owners' for legal purposes, but the norms ignore other types of relationships, such as homosexual ones, or even heterosexual ones, between Aborigines and non-Aborigines, which in Aboriginal eyes also establish legitimate claims to clan land. In effect, a subtle regulation of what counts as legitimate sexuality (racially bounded, heterosexual) is used to police how land claims are made and, moreover, what counts as a 'real' Aborigine – not the offspring of a racially 'mixed' union, but, and more generally, a person saturated by the kind of constraints envisaged in the genealogical imaginary of liberalism, that is the image, in liberal ideology, of society and its people governed and constrained by longstanding links of kinship, nation, race, biology and inheritance (Povinelli 1997, 2002: ch. 5).

*   *   *

I started this chapter with models of racial domination that permit white men to dominate black women (and men) and thus gain sexual access to them; sex is used as a tool for racial oppression. This is a central and enduring insight, but we need to incorporate gender and patriarchy in a more decisive way and this led us on to models of the intersection and articulation of sex/gender and race, which looked at both sexist and racist modes of oppression together. This in turn led us directly to a Foucauldian approach which starts with the regulation of sex as a productive practice of governance in which moral orders are being built, as well as categories of people oppressed. In the hands of analysts such as Stoler, this approach is recast so as to bring us back, in effect, to questions of intersection and articulation, seeing race and sex as linked through their mutual entanglement, in strongly gendered ways, with modes of governance. Race is about an ideology and practice of hierarchy and inequality, but so too is sex; these domains operate on a common ground that spreads over colonial and postcolonial spaces. The linkage also works because both race and sex (and gender) deploy a language and concepts of body and human nature: a key feature of ideologies of race is that 'racial' traits are passed on through sexual reproduction (although not through that means alone, as Stoler's work shows); hence the abiding concern with 'mixed-race' people which Young (1995).

However, many of the approaches reviewed so far in my view fall short of really delving into the mechanics of erotic desire and the ambivalent operation of desire and fear. As Moore (2007: 44) says, 'what gets left out is the importance of understanding and analysing fantasy, desire and unconscious motivation'. Systems of oppression may require, or certainly encourage, processes of othering, but why does this focus so strongly on sexuality? And why does the denigration of a specific category of people also seem to produce such ambivalence, manifest in desire for that category? One can argue, along with much of the literature on rape, that sex between dominated and dominant groups is about power, not about sexual desire, but it is unconvincing to say that the sexualisation of black men and women in the Americas and the related sexual imagery around whites (and indigenous people, not to mention Asians and other ethnic-racial categories) does *not* include some aspects of the workings of desire – and of fear and hate.[4] Doris Sommer argues that white men were 'seduced as much by the absolute power of their racial and sexual advantage as by their partner's sexual charms' (1991: 128), but this separates out the elements of 'charm' and 'power' in a way that I find unhelpful. The point is that desire/fear and power are intimately conjoined in their very production, so to say that sex is about one *rather than* or *as much as* the other does not really work.

In order to understand the process of othering and the production of ambivalence – (sexual) desire alongside anxiety and fear – some scholars have turned to the dynamics of self and other formation, using insights from psychoanalytic theories. Such scholars tend to come from literary and film studies, philosophy and queer theory – fields I have already been dipping into and which some social scientists and historians may view with suspicion (Moore 2007: ch. 1) – but I think it is necessary to review these approaches and consider what they have to offer, generally in terms of connecting race and sex, but particularly in terms of explaining ambivalence.

Explaining Race and Sex 2: Self, Other and Ambivalence

Patricia Hill Collins, like many others, depends on a concept of othering in her account of the articulations of race, sexuality, gender and class. The basic idea is simple – perhaps, too simple. Any dominant group will create a notion of outsider, who is excluded from membership; more than this, outsiders are defined as other, that is, radically and essentially different from self, beyond the pale of inclusion. Once a category of people is defined as other, the way is opened to treat its members in all kinds of discriminatory ways, create negative and indeed fantastical images about them, and use them as a scapegoat for a host of real and imagined ills. Edward Said's classic work on Orientalism (1985) describes at length the way the West constructed an image of the Orient as other, through a range of deployments of academic and popular knowledge, knowledge which often purported to be 'true' and objective, but which actually participated in the discursive construction of 'the Orient'. In this process, the West was consistently cast not just as superior, but as the norm (rational, masculine, morally upright), while the Orient was seen as irrational, feminised, eroticised and morally suspect.

One of the problems with Said is his tendency to over-generalise the othering process: all of the Orient is included, despite huge variations in the history of colonialism in and scholarship about different regions; there is a tendency to conflate not only different types of academic scholarship and very different perspectives within it, but also academic and popular representations of the Orient. In addition, the colonial studies perspective that takes much of its inspiration from Said may focus too strongly on the white man/native female relationship, marginalising other relationships and giving too much power to the white, male, colonial gaze or discourse (Manderson and Jolly 1997a: 7–9).

Yet the basic concept of othering remains a powerful one, as it taps into some key processes of identity formation. One aspect, frequently noted by scholars who trace practices of othering, is that, while the other is defined as different and inferior and thus as actually or potentially dangerous and threatening, the other may also be seen as mysteriously attractive, fascinating and powerful. That power may be perceived as operating in various spheres: the healing of mind and body, the intuitive understanding and manipulation of nature and the supernatural, the physical embodiment of special skills (e.g. in music, dance, sport) – and, of course, sexuality (sexual prowess, erotic intensity, desirability).[5] This ambivalence has been widely observed, but less often explained robustly. Stoler (1995: 171–6) notes that a common tendency in colonial studies is to deploy Freudian-derived notions of displacement and projection. White men, European colonial powers or the West generally have 'repressed' their (male) sexuality in the process of becoming 'civilised' (which involved the domination and control of 'nature', including, in the Western view, sexuality), but these repressed feelings and desires are 'projected' and 'displaced' onto others, who may include women, the working classes, colonised peoples and regions, and racialised categories. Thus these others become the locus of ideas about natural powers in general, and specifically sexual powers. These ideas of repression raise the spectre of psychoanalytic approaches, but do not really help us to understand them.

Frantz Fanon on Race and Sex

Frantz Fanon has been an important influence on theorists who seek to bring psychoanalytic insights into understanding race and sex. This Martinican psychiatrist who worked for a long time in French Algeria focused on processes of self-formation in colonial contexts and tried to link a psychoanalytic focus on the individual to a social analysis of power and politics. In some ways, his analysis is quite simple: for example, in his account of the relation between black women and white men, he says that black Antillean women are obsessed with finding a white, or light-skinned, man. This racial self-denial is a direct product of racial hierarchy and results in a neurosis of alienation (Fanon 1986 [1952]: ch. 2). The chapter he dedicates to black men and white women is very similar: black men are desperate for white approval (at least in the case Fanon analyses, an Antillean-born man, raised in France) and thus obsessively seek white women with whom they cannot, however, form satisfactory relationships, resulting in a neurosis rooted in the anguish of 'abandonment' (of the black man primarily by white society and white women, but also by his own black society and his black mother) and manifested in a lack of self-esteem and a defensive-aggressive posture (ibid.: 72–8).

While this account may over-generalise about black men and women, it does explain something about ambivalence: racially subordinate men and women desire a relationship with a person who is racially dominant, but are either denied it or must deny themselves having it; hence ambivalent feelings emerge. This is useful partly because it addresses ambivalence among the subordinates: the combination of desire and fear is not only characteristic of dominant people's affective reactions to their others; ambivalence may be linked to hierarchy, but not necessarily to dominance.

But if we want to know more generally why race and sex 'go together' so powerfully, we are left with an analysis that is close to Bastide's, with which we started, except that Fanon is focusing on the desires of black men and women: as social subordinates they want recognition and status and seek to achieve it through sexual relationships. 'I wish to be acknowledged not as *black* but as *white*. … When my restless hands caress those white breasts, they grasp civilisation and dignity and make them mine' (1986 [1952]: 63). Desire is a direct product of (the lack of) power.

Fanon goes deeper into the reasons for the mutuality of race and sex when he tries to understand 'The Negro and Psychopathology'. The context is again a colonial one in which black people are instilled with a sense of their own inferiority, but here Fanon is specifically interested in white racism and the black person as 'phobogenic' (liable to produce phobias in others). Fanon notes that phobias often hide repressed sexual desires: 'the Negrophobic woman is in fact nothing but a putative partner [i.e. desires sex with black men] – just as the Negrophobic man is a repressed homosexual' (ibid.: 156). He explains this in two main ways.

First, in a long footnote, he states that 'the real Other for the white man is and will continue to be the black man' (ibid.: 161). This Fanon explains, very loosely, in terms of the psychoanalyst Jacques Lacan's mirror stage, a period between the age of six and 18 months in which, Lacan said, the child sees itself in the mirror and (mis)recognises itself as a whole, independent being, while still experiencing its own body as uncoordinated and fragmented (Lacan 2001: 1–7). The child loves the image as an ideal and can identify with it (and thus look back on him- or herself from the position of the mirror-image), but also feels aggression and envy towards it because it highlights the child's own sense of fragmentation. This image is 'other', but is actually a projection of the Ego and expresses a dual relationship, a splitting of the self: the child experiences itself as self by seeing itself as other (and as others would see it). Fanon proposes that the 'appearance of the Negro' causes – for reasons he does not explain – 'the young white at the usual age [to] undergo an imaginary aggression' (1986 [1952]: 161). Somehow, the black person automatically takes on the role of the 'other' – and the other of the self now becomes radically separate. The white man also takes on this role for the black man, but the difference is that for the white man 'the Other is perceived … absolutely as the not-self … the unassimilable', whereas for the black man 'historical and economic realities come into the picture' (ibid.: 161–3), that is, colonialism creates a context in which the black man is denied subjectivity and made into an object for the white man, but judges himself in relation to the white and wishes to identify with him (see also Fuss 1994: 21). As such a radical other, the black man (and Fanon is usually talking about men here) serves as an object onto which to project all kinds of feelings and images, including ones about sex and particularly anxiety about sex: 'the Negro, because of his body, impedes the postural schema of the white man' (1986 [1952]: 160) and this is manifested in 'the fear of the sexual potency of the Negro' (ibid.: 164).[6]

Second, Fanon makes the Freudian argument that 'every intellectual gain requires a loss in sexual potency': the 'civilised' white man retains a longing for that lost potency and projects 'his own desires onto the Negro'.[7] But this is partly because, for Fanon, 'the Negro' has already been 'fixated at the genital' – for reasons that he does not explain (ibid.: 165).[8]

Fanon has been criticised for his lack of attention to black women, his homophobia and his tendency to overdraw the oppositions between black and white, creating a dualism that does not capture the ambivalences of the colonial situation.[9] My concern is that, in the end, he does not give us a very coherent explanation of how race and sex work together at the points of convergence between colonialism and subject formation. He relies on Freudian ideas that 'civilisation' entails the repression of sexuality and on rather ill-defined mechanisms of projection and displacement in which the black man is somehow peculiarly suited to take on the role of other for the white man (and presumably woman too). That this othering takes a specifically sexual form – compared to the othering of the Jew, which Fanon says centres on images of money – is only explained by the fact that 'in relation to the Negro everything takes place on the genital level' (1986 [1952]: 157). This genital fixation itself is never explained, although Fanon does set great store by the black body, its *visibility*, its very blackness. The black man has undergone the 'epidermalisation' (ibid.: 13) of his economic inferiority; the experience of racism for Fanon – 'Look, a Negro!' – meant that 'the corporeal schema crumbled, its place taken by a racial epidermal schema' (ibid.: 112). It may be that the importance of the physical body, for Fanon, led to the importance of sexuality in images of black men.

Psychoanalysis, Gender and Ambivalence

To understand better the way race and sex relate in the process of othering and specifically how ambivalence emerges, let us start with the basic process of self-formation. We shall assume for the moment that this takes place (for argument's sake, in a 'Western' context')[10] in a way that, in keeping with some widely shared tenets of psychoanalytic theory, gives rise to tensions and ambivalence. The developing child has to separate itself from the mother (or adult carer), and this is achieved by recognising the mother as a being distinct from oneself, and also by seeing oneself as an independent being. According to Lacan (2001: 1–7), this happens during the mirror phase, in which one perceives one's own individuality – and this is legitimated by a caring adult. In a key sense, one gains a sense of self by seeing from the point of view of another: I have already alluded to this splitting or doubling of the self, which Homi Bhabha (1986: xiv) calls the Otherness of the Self, and which is not just an infantile phase but a condition of being human. (Lacan himself saw the mirror 'phase' as something that did not just happen at a certain period of infancy, but was a protracted process.) This makes the self an inherently ambivalent construction: the self is an ideal illusion of stability and mastery, dependent on recognition by others (and oneself as other); having an illusive coherence, it is inevitably threatened by fragmentation. A relation of aggressive tension exists between self as embodied being (an experience of potential fragmentation and loss of mastery) and self as Ego or self as other (an image of coherence and control).

The self also emerges from the loss of original unity with the world/mother and is forever marked by that loss, adding to the ambivalence (Tyler 1994). From a Lacanian perspective, desire then is the wish to return to the original unitary wholeness and oneness with the world/mother, banishing the loss or lack caused by the basic rupture which constituted selfhood and, indeed, the emergence into language and culture. Desire is unconscious, but it is not a primal instinct: it is structured by and expressed in the language and symbols that the emergent self acquires. The original unitary wholeness is conceived as 'Other', even though, when the child was in it, no concept of Other existed, because it is only by rupturing with that oneness that its existence can be conceived. The return to oneness is impossible once selfhood has been achieved, but it is also prohibited, as it would imply an incestuous relation with the mother (in Freudian terms) or, understanding this metaphorically (and in more Lacanian terms), a refusal of entry into language and culture, a refusal to obey their laws (which in a patriarchal society are symbolically the Law of the Father). Thus the desire for oneness is repressed and this results in ambivalence: the Other is desired, but that desire is repressed; the Other is forbidden and aggression is directed against it. The Other is at once the original libidinal unity with the world/mother and the repressive Law of the Father, the system of linguistic and cultural rules that make possible the self and thus also make it possible to conceive the Other in the first place. The Other in this sense is not an actual person, but a concept of Otherness, which is informed by and informs relationships with actual others.[11] In short, desire has ambivalence at its core: it expresses a wish to submerge oneself, but also a fear of doing so, because it will lead to loss of self in the social world.

Jessica Benjamin provides a similar way to understand the roots of ambivalence. In a critical reformulation of Freudian, Lacanian and other currents in psychoanalysis, and drawing especially on what is known as object relations theory, Benjamin outlines a key tension in self formation between 'the need to establish autonomy and the need to be recognised by the other' (1984: 293). The paradoxical link between these two is that in order to feel autonomous, we want to be recognised as such by others, typically the ones on whom we are most dependent. This is a version of the Otherness of the Self: seeing oneself through the eyes of others. Benjamin's formulation differs in some respects from the Lacanian and Oedipal emphasis on desire as linked primarily to regaining a lost primordial unity; desire is instead linked to a struggle for autonomy, which necessarily entails dependence. Total dependence means death of self, which is to be feared; total autonomy, also to be feared, means isolation and lack of the very recognition that makes autonomy meaningful. Successful 'differentiation' (i.e. the process of acquiring a self) means balancing between these two.[12] Ambivalence lies in the fact that the things one wants (autonomy, recognition) are also to be feared.

This is no more than an outline sketch, which glosses over important differences in psychoanalytic approaches, but it can help to understand ambivalence. From a psychoanalytic perspective, the fundamental processes through which the self is formed entail a basic ambivalence of desire and aggression, of identification and denial. Although it is perhaps not self-evident why this should involve *sexual* feelings (desire is not only sexual), it is fundamental to the whole of psychoanalysis that these processes of self-formation are also processes of the formation of sexed, gendered and sexual selves: 'becoming a sexed being is a condition for subjecthood', although this happens in culturally diverse ways (Moore 1994: 17). Benjamin asserts that 'the common psychological root of ... erotic experiences can be found in the earliest issues of intimacy and separation in infancy' (1984: 292). More specifically, she argues, following Bataille, that eroticism centres on the fundamental tension between autonomy and dependence, because eroticism, and especially erotic dominance, 'breaks the taboo between life [autonomy] and death [total loss of self in the other, total dependence] and breaks through our discontinuity from the other'. She adds: 'Perhaps the most important way in which human beings experiment with loss of differentiation is through sex' (ibid.: 296, 97).

I have been working through these ideas about self formation because I think they can help us to grasp how the formation of self is a fundamentally ambivalent process, which is intimately related to the other and which generates powerful dynamics of both desire and fear, attraction and threat, realisation of mastery and profound dependence, all of which are deeply linked to sex and gender. Thus far, I have discussed these processes in a rather abstract way, divorced from their social context, but of course self formation takes place in a social world, which, in the West and in many other contexts, is divided by hierarchy and infused with power relations. For psychoanalysis, the key hierarchy involved has been gender itself and this has been the subject of extensive debate. To start with, the work of Freud (and, for some, Lacan) is strongly gendered in a patriarchal style and is also heterosexist: it takes a Western sex/gender hierarchy as given. The primary adult from whom the child separates is the mother; a return to original oneness is a return to the mother; the person who forbids the incest of the son with the mother is the father; the emergence of self into language and law is submission to the Law of the Father; a 'healthy' sexual development is seen as heterosexual; homosexuality occurs when 'normal' Oedipal processes go awry.

Feminist and queer theorists have been critical of these patriarchal and heteronormative formulations while also building on and reformulating them in many different directions, which still see sexual difference as key to the formation of self.[13] This extensive literature is beyond the scope of the present chapter, but the underlying point is to see these processes of self and other formation as structured differently for males and females in Western society, not only because sexual difference itself is posited as foundational in the emergence of self, but also because selves are formed in a society in which marked gender divisions already exist (e.g. women tend to do the childcare) and are strongly hierarchical (e.g. childcare is low-paid and low-status work).

Very briefly, the formation of self for a boy requires a more radical separation from the mother (who is usually the key other in relation to whom the self takes shape) than for a girl who, although she also has to separate from the concept of the mother, does not have to constitute herself as a different, socially defined category of sex/gender in the process. In his effort to construct a solid masculine identity, the boy objectifies the mother and – and this is the key point – given the gender hierarchies that already exist, denigrates her too (or at least consigns her to a subordinate role). Girls tend to identify more with the mother and the feminine gender role. Some formulations of this male/female difference thus see men who have grown up in male-dominated (usually Western) societies as having more insecure sex/gender identities than women, a greater drive towards self-sufficiency, autonomy and control, less predisposition to emotional nurturance and a tendency to objectify women (Chodorow 1978; Giddens 1992: 115–17). In short, when selves are fashioned in the context of gender hierarchy, women can emerge as a category of other (for men), surrounded by ambivalence. Likewise, as gay, lesbian and queer theorists have pointed out, when self formation takes place in a context in which sexuality is subject to powerful hierarchies and norms, homosexuals are labelled as other (Butler 1993; De Lauretis 1994a; Warner 1999; Weed and Schor 1997).

Self, Other and Hierarchy

Seeing self and other formation in the context of gender hierarchy is a key step in linking ambivalent emotions to a political-economic formation – it means locating these psychoanalytic processes in their social context, rather then seeing them simply as self-propelling processes that arise automatically from the fact of growing up as a child. We can now ask what happens with other forms of hierarchy, without assuming that these are secondary to gender in a temporal or theoretical sense.[14]

In a class and/or racial hierarchy, the basic processes of othering, with their associated emotions of desire and fear, are strongly mediated by the experience of class and racial difference. As a person encounters or simply learns about certain categories of people who are socially defined as different in important ways, s/he is likely to experience that category as a form of the other in relation to which a sense of self has always been formulated from a very early age, even if those categories of people were not part of those early processes of self formation. Othering is an ongoing process that continues into adult life as individuals struggle to balance autonomy and recognition. But it is also clear that othering and self formation are founded on early experiences which shape, partly unconsciously, the way that the ongoing process plays out. This is, in effect, the phenomenon known as displacement, by which I mean the way that early processes of self and other formation shape unconscious or subconscious processes later. Stoler's critique of easy formulations of quasi-Freudian notions of projection and displacement, applied to 'white men' or 'the West', is relevant here, because it cautions us against over-generalised applications of the idea of displacement. But it is still possible to think in terms of how the early experiences of a person – say, a white middle-class male growing up in Europe or a black working-class boy in Colombia – in terms of gaining a sense of self vis-à-vis others will set up patterns that shape how that person deals with different categories of others later in life.

My argument is that, if ambivalence is a basic feature of the emergence of self, vis-à-vis others, then one would expect some ambivalence in the way people think about and interact with those who, in the existing hierarchies of the social order, are classified as others in class or racial terms – one would expect the combination of fear or contempt, plus attraction or fascination. This ambivalence is not necessarily confined to the feelings of the dominant towards the subordinate, but can operate in the other direction too, as Fanon notes. Given the conditions in which ambivalence is formed, it would be almost bound to have sexual dimensions, even if not overtly so.

McClintock (1995: 75–131) has an excellent example of how these kinds of dynamics work, which is also useful in exploring racial aspects in the discussion of othering in a hierarchical context. She examines the well-known case of Arthur Munby, a Victorian barrister in England, who had a sexual obsession with working-class women, which he detailed at great length in his diaries. He secretly married his servant, Hannah Cullwick, and lived with her in a relationship that was both husband–wife and master–maid, replete with many ritualised erotic dramas of dominance and submission, many of which had distinctly racial overtones (e.g. Cullwick posed as a slave). McClintock points out that Freud, while he talked a lot in his letters about his own nanny, including sexual aspects of his relationship with her, does not mention the figure of the nanny in his theories about Oedipus and sexuality, despite the pervasive spread of this person throughout middle- and upper-class Europe as part of the growing institution-alisation of domestic service in the nineteenth century. Yet it seems undeniably relevant that most middle-class men (McClintock does not address the role of the nanny in girls' lives) had two mother figures, radically separated by class: the mother and the nanny. Freudian ideas about how a boy competes with the father for the mother as part of the playing out of the Oedipus complex do not really work with the nanny, who is an employee. McClintock contends that the split image of the woman as Madonna and whore, perfect and sullied, emerges from this historical reality – or more generally from the way class differences entered the domestic sphere at this time – rather than being a psychological archetype. Making recourse to what is in effect a notion of displacement, McClintock argues that:

> The class and gender contradictions of late Victorian society entered Munby's life with the force of an insoluble riddle. Mastering the riddle of doubled gender became the obsession that consumed his life. His chief

strategy for managing the contradictions was, I suggest, the imperial discourse on race. In this respect, Munby was no eccentric, but was fully representative of his class. (McClintock 1995: 80)

The contradictions lay in the emotional and physical distance of the mother compared to the closeness of the nanny; and in the class status of the mother, compared to the clearly subordinate status of the nanny, whose word was, however, law for the child. Although McClintock does not deal with the material in exactly this way, one can certainly see the scope for complex processes of self and other formation in relation to a distant mother who is a social equal and a close nanny who is clearly defined as other in class terms. This seems especially relevant to Latin America, where domestic service is still a key institution, in which working-class women, often black, indigenous or mixed-race, work in middle- and upper-class homes (Gill 1994; Radcliffe 1990).

The tension between autonomy and dependence in this peculiarly intimate conjuncture of the class structure is complicated by the fact that the nanny mother figure, who acts as a key legitimator of the child's self and as the intimate, physically close protector in which that self can find respite, is herself *already* other in class terms to the child and the family. Ambivalence towards this other is likely to be intensified. McClintock uses the idea of 'managing' this bundle of contradictions: not resolving them, but somehow coping with them, or at least expressing them, by engaging in various strategies. For Munby, it was fetishising working-class women – and the rougher, the better for his tastes. He also masculinised them and racialised them (as black and primitive) in writing about and drawing them.

For Cullwick herself, who also left extensive diaries, McClintock's argument is similar. Cullwick chose to continue her life as a working servant even after marrying Munby: she insisted on and took pride in her labours, which she described in endless detail; she refused to be a middle-class wife. McClintock argues that Cullwick craved recognition by the upper classes, which she could achieve only through self-negation and service – and then not always, as she, like all domestic servants, was often ignored and made invisible. If the upper classes constituted the other for her, she clearly had ambivalent feelings, craving their recognition, marrying a middle-class man, but insisting on her drudgery, which became a sexual fetish for her as it was for Munby. She stamped her working-class status upon herself, but it was also dramatised and valued by Munby's obsession. Cullwick also wore a 'slave band' (a leather wrist strap) and a padlock and chain around her neck; she blacked her face and wrote of Munby as her 'Massa'. Race served Cullwick as a means to express her subservience, which in her case was at least in part voluntary (i.e. she chose to continue as a servant): for Cullwick, too, differences of class and gender were cast in a racial idiom.

The function of racialisation in McClintock's argument is a little under-specified: 'dangerous crossings of gender and class are negotiated by projecting onto them the rhetoric of race' (1995: 108); 'class and gender distinctions were displaced and represented as natural racial differences' (ibid.: 154).[15] The implication is that this racialisation helped to mask and/or naturalise and thus legitimate distinctions of class and gender (even though gender was already seen as an essentially natural difference). McClintock also argues that fetishes, whether racial or sexual, worked by 'displacing what the modern imagination could not incorporate onto the invented domain of the primitive' (ibid.: 182). More generally, they act as a recipient into which are displaced 'contradictions' which cannot be resolved on a personal level (ibid.: 184). In McClintock's view, the modern imagination had particular trouble incorporating the simple fact of women's paid labour in a world in which the cult of domesticity defined women as purely domestic. Working women were thus subject to fetishisation as sexually and racially other: they were ambivalently loathed and desired, invisibilised and loved. This generated ambivalence among those women too.

In McClintock's argument, then, the reason why race and sex interrelate in such a close fashion is linked – rather like in Stoler's approach – to the functions empire and race played in dealing with emerging issues around class and gender in bourgeois European society. The difference from Stoler is that McClintock uses psychoanalytic insights to understand the generation of desire in this context, as well as focusing on the regulation of sexuality, gender and class (which is not to say that Stoler is not interested in questions of desire, as I shall show later). Processes of self formation, for the white, middle-class men on whom McClintock concentrates in this part of her book, created others in gender and class terms, who were desired and even fetishised in ways that were displaced onto a discourse of race. What McClintock does not really address, however, is that this discourse of race existed and was already sexualised by the period she is talking about. In the end, race is introduced to the argument as a secondary issue and some questions about why race and sex go together are left unanswered. The sexualisation of race cannot be seen just as the result of the displacement of specific class and gender contradictions in a nineteenth-century imperial context. It runs deeper than that.

McClintock is, however, very useful for showing how processes of self and other formation generate sexual desire in a class hierarchy. Categories that are defined as other in a concrete social context of hierarchy become targets, receptacles or conceptual spaces for the emotional and sexual ambivalences that arise from the gendered processes of self and other formation: the relationship with other, in the structural sense, shapes and is shaped by the relationships with actual others, many of whom are predefined as other by hierarchical social categorisation. In that sense, it is easy to see how a category defined as racially other could as easily get entangled in all those processes as a category defined in class terms, especially as racial otherness very often overlaps with class otherness. There is a central truth to this, in my view, yet it brings us back to our central problem, which is that, while class has undoubtedly been sexualised, as McClintock shows, there seems to be a particularly powerful affinity between race and sex, which means that to analyse race simply as a parallel case to class or as secondary adjunct to class is not sufficient. Fanon clearly recognises this, but, as we have seen, he does not explain it beyond asserting that 'in relation to the Negro everything takes place on the genital level' (1986 [1952]: 157).

Homi Bhabha, Colonialism and Ambivalence

Homi Bhabha, who draws on Fanon, make a useful intervention in this respect, in part because he is interested in psychoanalysis, but also because he focuses on the colonial (and postcolonial) racialised situation as *sui generis*, as one in which the dramas of the ambivalence and the Otherness of the Self get played out with peculiar intensity. Bhabha interrogates the phenomenon of ambivalence: this is characteristic of self formation in general, but it is especially powerful in the colonial context, with its 'extremity of ... alienation', 'its displacement of time and person, its defilement of culture and territory' and the 'peculiar visibility' of power (1994: 41, 83): 'It is not the colonialist Self or the colonised Other, but the disturbing distance in-between that constitutes the figure of colonial otherness' (ibid.: 45). Part of that distance in-between is captured by the ambivalence of desire and derision that characterises relationships between coloniser and colonised and Bhabha has a specific argument about how and why racial and sexual discourses combine to express that ambivalence. He sees a structural and functional parallel between the figure of the colonial racial stereotype and the figure of the sexual fetish, which allows the former to be read as the latter (ibid.: 74).

Following Freud, Bhabha argues that the sexual fetish is a substitute. A boy – and in Freud's theory this does apply only to boys, not girls (McClintock 1995: 190) – desires oneness with the mother, but this threatens his sexual identity as a boy, because he has seen that his mother is not a male, as she has no penis. Oneness with her would for him entail 'castration', or loss of masculine identity. A fetish is an object of (sexual) worship that substitutes for the mother, allowing desire while allaying the threat of castration. According to Bhabha, the fetish normalises the threat of sexual difference (between men and women) and the anxiety of castration. Simplifying somewhat, it is a way of engaging with sexual desire, while avoiding some of the basic realities of the differences between men and women.

The colonial racial stereotype, says Bhabha, depends on a myth of racial purity that normalises the internal diversity of a putative racial category and presents a simple image of identity – 'whites/blacks are like *this*'. Thus both the sexual fetish and the colonial stereotype normalise difference. There is more than just a structural parallel, however, there is also a functional link: the sexual fetish 'plays' between the anxiety about sexual difference and the untroubled affirmation of no difference; the stereotype 'plays' between anxiety about racial difference and the affirmation of racial purity and unmixed origins. Thus: 'Discourses of sexuality and race relate in a process of *functional overdetermination*' (1994: 74, emphasis in original). This, then, allows Bhabha to analyse the colonial stereotype and how it operates in relation to basic processes of self and other formation that are deeply entangled in sexuality. The self emerges through the mirror phase, which gives rise to both narcissism (love of the coherent self) and aggression (towards the self as other, potentially fragmenting). This love/hate ambivalence is also found in colonial strategies of domination in which stereotypes both mask difference (narcis- sistically holding up an image of racial purity) and acknowledge it (aggressively pointing to racial difference) (ibid.: 77). The insecurity and ambivalence of the stereotype lead to its obsessive and endless repetition – in jokes, sayings and other iterations – and also to contradictory qualities: the black man as savage yet obedient, as sexually rampant yet child-like, as cunning yet innocent (ibid.: 82).

Bhabha's account is complex and even opaque, but stripped to its bare bones, he is saying that the ambivalences that emerge out of self and other formation become harnessed to a colonial project of racial domination and alienation in which the tense dependencies between ruler and ruled parallel the ambivalences of self and other. Race and sex fit together because they work in similar ways: this is a functional 'over-determination', not only because the basic ambivalences of self and other are transferred to the colonial situation and shape it, nor only because the colonial situation creates a fertile environment in which self/other ambivalences emerge, but because both those things happen at the same time and determine each other. One could speculate that the same thing could be true for any context of domination, such as a class hierarchy, but, although he does not address exactly this question, Bhabha, like Fanon, does see something specific about the racial colonial situation. This lies in the *visibility* of racialisation – not a natural fact, but one in which skin is 'produced or processed as visible' (1994: 79) – which links to the 'peculiar visibility of colonial power' (ibid.: 83). Bhabha states: 'The visibility of the racial/colonial Other is at once a *point* of identity ("Look, a Negro") and at the same time a *problem* for the attempted closure within discourse' (ibid.: 81). That is, the intensely scopic nature of racial/colonial domination – its reliance on *looking* – accentuates the ambivalent nature of the stereotype, which is stretched between asserting simple racial purities and recognising the complexities of racial heterogeneity (cf. Seshadri-Crooks 2000: 1–11). Although Bhabha does not make this specific point, one could conclude that, because of this, there is a particularly intense relationship between race and sex: the ambivalences of racial/colonial domination fit particularly well with the ambivalences of sexualised, gendered processes of self-other formation.[16]

Domination, Regulation and Ambivalence: Combining Psychoanalysis and Social Science

The introduction of a psychoanalytic element is, in my view, potentially useful because it holds the promise of explaining why systems of domination seem to generate sexualised imaginaries and discourses, in which sexuality is not only an instrument of power and a target for regulation and governance, but is also involved in an ambivalent play of fear and desire, of hate and love. Psychoanalysis suggests that the process of forming a self, in a necessary but necessarily agonistic relation to others, produces ambivalence; in a situation of social hierarchy, the categories that are defined as subordinate and inferior (women, working classes, non-whites) come to occupy the position of other and become the subject of ambivalent emotions which are deeply entangled with sexuality. It is worth noting that the promise of psychoanalysis lies partly in the fact that gender difference is introduced at the very heart of the approach (which is not to say that gender is confined to simple differences between 'men' and 'women', as feminist and queer reformulations of classic psychoanalysis have stressed): othering occurs in a gendered way right from the start and this is inherently linked to sexuality.

A second contribution of an approach open to the insights of psychoanalysis is that it may also help us to understand why *racial* domination seems to have such an elective affinity for sex: this is linked to the strong parallels between sex/gendered processes of self and other formation and racialised processes of othering, in which relations with a gendered/sexed other easily morph into relations with a racialised other, due to the role played by differences perceived, in a scopic regime, as 'natural' and embodied.

However, we need to be aware of the strong critiques to which psychoanalytic accounts of desire have been subjected – even as they have been reformulated by feminist and queer theorists. The French philosophers Gilles Deleuze and Michel Foucault have both, in different ways, challenged the very basis of Freudian and Lacanian approaches to understanding desire (Butler 1987: ch. 4; Campbell 2000; Young 1995: ch. 7), or pleasure to use Foucault's preferred term (see Deleuze 1994). In *Anti-Oedipus*, Deleuze and Guattari (1983) argue that Freud's Oedipus complex – which is the key to Freud's ideas about the emergence of sex/gender and desire – does exist, but only under the specific conditions of Western capitalism. It is not, as Freud implied, a universal dynamic which grows out of the basic family unit and the experience of any child in relation to its mother and father (Bertold 1998). Sexuality thus has to be seen as the 'libidinal unconscious of political economy' (Deleuze and Guattari, cited in Young 1995: 168). Freud saw sexual desire as socially constructed, through the mechanism of the Oedipus complex, but Deleuze and Guattari propose a much more radically socialised approach to desire (and not just sexual desire): the whole notion of lack, which is basic to the Lacanian notion of desire as originating in loss of primal oneness, is rejected by Deleuze and Guattari, who argue that desire-as-lack is linked to capitalism's material need for 'scarcity'. Colonialism, however, does impose the Oedipus complex as a psychic structure on the West's colonies: 'Oedipus is always colonisation pursued by other means, it is the interior colony, and ... at home, where we Europeans are concerned, it is our intimate colonial education' (Deleuze and Guattari 1975: 173). Failure to recognise this, simply to analyse psychopathologies from the point of view of the Oedipus complex, is to make psychoanalysis itself part of the mechanisms by which capitalism and colonialism are reproduced.

Foucault also argues that desire is produced by power-laden discourses that seek to regulate it and cannot be seen as the product of universal psychic dynamics of self formation. Desire only emerges in and through discourse. Foucault takes issue with the Freudian and Lacanian notion of repression: that desire, although seen by Freud and Lacan as socially constructed and not a simple instinct, is nonetheless a product of denial, loss and repression. For Foucault, in his analysis of sexuality in modern Western society, bio-power positively *produces* desire, especially sexual desire, as a key mechanism for the production and regulation of life itself. Psychoanalysis is a discursive domain that constructs sexuality and repression as keys to modern identity and well-being; it thus produces the desires it purports to reveal. It is an object of, not a tool for, sociological and historical analysis.

Campbell (2000) argues that psychoanalytic approaches that rely on Oedipal narratives – whether in Freud, Lacan or a host of theories derived from them, including by some feminists and queer theorists – remain mired in 'a white, ethnocentric imaginary' and are 'part of a Western colonising discourse that imposes itself as a universal cultural narrative'. (It is notable that Bhabha's analysis only really applies to colonisers, not the colonised.) For Campbell, Oedipal narratives can and do operate in the West, but the unconscious may function according to other logics too.

These critiques indicate the need to be cautious with psychoanalysis and, of course, direct us back to the kinds of approaches I reviewed in the first section of this chapter, which focus on power. Yet my view is that these approaches do not get us far enough in their account of the ambivalence around sex and race, and the role that desire plays. For example, in his book *Colonial Desire*, Robert Young, while acknowledging Bhabha, generally adopts an approach that owes little to psychoanalysis and more to theories of social power and domination. He notes that much postcolonial criticism focuses on the coloniser/colonised opposition, and less on the processes of mixture and cultural contact. He therefore proposes to use sex as a model for understanding contact and to focus on the questions of hybridity and mixedness that concerned both colonisers and colonised (1995: 5). Racism worked partly by policing the crossing of sexual boundaries: 'bastard and mixed-blood are the true names of race' (ibid.: 180, citing Deleuze and Guattari) and notes the fascination of nineteenth-century racial theory with 'a Malthusian fantasy of uncontrollable, frenetic fornication producing countless motley varieties of interbreeding' (ibid.: 181). Sexual exchange, Young says, mirrored colonial economic exchange and 'it was therefore wholly appropriate that sexual exchange, and its miscegenated product ... should become the dominant paradigm through which ... colonialism was conceived' (ibid.: 182). But, while he recognises the ambivalence of desire and fear in colonial contexts, Young never explains this, nor does he delve into why race and sex intertwine, other than to imply that if divisions of power and hierarchy exist between two categories, then any relationship across that division would be of concern – *a fortiori* a sexual one. This is crucial, to be sure, but leaves a certain amount unexplained: that sexual exchange went hand in hand with economic exchange does not really account for why sexual exchange became the 'dominant paradigm' for colonialism.

Stoler takes a more promising approach. As we have seen, she has a critical view of appropriations of Freud by historical studies, with their notions of the displacement and projection of white male anxieties onto colonial others. According to her, this actually leaves unexplained the workings of sexual desire, which figures only as a repressed biological instinct that flows in a 'hydraulic model of sexuality' and seeps or bursts out in unexpected places (1995: 173, citing Martha Vicinus). Taking a Foucauldian line,

Stoler understands colonial discourses of sexuality as 'productive of class and racial power, not mere reflections of them' (ibid.: 176). She challenges 'the story that colonialism was that quintessential project in which desire was always about sex, that sex was always about power, and that both were contingent on a particular representation of non-white women's bodies' (ibid.: 189). Sexuality in the colonies embraced a range of desires and subjects (mothers, children, maids) and had as much to say about broader moral values and propriety as it did about the direct exercise of prurient power by white men over native women. As one would expect from the Foucauldian angle, sexuality is seen as part of the overall regulation and administration of the social order in the colonies; and in this, sex was not necessarily the key aspect Foucault made it out to be. Stoler argues that relationships of affect, kinship and nurturance, which cannot be reduced to sexuality itself, were also important ties that had to be regulated (ibid.: 191).

In all this, though, the affirmation of the bourgeois self, both in Europe and in the colonies, was central and this was always 'contingent on a changing set of Others' (ibid.: 193) who acted as mirrors and mimics. 'If desire is about both externalisation and mimesis as so much of the philosophical literature on desire suggests, then no political story is more relevant to the production of western desire than colonialism' (ibid.: 192). Despite the reference to 'philosophy' rather than psychoanalysis, externalisation is also a Freudian concept (meaning projection or displacement) and Stoler is clearly saying not only that constructions of self in relation to Others were important, but that colonialism set a special stage for these processes of the 'education of desire' – that is, that race and sex intertwined in particular ways on this stage. One must agree that these processes should not be assumed to be the result of 'hydraulic' manifestations of a pre-established (male) desire, nor reduced to white male exploitation of non-white females in a straight exercise of power and domination, but this still leaves room for considering processes of self and other formation in their social context.

In some ways, this converges with McClintock's aim to 'refuse the clinical separation of psychoanalysis and history', a distinction that 'was germane to imperial modernity itself' in its opposition of the private and the public. She aims to link up family, sexuality and fantasy with labour, money and the market (1995: 8). De Lauretis (1994a) says that 'we cannot think the sexual outside of psychoanalytic categories', but she wants to combine Freud and Foucault – 'unwonted bedfellows' – in a 'theoretical articulation of Freud's psychosexual view of the internal world with Foucault's sociosexual view'. Likewise, trying to reconcile anthropology and psychoanalytic approaches, Moore sees the latter as seeking 'to understand the entrance of the human subject into the existing networks and discourses of social and cultural relations', a process that 'needs to be accounted for in historically specific ways' (2007: 44–5). Campbell (2000: ch. 8) also seeks to situate the cultural unconscious historically and socially, tracing how embodied experience in a given social context shapes the unconscious, which in turn, through its creative and representational capacities, institutes cultural myths and regimes of symbolic difference.

Conclusion

The problem with which I started – why do race and sex intertwine in contexts of domination and hierarchy? – can appear to be resolved with disarming simplicity. Sex can be used as a direct instrument of domination, of course, but more generally, if race 'stands for' hierarchical position and sexual reproduction is key to maintaining hierarchy, then the two domains will converge. Stolcke sums up with admirable clarity the 'reason race and sex as criteria of discrimination intersect':

> In fact, racialist classifications invariably entail the control of women's sexuality because ideologies of race attribute social placement in an unequal social order to heredity, that is, to genealogy. It is this genealogical thinking that endows sex with sociopolitical significance. Because the entire society is caught in this genealogical logic, for the white elites to ensure

their preeminence they need to control their own women's bodies and sexuality, whereas, for example, Indian maids fall prey to white men's sexual depredations. (Stolcke 2002: 680)

Stolcke captures a central truth here, but further considerations are needed. First, there is a tendency here to start with the existence of a society stratified in terms of genealogy and then see the control of women's sexuality as a consequence of that. This tends to skate over how the society came to be stratified in genealogical terms in the first place, which must have happened partly through mechanisms of control of property and inheritance, which themselves depended on controlling (women's) marriage and reproduction.

Second, and linked to the first point, prior to the conquest of the Americas, several native American and African societies had unequal social orders, characterised by noble and aristocratic lineages, which depended in different ways on genealogy (as we shall see in the next chapter). Yet how men controlled female sexuality there was different from the situation in Europe. There was much less concern with premarital virginity, for example. In short, there are different modes of genealogical thinking, which link to stratification and to sexuality in different ways.

Third, during this pre-conquest period, Iberian and other European men were very concerned with 'their own women's bodies and sexuality' – specifically, their premarital virginity and marital fidelity – and genealogy was certainly important to the hierarchical organisation of society, but it is a very open question whether 'racialist classifications' were operating at that time. Thus 'genealogical thinking' need not be racial thinking.

Fourth, the control of sexuality invoked by Stolcke is linked directly to white elite male domination, whereas a more Foucauldian approach expands the idea of the regulation of sexuality to a broader domain in which sexuality is seen as key to the construction of a European moral order, based on twin pillars of hierarchy in Europe and in the colonies. White men are dominant in this order, but there is a broader project of moral construction at work.

Finally, this moral order is one in which selves are formed in relation to others, and in order to really explain the characteristic ambivalence of desire and fear, love and loathing – and perhaps to explain the peculiar intensity with which race and sex converge – it seems necessary to add to the picture of domination and regulation of sexuality some element of attention to processes of self and other formation, always, however, in their social context and not assumed as universal or automatic dynamics.

3

RACE AND SEX IN COLONIAL LATIN AMERICA

Introduction

If we want to understand how and why race and sex articulate with each other in the formation of colonial societies in Latin America, we have to start with an outline of sex and sexuality in both the Iberian and indigenous American social orders around the time of the conquest of the Americas, with some brief comments about West Africa too. We also need a sketch of Spanish and Portuguese thinking about the differences between themselves, indigenous peoples and Africans – thinking that we can gloss as 'racial' only once we have grasped its historical specificity.

Sex and Gender in Iberia and the Americas

Iberia at the time of the conquest formed part of what Jack Goody called Eurasian societies, which relied on plough agriculture controlled by men, had stratified systems based on the holding of landed properties, which were passed on through 'diverging devolution', a mode of inheritance that gave property both to sons and, via dowries, to daughters (Goody 1976).[1] In such systems, great importance was attached to the marriage of daughters and the legitimacy of their offspring, because these matters impinged directly on where a family's property ended up; women's sexuality was bound up with notions of virtue and premarital chastity was highly valued. These questions were of particular importance to the elite families which controlled large landed properties; plebeian families were less concerned with controlling marriages, but the ideology of female virtue was more widespread. Great importance was attached to notions of honour and shame. I shall discuss these in more detail later in the context of Latin America, but in outline a man's status was centrally defined by his honour, that is, his reputation as a man and his standing in political and economic terms (by nobility of birth, personal wealth). Reputation was a tricky matter, as it depended on recognition by others, but it was influenced by perceptions of bravery, integrity, sexuality (heterosexual prowess helped; accusations of homosexuality, or sodomy as it was called, harmed) and – crucially – the sexual reputation of the women publicly linked to the man by kinship and marriage. A woman could bring shame (*vergüenza* in Spanish, *vergonha* in Portuguese) on herself, her family and her husband by publicly tarnishing – or being thought to have tarnished – her sexual virtue, that is, her premarital chastity or her marital fidelity. Women, especially elite women, were subject to close vigilance and, in general, were seen as under the control of their fathers, brothers and husbands. Legally, they were considered minors and could not hold public positions of authority (Powers 2005: 40–1; Seed 1988: ch. 4).

In relation to sexuality, the difference between being active and passive was important and sex generally was more a matter of doing or being done to, rather than doing together.[2] Being an active penetrator was seen as masculine, while being penetrated was feminine; the Church defined sex with the woman on top as counter to nature. Broadly speaking, the active/passive distinction applied to homosexual acts as well, although any suggestion of sodomy was potentially feminising; often, too, charges of homosexuality, without a clear passive/active distinction, were made against those seen as outsiders, enemies or others, typically Moors, but also Italians.[3] The Church saw all sodomy – even anal sex in the context of marriage – as a sin against nature and punished it severely, although it seems to have been fairly common (Borja Gómez 2001; Karras 2005; Nesvig 2001; Sigal 2003c; Trexler 1995: ch. 2). Lesbian acts were included as a type of sodomy, but were seen as less sinful than male sodomy.[4] Penetration was a masculine activity linked to dominance and power: this was evident also in the field of war and conquest, which had been a key aspect of Iberian society during 750 years of on-and-off fighting between Muslims and Christians for control of the Iberian peninsular. Dominating through force also meant feminising the opponent: rape of both males and females who had been vanquished was an extension of this logic (Trexler 1995; Wood 1998).

Indigenous American gender and sex arrangements around the time of the conquest were very varied across an entire continent, but those of the Incas and the Aztecs have received the most attention. Historians have emphasised gender parallelism and gender complementarity (Gutiérrez 1991; Horswell 2005; Powers 2005: ch. 1; Silverblatt 1987, 1994). Gender parallelism is defined by Silverblatt as 'the conceptualization of social relations in terms of parallel, gender-marked lines of descent' and this 'moulded Andean kin ties, land rights and religious practice' (1994: 260). 'Chains of women paralleled by chains of men formed the kinship channels along which flowed rights to the use of community resources' (1987: 20). Powers extends this picture to the Aztecs and notes that women and men operated in 'two separate but equal spheres'; these were complementary insofar as 'each gender's roles were perceived as equally important to the successful operation of the society, whether performed by men or women' (Powers 2005: 15, 16). Women could inherit property and ritual status from their mothers, and they occupied important positions of religious and political leadership over other women.

Although both Inca and Aztec societies were hierarchical, with a noble elite in control. The political economy underlying this was driven by taxes and tributes of labour and goods which sustained the elite, while stockpiles of goods were redistributed to needy non-elites as a kind of welfare. Although genealogical connections were important in determining nobility (Garrett 2005), large landholdings were not owned by families who passed on that control from one generation to another using dowry as one channel of transmission, as was the case in Europe. Accordingly, the whole complex of controlling the sexuality and marriage of daughters was different. Women were involved in marriages of political alliance, and Silverblatt (1987: ch. 4; 1994: 260) notes that, alongside gender parallelism in the Andes, there was also a 'conquest hierarchy' that expressed male dominance over women by associating victorious warriors with the right to marry the women of vanquished groups. Inca noblemen could take the women of conquered groups as wives, or distribute them to other men. Trexler (1995) also argues that, among native Americans, conquest of one group by another involved the feminisation of the defeated men, including by the use of male rape.[5] These patterns of male dominance need to be taken into account alongside patterns of gender complementarity. Silverblatt says, however, that ideologies of conquest hierarchy did not prescribe the 'direct manipulation of women by men' (1994: 260). Moreover, there was little concern with the control of virginity and premarital sex was not forbidden; indeed, it was considered normal. Describing the Pueblo indigenous people of what is now New Mexico in the southern US, Gutiérrez says that 'female sexuality was theirs [women's] to give and withhold'. Furthermore, 'modesty and shame were not sentiments the Pueblo Indians knew in relationship to their bodies' and 'erotic behaviour in its myriad forms (heterosexuality, homosexuality, bisexuality) knew no bounds of sex or age' (Gutiérrez 1991: 17, 18).

Questions have been raised about Gutiérrez's representations of Pueblo sexuality (see below) and, in particular, there is debate about the role of male homosexuality in native American cultures, with some observers emphasising its presence and tolerance of it (albeit often in prescribed contexts) and others emphasising its despised status (Sigal 2003c). Discussion often centres on the figure of the berdache, commonly understood as a transvestite male gendered as female.[6] Broadly, it seems that male homosexual practice had a varied, but acceptable place in some areas in specific ritual and political contexts, but was not generally accepted and that a distinction was commonly drawn between the penetrator (masculine, powerful) and the penetrated (feminine, subordinate).

African sex/gender arrangements arguably had less impact on the Americas than those of either the Iberians or the indigenous

Americans. Africans refashioned new cultural and social forms in the Americas and African cultural principles were one of the key drivers in that process (Mintz and Price 1992 [1976]; Price and Price 1999). Yet, as uprooted slaves, they were clearly in a highly constrained position. When they escaped and set up their own communities or when they gained their individual freedom, they were in a better, though still constricted, position to shape their own ways of life. Pre-colonial African societies in the western areas that supplied the majority of the slaves transported to the Americas were, like the indigenous American societies, a very mixed set. For our purposes, I want to highlight only a couple of features. Many societies were highly stratified, with royal and noble elites, but the political economy underlying this was based on taxes and tributes, control of trade and, increasingly with the advent of European weapons, conquest of neighbouring groups (with enslavement of the vanquished). Like the native American societies, sub-Saharan African societies generally differed from European ones in that, while genealogy and descent were part of what defined royal and noble elites, there was an absence of landed properties owned by elite families who passed on their property by means of dowry and inheritance to both daughters and sons and for whom the control of daughters' virginity, sexuality and marriage choice was absolutely central (Goody 1976). (Muslim societies, which were mainly in North Africa but had important influences in areas of sub-Saharan West Africa, were distinct in this respect and, like European societies, were based on plough agriculture, family-owned landed properties, diverging devolution with dowries and an intense concern with control of female virginity, honour and shame.)

Sub-Saharan cultures had a well-defined sexual division of labour, but women performed a lot of agricultural labour and, often, trading. Women could also occupy important roles in the religious and political spheres as ritual specialists and royalty. Gender relations in Africa have, as for indigenous America, been characterised as showing complementarity and cooperation between women and men (Cornwall 2005).[7] In some areas, gender roles were flexible and not determined by biological sex: hence in pre-colonial Igbo society (Nigeria), there were 'male daughters and female sons': if a man had no son, his daughter could inherit property and goods and assume a powerful position, including the acquisition of wives. Gender and power were still linked, however, as these powerful women assumed aspects of male gender roles (Amadiume 1987; see also Matory 1994). Women could also be constrained by patriarchal demands and pressured to marry according to clan elders' demands (Greene 1996).

There is evidence that homosexuality was present and, as in the native American case, same-sex practices and transvestism also existed in ritual contexts (Matory 1994; Sweet 2003). It is less clear how institutionalised or tolerated sexual acts between people of the same sex were, although it seems that European colonialism certainly stigmatised homosexuality in powerful ways (Murray and Roscoe 1998). Generalising about Africa, Bhana et al. say:

> It is not the case that women were outside the circle of male power and, in some contexts, women's reproductive capacity itself became the currency of gender struggle .... Yet for the most part an African gender order did not systematically discriminate and subordinate African women nor did it seek to regulate the expression of sexuality other than in contexts where this resulted in pregnancy and childbirth. (Bhana et al. 2007: 132)

In sum, if we think back to the end of the last chapter and Stolcke's concise reasoning about why race and sex intersect, it is clear that for Iberian, native American and West African regions, stratified societies existed in which elite status was defined, to a greater or lesser degree, by 'genealogical thinking'. Yet the mode and degree of control of women's sexuality varied considerably, especially around the issue of premarital virginity. This indicates that the way race and sex came to articulate in Latin America was the result of particular modes of genealogical thinking, rather than genealogical thinking *per se*. The next question, then, concerns the character of Iberian genealogical thinking and its relation to racial thinking.

Ideologies of Race and *Limpieza de Sangre*

The terms *raza* in Spanish and *raça* in Portuguese appear occasionally from the thirteenth century and become more common by the sixteenth century (Stolcke 1994: 276). As Banton has argued (1987), the terms referred to 'race as lineage': all the descendants of a single ancestor or group of ancestors were connected genealogically and thus of the same lineage or race. What all these descendants looked like was not necessarily definitive; physical appearance came to play a much greater role from the late eighteenth century in European conceptions of race as a biological type. Nevertheless, *raza* in its early sense still invoked ideas of inherited qualities that were 'in the blood' and the concepts of race, blood and genealogy were used in a discriminatory way in Spain, primarily in the notion of *limpieza de sangre* (cleanliness or purity of blood) (Martínez 2008; Poole 1999; Stolcke 1994; Twinam 1999: 41).

In Spain and Portugal, this was connected to discrimination against Jews and Muslims. For centuries Christians had been involved in expanding their territory in the Iberian peninsula, against Muslim control. Christians lived in a tolerant, though not fully equal, relationship with the Jewish population until the late 1300s, when anti-Semitic riots broke out in several cities. Jews began to convert to Christianity in greater numbers and this current swelled in 1492, when not only were the Muslims formally ousted from Iberia, but the Jews were also expelled from Spain – being expelled from Portugal in 1497 – or were obliged to convert to Christianity. Remaining Muslims were also persecuted and pressured to convert. In the early 1600s, converts from Islam, the *moriscos*, were also expelled. Prejudice had long existed against the *conversos*, the newly converted, who were suspected of continuing to practise their old religion in secret. From 1449, these prejudices were institutionalised in statutes of *limpieza de sangre*, which, for example, banned Christians of Jewish and Muslim descent from holding public office. The founding of the Inquisition in 1478 intensified the persecution of the *conversos* and use of ideas of *limpieza de sangre*, which was extended to include the descendants of people already found guilty by the Inquisition. In Portugal, statutes on *limpeza de sangue* were enforced from the late sixteenth century.

The 'racial' character of these statutes was particular: on the one hand, lack of *limpieza* was clearly linked to descent and genealogy; on the other, 'descent' was often limited to two generations (Twinam 1999: 43) and in 1550 Charles V specifically said that the children of Jews and Muslims should not be included in the statutes (Poole 1999). Also, for purposes of gaining public office, an individual could be declared 'clean' by royal dispensation. In that sense, *limpieza de sangre* involved a combination of criteria of religious practice (did a person secretly practise Judaism?) and race-as-descent (did a person have Jewish or Muslim 'blood'?). The statutes and the Inquisition targeted heterodox religious belief, but they did so using genealogical criteria. These criteria varied in their application, but they were an important component. In fourteenth-century Spain, Judaism was seen as a biologically heritable trait and Jews were talked about as being a *raza* and having *sangre infecta* (infected blood) (Manrique 1993). And while there was some debate early on about the status of the children of converts, ideas of blood and heredity soon came to dominate (Stolcke 1994).

The encounter of the Iberians with indigenous Americans was distinct from that with Africans. North Africans had, of course, been living in the Iberian peninsula for centuries. Sub-Saharan Africans were known through classical texts and, from the 1430s, through voyages down the West African coast. By the sixteenth century, African slaves were numerous in cities such as Seville and Lisbon. Africa in general was seen as infidel (.e. Muslim) territory and the Pope confirmed this in several papal bulls in the fifteenth century (Saunders 1982). It was partly this status that was used to legitimise the enslavement of Africans which went more or less unquestioned until the eighteenth century – and even then only by religious minorities in the first instance. Indigenous Americans were more problematic and there were debates about their status: whether they were rational beings, whether they were barely human savages or unspoiled innocents, and whether they could be enslaved or not (Hulme 1986; Mason 1990; Pagden 1982; Wade 1997: 25–7). Formally, it was decided in 1542 for Spanish colonies and 1570 in Brazil that indigenous people should not be enslaved (although informally colonists continued to enslave them in many areas). The Spanish Crown also conceded to indigenous people the quality of *limpieza de sangre* if they converted to Christianity (Stolcke 1994: 279); this was never conceded to Africans.

In the Americas, ideas of *limpieza de sangre* and the purity of blood were adapted to new circumstances. The exclusion and persecution of new converts continued, but it was supplemented by the exclusion of people who had, or couldn't prove that they did not have, any indigenous or black heritage, which made a mockery of the official concession of 'cleanliness' of blood to indigenous people (Martínez 2004, 2008; Silverblatt 2004: 117–40). As we shall see, sexual unions between Spaniards, Africans and indigenous people started early on and the offspring of these unions were generally recognised as distinct from either of their parents: they were *mestizos* (*mestiços* in Portuguese) – although in practice a whole host of terms was used to label different kinds of mixture. A lot of attention was paid, above all by the elite, to a person's ancestry and any 'taint' of mixture could create suspicion and possibly exclude a person from public office, university entrance or ordination in the Church. Also the stigma of illegitimacy became tightly entwined with ideas about purity of blood (Twinam 1999: 45). In Spain, illegitimacy had been defined as an impediment to political and economic power and, already in the fifteenth century, had been linked to purity of blood. In the Americas, people of mixed descent were very often illegitimate, so much so that '*mestizo*' and 'illegitimate' were practically synonymous. People of illegitimate birth might know their parents, but very often they did not (or would not be recognised by them) and this meant they could not formally prove their purity of blood. In general, the so-called *castas*, the non-white classes, because of their 'unclean' blood and the reputation of illegitimacy, found it very difficult to aspire to honour, even if they might seek to live honourably (Johnson and Lipsett-Rivera 1998b: 8).

This was far from a rigid system, however. Generally, people had to prove *limpieza* going back two generations and any earlier mixture was ignored for legal purposes (even if in popular memory it might be recalled). A great deal also depended on reputation: a person was 'white' if he was accepted publicly as such; if another person insulted him – besmirched his honour – by publicly calling him (or his ancestors) a *mestizo* or a mulatto, long litigations might ensue as the insulted person tried to prove his whiteness, which was done in part by showing that other people accepted him as such, a rather circular sort of proof. In addition, individuals could also gain a royal dispensation – a *gracias al sacar* – which decreed them white (or legitimate) for public purposes (Twinam 1999). Finally, Brazil had even more flexibility in terms of how mixed heritage affected public honour. While the Brazilian elite was also highly preoccupied with its own purity of blood, *limpeza de sangue* statutes were passed later in Portugal (1588) than in Spain and were abrogated in Brazil in 1773 by the Marquis de Pombal, at a time when they were still highly significant in Spanish America.

Despite these flexibilities, it is clear that, whatever the ambiguities about the 'racial' character of Iberian concepts of purity of blood, by the time these became ensconced in the Americas their character was recognisably racial (and racist) in the sense in which these terms are used in this book. As Twinam (1999: 76–7) puts it for Spanish America, and the same holds for Portuguese America: 'the American colonies added an explicit racism to prejudices of birth and religion encompassed in the classic Spanish concept of limpieza de sangre … the colonial limpieza ordinances became targeted almost exclusively against the illegitimate and the racially mixed'. Silverblatt emphasises that colonial bureaucrats were actively constructing racial categories as their work led them to ask how to deal with and categorise known classes of people in a new context – new Christians, for example – and less familiar classes of people – indigenous people, Africans, *mestizos*: 'as they went about their daily chores of statecraft, they were helping make race into a calculable thing' (2004: 25).

Race, Sex and Conquest in Latin America

In Chapter 1, I started with an approach to the articulation of race and sex that focused, first and foremost, on sheer domination and coercion. This view emphasises that the race/sex articulation stems above all from sex being used as an instrument of direct subjugation and humiliation and from the ability of conquering (white) men to satisfy their lusts on conquered (black and indigenous) women, and in some cases men, who are sexually accessible – and perhaps even 'willing' in a constrained way – because of their subordinate status. The history of the conquest of what we now call Latin America provides a good deal of substance for this view.

Historians have long recognised that sexual relations between Iberian men and indigenous and African women occurred from early on. The first African slaves who were part of the conquest tended to be men, but significant numbers of African women were soon present in many areas of the Iberian colonies. As legal property of their masters, slave women were subject to extensive sexual abuse and enjoyed little practical protection from the courts or the Church. In 1580, one slave owner stated: 'It is not a sin to have sex with my slave woman because she is my property' (Powers 2005: 97). Municipal authorities 'totally ignored the sexual exploitation and abuse that occurred within the master's house' (Socolow 2000: 134).[8] Male slaves also suffered abuse: 'To rape a male slave was to feminise him – to conquer him both physically and psychologically' (Sweet 2003: 74).

While the overall picture drawn by historians tends to be one of sex as domination and female slaves as victims, these women could sometimes use sexual relations with a white man to gain some influence over their own destinies in what was a highly constrained and unequal situation. In relation to colonial Jamaica, Bush has argued that: 'White men created a black woman who essentially reflected their needs, economic or sexual' – this was a woman basically stereotyped as a sexual 'Sable Venus' or a working 'drudge', but who could be a 'she devil' if she stepped outside those roles. However, white men's fascination with the Sable Venus meant that 'paradoxically, women were able to "get on" in slave societies through using their sexuality as the "wives" of white men'; thus by the 1800s 'concubinage had become an essential survival strategy for some younger slave women' (Bush 2000: 762, 69). In Latin American too, 'sexual liaisons could benefit slave women' (Socolow 2000: 135).

With relations between Iberian men and indigenous women, there has been more debate about coercion and consent. Some scholars have downplayed the role of sexual abuse in these relations. It was the *membrus febrilis* (the fevered member) of the Spaniards that conquered Mexico rather than the sword or the microbe; it was the 'love-making' of these 'donjuanistas' that created a colonial society (R. C. Padden, cited in Wood 1998: 9). Mörner is a little more balanced in his assessment that the 'Spanish conquest of the Americas was a conquest of women' when he says that the Spaniards took 'the Indian girls by force and by peaceful means'; however, he goes on to say that 'the element of rape should not be overemphasised' and that 'probably the Indian women very often docilely complied with the conquistadores' desires' (Mörner 1967: 22, 23).

Other scholars contest these views, even while admitting that some unions were consensual. For them, 'sexual force was the primary relationship' between conquering men and conquered women, whether indigenous or African (Powers 2005: 96). Contemporary accounts by European men make plain that they rhapsodised about native female charms and described seductions or, quite possibly, rapes (Wood 1998). Around Quito, indigenous women were abducted in large numbers and forced into 'service' – economic but doubtless also sexual – in the homes of the city's Spanish population; indigenous women servants might also be 'gifted' in exchanges between notable Spaniards (Powers 2005). Gifts also occurred between indigenous communities and conquering forces as part of exchange relationships that cemented political alliances: noble-born Aztec or Inca women might actually marry elite Spanish men, in unions that often gave such men access to land and indigenous labour, while also promising protection and advancement for indigenous communities. These unions were consensual in one sense, but not only were the women apparently marrying at the behest of indigenous men, but also records left by Náhuatal-speaking men in Mexico show that they thought that it was 'prudent that we give ourselves to the men of Castile to see if that way they do not kill us' (cited in Wood 1998: 20). The famous case of 'La Malinche' probably fits into this category. A classic symbol in Mexican nationalist discourse of 'betrayal' by indigenous women when they consorted with the conquistadores, she was one of 20 women given to Cortés, the leader of the Spanish conquerors, in 1519. Doña Marina, as she is also known, became an interpreter and lover to Cortés and bore him a child, but it is also very likely that her choices were highly constrained: 'Her best hope for survival was to accept whatever situation was assigned to her and try to make herself useful and agreeable' (Frances Karttunen, cited in Wood 1998: 18).

Sexual abuse by clergy was also a significant problem that indigenous and other women (and young men) complained about. It was prosecuted by the Church and courts – but not always with great rigour: in 1587 one Inquisition official was arraigned in Lima on 216 charges of sexual misconduct and found guilty on five counts; he was later promoted to a higher Church office (Powers 2005: 99). Even in cases where the relationships were apparently consensual, the role of constraint and power differences is clear. Spurling documents the case of an elite cleric, accused of sodomy in 1595 and 1608. The first case concerned a young man who worked in an apothecary shop and with whom Dr González apparently took the active role; the younger man was executed, while the cleric was eventually released after a series of appeals to higher ecclesiastical authorities. In 1608, Dr González began a long relationship with a poor young man whom González looked after and indeed cohabited with over a long period and on whom he bestowed the title of Don. This man was tortured, imprisoned and exiled, while González again used successive appeals to higher courts to avoid punishment (Spurling 1998).

Spurling does not tell us whether Dr González's lovers were white or not, but Mott, using Inquisition records on accusations of sodomy for Brazil between 1591 and 1620, argues that white men used their status to dominate non-white men (Mott 1985). White men were the majority of those accused (61 per cent) and a majority of cases involved a relation between people of different colours. These small numbers do not indicate a clear trend: eight mulatto men were a passive partner for whites, while four were the active partner; other data show that white men could be passive partners (Nesvig 2001: 706–7). Mott (1994) admits that 'there are various examples of indigenous men and blacks who played the active role'. Lesbian relations do not seem to show a clear sexual-racial pattern.[9]

Trexler (1995) also focuses strongly on the use of sex as a tool of domination, but he argues that sex was used to feminise subordinate men, by forcing them into the role of passive recipients of active, conquering penetration. The use of anal rape and other techniques of literal and symbolic emasculation was, says Trexler, common to both Mediterranean and native American cultures. In the latter area, institutionalised cross-dressing and homosexuality – often centred on the figure of the berdache – were structured by political power: in Trexler's view, younger berdaches were sexual, economic and political resources for older men of power.[10] Among the Maya, too, native conquest discourse 'was centred around a portrayal of masculinity and power through the symbolic penetration of the defeated warriors by the victorious' (Sigal 2003a: 123).[11] Despite parallels between Iberian and some native American views on sodomy, the Iberians often viewed native American men as sodomites – partly due to their interpretation of widespread cross-dressing behaviour and partly due to seeing ethnic-racial others as sodomites. As sodomy was a 'nefarious sin', this provided a justification for conquest as well as effectively feminising the vanquished (Trexler 1995: 84).

Race, Sex and Desire in Conquest

Trexler comes up against the problem – of which he is aware – that many of his sources on native American practices of homosexuality were written by Spanish or American-born white observers (Horswell 2003, 2005). This raises the issue of representation: some observers did not 'see' much homosexual practice, although they did 'see' cross-dressing; some downplayed the issue of homosexuality in an effort to dignify indigenous cultures. Others saw homosexuality everywhere. The same problem arises with the question of coercion and consent in heterosexual, inter-ethnic relations: where does the balance lie between native women's 'docile compliance' and their coercion?

Gutiérrez (1991) runs into this question in his account of Pueblo sexuality and how it figured during conquest. As we saw above, he describes Pueblo sexual practices as open and relaxed. He also shows that the Spanish soldiers saw Pueblo women as licentious and unfaithful to their men, whom they saw as sodomites and unprotective of their women; the Franciscan friars documented the sexual abuses practised by the soldiers, but tried to impose European sexual and gender norms on the Pueblo. However, he also argues that 'because sanctity and sex were so closely related in the Pueblo world, it was common for men and women to give their bodies to persons they deemed holy' (Gutiérrez 1991: 50) and that native practices of dealing with angry spirits induced women to offer themselves sexually to the conquistadores who were initially seen as visiting spirits:

> The Pueblo women cooled the passion of the fierce fire-brandishing Spanish katsina [spirits] through intercourse, and by so doing, tried to transform and domesticate the malevolence of these foreign gods. But the Spaniards as a group would interpret their subjugation of the Pueblos as a supreme assertion of masculine virility, and, as such, would see 1598 as a sexual conquest of women. (Gutiérrez 1991: 51)

Gutiérrez has been accused of seeing Pueblo sexuality through the eyes of the conquistadores and the priests.[12] It is clear, however, that he is aware of the biased representation of indigenous sexuality by the Spanish; what is less clear is the extent to which this shapes his own description of the Pueblo of whom he says that, although they did not live a life of 'unbridled lust' as portrayed by the Spanish, they were 'sexually spirited' (Gutiérrez 1991: 72).

The important point is that Iberian preconceptions and fantasies clearly shaped the way they perceived indigenous peoples as Others: an important aspect of that othering was to see these peoples as sexually uncontrolled, which was both barbaric and exciting. As I argued in Chapter 2, in understanding the articulation of race and sex, it is useful to pay attention to the processes that shape desire and hate: the way the Iberians saw Others as sexually despicable but also desirable is important in grasping the role that sex played in racialised domination. Now, it is very possible that native sexual behaviour towards the conquistadores – whether due to local understandings of how to deal with unknown incomers through the exchange of services and gifts or to local (female) strategies of survival in the face of violent (male) dominance – fanned Iberian ideas about native licentiousness, but it seems clear that these ideas already existed in thinking about non-European others.

In Europe, 'medieval, like ancient Roman, thinkers conceived barbarians and wild men to be enslaved to nature, to be, like animals, slaves to desire and unable to control their passions' (White 1972: 20). There was a distinction between barbarians, who were thought to live collectively in some kind of social order outside the borders of civilised society, and wild men (or women), who were seen as solitary creatures, animal-like, usually living in the interstices of the civilised world (the forests, the mountains) and subject to no social order at all. Yet in practice barbarism and wildness were often interwoven ideas (ibid.: 19–20). Certainly, both categories shared in being the opposite of civilised. Unbridled sexuality was a key feature, as it was for the ancient Greeks: 'it is barbarians or non-Greeks who flaunt their sexuality quite shamelessly: and so Herodotus reports that the natives of the Caucasus region copulate in the open like animals' (Walcot 1998: 172).

In the same way, European ideas about Africa depicted it as a region saturated with lust (Bush 2000; Nederveen Pieterse 1992). Leo Africanus, a 'Spanish Moroccan Moor converted to Christianity', in about 1526 described the 'land of Negroes' thus: 'there is no Nation under Heaven more prone to Venery …

They have great swarms of Harlots among them; whereupon a man may easily conjecture their manner of living' (Jordan 1977: 33–4). Depictions of Moors were similarly sexualised throughout Europe, from Shakespeare's *Othello* to Iberian medieval poetry: 'the voyeuristic fantasy of imagined Oriental female sexuality is prevalent in Hispanic poems about *moras* [Moorish women]' (Vasvári 1999: 33).

Figure 1 Amerigo [Vespucci] discovers America. Drawing by Jan van der Straeten, circa 1580, after an engraving by Théodore Galle. © National Maritime Museum, Greenwich, London.

By the time of the conquest of the Americas, the wild man had come to symbolise not just fear and threat, but also the possible virtues of living at one with nature and, especially, the pleasures of erotic freedom, which the Greeks had projected onto mythical fauns and satyrs (White 1972: 25). Europeans approached indigenous Americans with the intertwined categories of barbarian and wild man in mind: images of native cannibals vied with images of innocents living in an Edenic paradise, but both linked to different facets of contemporary notions of wildness

(Robe 1972: 45–6). Existing ideas and fantasies about exotic and racialised Others – Moorish, African, wild, barbarian – informed and shaped Iberians' perceptions of indigenous Americans and predisposed them to see the natives as licentious. One foot soldier (actually a German mercenary) in the conquest of the Río de la Plata region[13] said of the local Jarayes women that they were 'very handsome and great lovers, affectionate and with ardent bodies, in my opinion' (Ulrich Schmidel, cited in Mörner 1967: 22).[14] Other contemporary sources reveal a powerful interest in indigenous women's nakedness, sexual attractiveness and supposed lust. The image of the explorer Amerigo Vespucci 'discovering' America has strong sexual overtones (Figure 1), while Vespucci himself asserted that the local women in the Caribbean were so fond of Christians that they 'debauch and prostitute themselves', while a Portuguese invader 'went into raptures about the local Brazilian women's "privy parts" (described in intimate detail) and how, "even when we examined them very closely, they did not become embarrassed"' (Wood 1998: 12, 14). A colonial drawing, first published in 1509 (Figure 2), shows an incident recounted by Vespucci in which a Spaniard is distracted by three naked indigenous women, while another woman is about to club him over the head from behind (ibid.). In this, and more generally, we can see the classic ambivalence attached to others, explored in Chapter 2: disgust (at perceived sexual excess) and fear (of cannibalism), but also fascination and desire (particularly around sexuality).

Sex was certainly an instrument of conquest, but one problem with an exclusive emphasis on sex as racialised domination is that it tends to assume that male desire emerges straightforwardly from the practice of domination itself and from the access to subordinate women (and men) that ensues. It is important to note that the male desire that drove sexual conquest did not emerge simply from the encounter between conquering males' instinctual lusts and the actual availability of subjugated people, but was already present in socially constructed dynamics of desire around exotic others who were 'naturally' different and were seen as both disgusting and desirable. The ambivalence of otherness in a context of hierarchy gave rise to pre-existing conceptions, which structured the process of conquest itself by shaping the way Iberian soldiers, priests and other invaders understood the people whose territories they were conquering.

Figure 2   Engraving from Amerigo Vespucci's *Quatuor Navigationes* (1509), reproduced from Todorov (1991: Fig. 8). By permission of Éditions Grasset et Fasquelle.

This brief look at the character of (male) Iberian sexual images and fantasies about others raises the question of indigenous and

black women's (and men's) desires and feelings about sexual
relations with ethnic others, which is unfortunately a subject on
which there is much less evidence. Rape, coercion and abuse were
widespread and the context in which all relationships existed
was, of course, structured by racial and gender hierarchy, but
various kinds of consensual relationships did exist: marriage,
concubinage, casual consensual sex.[15] The longevity of some of
the relations between Spanish conquistadores and their indigenous
lovers indicates that 'they combined mutual endearment with
mutual opportunity for both man and woman' (Socolow 2000:
35), although we have to be very cautious about evoking an
unrealistic image of racial and gender equality, given the power
differences involved. Homosexual relations between white masters
and their black slaves could be 'surprisingly affectionate' even if
they generally did not avoid the 'violence and coercion typical
of the system' (Vainfas 2008 [1997]: 11). On the other hand,
indigenous women in early colonial interracial unions, whether
coerced or chosen, often had to painfully negotiate two cultural
worlds and conflicting loyalties. One example of this was the
common practice of removing *mestizo* children from the care of
indigenous mothers deemed not suitable for raising the offspring
of Spanish men (Powers 2005: 76–8).

Formal marriages between Spaniards and indigenous women
became less frequent in the context of the increasing immigration
of Spanish women and patterns of informal concubinage became
the norm, unions which were 'the product of power relations
in which white men held the upper hand'; the women were the
victims of rape or they consented out of fear (Powers 2005: 91).
There remained the possibility that they might also consent from
desire or because they sought to improve their status and that of
their children. Indeed, some indigenous men saw this as the norm:
Guaman Poma, the indigenous Peruvian chronicler who reported
at length to the Spanish king on the state of the colonies in 1615,
said that 'All Indian women are ... above all great whores.... They
prefer to live as concubines of the Spaniards, and on occasion
with black and mulatto men, than marry an Indian commoner'

(cited in Powers 2005: 69). One senses that resentment may have coloured Guaman Poma's views!

In any event, it seems likely that indigenous and black women must have had very varied motives. An interesting example is that of a slave woman called Paula de Eguiluz, whose history appears in the Inquisitorial records of people accused of witchcraft (Maya Restrepo 2005: 599–615). She was a black slave born in Santo Domingo and, at age 13, given to a Spaniard, Otaco, who took her to Puerto Rico. Otaco's wife became jealous of her and she was sold to Joan de Eguiluz in Havana, moving with him to the copper mines near the city of Santiago in eastern Cuba. She had three children with him and was given privileges, such as the right to wear certain clothes reserved for whites and go to mass with the local whites. She was accused of witchcraft in 1624 and taken for trial to Cartagena (a city on the Caribbean coast of what is now Colombia), where she lived for many years. In her testimony to the Inquisition, she made it clear that she loved her owner, missed him when he was away and that some of her 'witchcraft' consisted in making cures for his ailments, by drawing on African and indigenous knowledge of magic and curing.

However much she loved her owner, the freedom she had to move around also allowed her to get together with other black and white men and women in celebrations held in isolated locations, where she danced and ate and where her companion *diablillo* (little devil) 'knew her carnally', a sexual experience which she said she did not enjoy. Paula also admitted to having sexual relations with other men whom she actively sought out, some of whom she had cured with herbal and magical remedies. It is difficult to interpret such Inquisitorial records for motive and emotion, but clearly Paula had a number of sexual relationships in which she, despite her slave status, managed a certain amount of autonomous action.

In contrast to Paula's case, the seventeenth-century Andean 'virgins' abjured all sexual relations and became sacred representatives of Andean gods in ways that evoked both the *aclla*, the virginal wives of the Inca sun god, and the Catholic Madonna. As sacred priestesses, they became active in nativist movements to challenge Church dominance and to reassert traditional Andean religious practices (Silverblatt 1994).

*   *   *

To summarise this section: sex was an instrument of conquest and a means by which domination was effected, above all by white men on indigenous, black and mixed-race women, but also on men in these categories – and also by non-white men on women in these same categories, as in the cases where indigenous men 'gave' indigenous women to Iberian conquerors. In this sense, race and sex 'fitted together' because sex was being used as a means of dominating categories that were racialised (in a seventeenth-century meaning of the term) and this occurred because existing patterns of gender inequality in Iberian societies meant that conquest included the domination of women and sexual access to their bodies. But I argued that race and sex also fitted together because Iberian notions of the other were deeply sexualised, even before the conquest, and those seen as 'naturally' and radically different were seen as sexually exciting as well as sexually degenerate.

The Regulation of Sexuality and Race: Building a New Social Order

Looking back to Chapter 2, other key aspects of the entanglement of sex with power were, first, the way in which white men maintained dominance through patriarchal control of white women and, second and closely related, the aspect that can broadly be called the regulation of sexuality. Sex was not only a means of conquest, but also a means of building and governing a new social and moral order, built out of basic ideas, drawn from Iberian life, about how a society should be run and the encounter of these ideas with the realities and resistances of indigenous social orders, African slavery and the emergence of new categories of mixed people (Borja Gómez 1996). It is, of course, impossible to draw a line between conquest and regulation, because power and control are intrinsic to both – and, as we shall see, white men's defence of 'their' women's sexuality operated in tandem with their privileged access to non-white women's sexuality – but it is possible to draw attention to the wider operations of power than those centred on rape, abuse and direct domination.

Creating a Moral Order: Religion, Witchcraft and Race

In Brazil, the Inquisition and the Crown worked hard to render the population more 'well-ordered' in a place widely viewed as a kind of 'purgatory', permeated by moral disorder (Mello e Souza 2003: 186). The Inquisition's 'attempt at moral organisation' in Brazil was based on a Manichean separation of good and evil in which the latter had to be rooted out (Piccini 1992: 76). In New Granada, the chronicler Brother Pedro Simón described indigenous settlements as 'ants' nests' rather than villages, because of lustfulness and the practice of polygamy, which gave rise to a 'multitude of people', among whom cannibalism and sodomy were widespread (cited in Borja Gómez 1996: 176). In this quest to organise and order a colony founded on the control of racialised others, sex was a key concern.

As we saw in Chapter 2, Foucault focuses on the period from the late eighteenth century as the time when an 'analytics of sexuality' became dominant and biopower began to centre on the regulation (and indeed invention) of 'sexuality' as a key to understanding social and personal life and a means of improving national populations. This does not mean that a concern with the regulation of sexuality did not predate that period. But rather than being expressed through a discourse of the science of sexuality, this concern focused instead on regulating marriage, kinship, the flesh and certain carnal acts, mainly through the operation of law and decree, with much less emphasis on the role of scientific knowledge.

From early on in colonial Latin America, the Church expressed a close interest in sex, as it did in Europe in this period: after all, adultery and lust were mortal sins (Lavrin 1989a; Wiesner-Hanks 1999). The Church 'insinuated itself into the domain of the family and sexuality, by controlling the rites of marriage and defining sexual and domestic sins'. Men and women brought problems in these realms to the Church, 'translating their domestic conflicts and sexual ambivalence into a religious discourse' (Behar 1989: 180). All residents of the colonies were subject to surveillance and denunciation and many white people were investigated, but the sexuality of indigenous, African and mixed-race people was a particular focus of interest. This was partly because the sexual morality of these people was deemed to be highly questionable, as we have seen: fornication, concubinage, adultery and sodomy were all sins believed to be widely practised among these classes of the population.

In addition, sexual misdemeanour was closely linked to religious deviance. Both the regular Church and the Inquisitions established in Lima and Mexico in 1569 and in Cartagena in 1610 – with occasional inquisitorial visits practised to Brazil – targeted many indigenous, black and mixed-race people, often women labelled as witches (a category which had already been a target of persecution in Europe). The key concern was with religious heterodoxy and, although a great deal of Inquisitorial attention was focused on *conversos* suspected of secretly practising Judaism or Islam, indigenous, African and mixed-race people were also likely to be prime suspects, because of presumed loyalties to 'pagan' beliefs and imperfect or rejected conversion to Christianity. In colonial Brazil, the term *mandingueiro* (from the West African ethnic name, Mandinka) became synonymous with sorcerer (Sansi-Roca 2007: 61 n. 1). Indigenous people in the Andes were subjected to the notorious 'extirpation of idolatry' campaigns of the seventeenth century, implemented by the bishops rather than the Inquisition. Specifically sexual offences were not necessarily a prime concern in all this: of the 350 offences investigated by the Inquisitorial official visiting northern Brazil in 1593, only 51 concerned bigamy and sodomy, while 299 concerned blasphemy, heresy and other religious matters (Mott 2003: 171). But religious heterodoxy and heresy were seen as closely intertwined with sexual misdemeanours. Many of the heresy and blasphemy cases in Brazil dealt with sexuality (Mott 2003) and, in colonial Mexico,

'Spaniards linked together the sexual and religious immorality of Indians', especially indigenous females (Lewis 2003: 111).

Witchcraft was a heavily sexualised realm. A lot of activity labelled as witchcraft involved attempts to attract a lover, control a spouse, and so on (Behar 1989; Sommer 2003). The witches who formed a key target of the Church's campaigns against idolatry were highly sexual beings; 'the Church explicated how woman's lust was the source from which the power of witches ultimately derived' (Silverblatt 1987: 166), and their supposed pacts with the devil often involved carnal knowledge (White 2005). Such witches were commonly indigenous, black or mixed-race women. In Brazil, little distinction was made between witchcraft and prostitution or sexual licence. At the 1610 trial of Maria Barbosa, a *parda* (mixed-race woman), the defendant's acts of sorcery were described alongside her acts of indecency: 'she turned her home into a bawdyhouse; procured women for men … She dishonoured her husband, "calling him a cuckold, and making him stay at the foot of the cot and sleeping with men in front of him"' (Mello e Souza 2003: 220). Much of the famous witch-finders' manual, the *Malleus Maleficarum* (1487), used by inquisitors in the colonies, was concerned with sexual matters (Piccini 1992: 80).

At the same time that colonial authorities were trying to create and run a colony which had a respectable moral and religious order, they were also attempting to govern a colony which depended on the subordinate labour of indigenous, black and mixed-race people. The original plan, especially in the Spanish colonies, was to create separate *repúblicas* for *indios* and *españoles*, physically and legally distinct spaces for each category; slaves formed another distinct category or 'caste'. From the beginning, this scheme was undermined by sexual relations between these three classes of people and the resulting offspring. *Mestizos* could initially be incorporated into the dominant category and for a time the offspring of whites and indigenous people were recognised as white and at times forcibly separated from their indigenous mothers (Mörner 1967: 27; Powers 2005: 78). But this threatened the exclusivity of the white category and its presumed purity of blood and was not a long-term option. The other option was to forcibly incorporate *mestizos* into the two subordinate categories and to some extent this also happened: the child of a slave mother was born a slave and the child of an indigenous mother could be classed as indigenous. In New Spain (Mexico) until the mid-1600s, the mixed population was generally incorporated into parental status categories (Seed 1988: 25).

But it required an enormous effort of repression and segregation to fully enforce a long-term system in which each racial category was clearly defined, most people were securely assigned to one category and the subordinate categories absorbed – in a classificatory sense – all the products of mixture. The pressures generated by subordinate people seeking to escape the strictures of oppression were very hard to contain fully. In the New World context, a system of segregated containment like this only really emerged in the US slave states and even then did not become fully-fledged until the nineteenth century (Foner and Genovese 1969; Harris 1974; Marx 1998). In the US, although sexual relations certainly occurred between whites, slaves and native Americans, the offspring of these unions were generally assigned to the subordinate category and, as a rule, not socially recognised by their white fathers. Although mixed-race people were at times accorded some institutional status as an intermediate social category, this possibility declined over time and the tendency was towards the maintenance of three separate and well-defined racial categories.

In the Iberian colonies, the conditions of colonial life – among other things, the relatively small numbers of whites, the early scarcity of white women, the lack of control over large areas of the territory, the legal measures that allowed slaves to buy their freedom – meant in the long term not only that *mestizos* of different kinds were socially recognised as distinct from either parent, but also that a whole variegated set of mixed people began to occupy an intermediate role in society and, indeed, become a majority in several areas by the eighteenth century.

This resulted in a stratified society, in which whites occupied the top place, *indios* and slaves were at the bottom (although these two categories were of distinct status, as *indio* was, on paper at least, a protected legal category), while the middle strata were occupied by a range of legally free, non-white and often mixed people, known in the Spanish colonies as *castas* (castes, breeds). The so-called *casta* paintings of eighteenth-century New Spain (Mexico) depicted an elaborate system, with named types of people and labels for different kinds of mixed offspring – a caption might read 'From Spaniard and Black Woman, Mulata' (Figure 3). Several complex tables existed, listing up to 16 degrees of mixture and their names (Katzew 2004; Mörner 1967: 58). These fanciful systems were reduced in practice to simpler classifications centred on terms such as *mestizo, mulato, pardo*, with many regional variants. In this social order, racialised genealogy was very important, but not definitive. Occupation and spouse's status could shape a person's racialised classification in Church and official records – a classification that was often referred to as part of a more general status judgement of *calidad* (quality) in Spanish America. And there were often disputes about whether a person was truly white or had some 'taint' of indigenous or African blood (Cope 1994; McCaa 1984).

The governance of this racialised social order, focused on protecting white elite positions and maintaining the subordination of indigenous, black and mixed-race people, was a complex process in which race and sex articulated – in the sense outlined in Chapter 2 – to produce a specific set of practices and structures of power. In colonial Peru, the bureaucracies of Church, Inquisition and Crown together tried to construct a political and moral order – which also entailed a sexual order – while instituting racial categories at the same time:

> Peru's inquisitors (as little gods) were producing the 'state' at the same time as they were inscribing race thinking into institutional practice. And the processes were remarkably similar. Just as the inquisitors (among others) were conjuring diverse government institutions into an abstract state, diverse social relationships were being conjured into abstract race categories. By the seventeenth century, magistrates and other functionaries were routinely dividing people into Spanish-Indian-black boxes as a matter of course. (Silverblatt 2004: 18)

The institutions that were pursuing witches or prosecuting religious heterodoxy were imposing a moral-sexual order and at the same time sorting people into racial categories, especially because those who fell into the categories of indigenous, black and mixed-race were commonly seen as religiously and sexually heterodox.

Figure 3   A *casta* painting from eighteenth-century New Spain. The caption reads 'De Español y Negra, Mulata' (From Spaniard and Black Woman, Mulata). By permission, Museo de América, Madrid.

Purity of Blood and Sexual Virtue: Honour in Marriage

The articulation of race and sex is most plainly seen in the way ideas about *limpieza de sangre* and racialised genealogy entwined with ideas about honour in the realm of marriage and the family. The empirical manifestation of this was the general practice of racial endogamy in Spanish and Portuguese America during the colonial period, above all for the elite (Kuznesof 1993; Nazzari 1996; Powers 2005: 90; Seed 1988: 25). In New Mexico between 1694 and 1846, the majority of people married someone of the same racial status (within the categories of Spanish, mixed and indigenous). However, within each racial status group, these patterns varied considerably: Spanish men were the most endogamous and, in 1750, their intermarriage rate was 21 per cent (dropping to 13 per cent in 1790); two categories of mixed-race men, *mulatos* and *coyotes*,[16] had rates of 72 per cent and 75 per cent, while those classified as *indio* had a rate of 37 per cent (Gutiérrez 1991: 288–91). In the Brazilian town of Vila Rica do Ouro Preto (Minas Gerais) in 1804, only 9 per cent of marriages were interracial (Ramos 1979: 501).

Of course, marriage was only part of the story and there were diverse patterns of informal unions, involving everything from rape to casual sex and long-term concubinage (the usual term for an informal union). Among the *castas*, formal marriage was less common and people frequently lived 'in sin', to the consternation of the Church. There were also many informal unions between white men and non-white women. During an ecclesiastical visit to Venezuela in the 1770s, Bishop Martí encountered 300 reports of fornication and concubinage, of which 174 involved a white man and a non-white woman; in contrast, the 1792 census showed that of 3500 formal marriages registered, only 100 involved white with non-white partners (Waldron 1989: 158, 63). In seventeenth-century São Paulo, interracial marriage was often of poor European men with rich *mestiza* women of the local elite, in which the man's racial status compensated for his poverty (Nazzari 1996: 107). In contrast, in Vila Rica in 1737–38, in cases of concubinage involving a slave, 75 per cent were between a slave woman and her own master (Kuznesof 1991: 247).

Racial endogamy in marriage combined with informal interracial unions outside marriage were not *primarily* a result of direct enforcement by the state or the Church, at least until the late eighteenth century, even if both sets of institutions did not generally approve of interracial marriage. Indeed, the fact that concubinage was both illegal and a sin should, theoretically, have encouraged racial intermarriage. Rather, the key driver underlying these patterns was the elite's concern with honour and purity of blood. This concern was highly gendered in the sense that a man's and a family's honour depended on the sexual virtue (chastity, continence) of wives, mothers and daughters, while a man's honour was not damaged simply by having sex with, or even having children by, women, white or non-white, outside marriage (Johnson and Lipsett-Rivera 1998a); although his honour easily could suffer if he was accused of having sex with men, even if he was the active partner. Honour was established not only by virtue, but also by status, including racial condition as manifest in genealogy and purity of blood. Honour as status was very hierarchical, with the uppermost strata, and ultimately the king, having the most. Honour as status and honour as virtue were intertwined: people of low status (and this included by default indigenous, black and most mixed-race people) were likely to have less virtue too: less formal marriage, more informal unions, less chastity; often they had less of the private property the control of which was so linked to the control of marriage and inheritance. Less controlled marriage practices also meant higher rates of illegitimacy.

Legitimacy of birth was a vital prerequisite of honour and the sexual virtue of women was necessary to establish legitimate offspring and heirs. Because of patterns of racial endogamy, being *mestizo* was strongly associated with being illegitimate, but, as noted earlier, there was also a longstanding Iberian tradition of being able to petition the Crown (or, in Brazil, the Palace of Justice) for a formal legitimation – the *gracias al sacar* – that made a person legitimate for public purposes (Nazzari 1989; Twinam 1999). There was also in the American colonies a practice by which a person could petition to be considered white for legal and public purposes, such as holding public offices that were not open to non-whites (Twinam 1999: 307). Not surprisingly, such petitions were usually made by people for whom such issues really mattered, that is, illegitimate white people or mixed-race people aspiring to high status. In this sense, a stain on someone's honour as virtue (illegitimacy, the result of dishonourable behaviour by parents) could be redressed by a public dispensation from above of honour as status. Another example is that of Dr Gonzalez, the homosexual cleric described earlier, whose honour as status allowed him to evade the dishonour of his unvirtuous sexual conduct (Spurling 1998).

These loopholes in the system introduced some flexibility, while people adopted other tactics to preserve honour, such as concealing an unwanted pregnancy. A compelling example is that of a woman of the eighteenth-century regional elite in Puebla, Mexico, who had an illegitimate child by an elite male (Twinam 1999: 147–50). She passed it off as the child of her maid, a *morisca* (a term used for black-white mixed-race), and this public fiction was maintained for 50 years, while in private and among close friends, the child was recognised as a white member of the family. In 1785, the by then middle-aged daughter received the official legitimation she had applied for, which redefined her as the legitimate child of her elite parents and thus also reclassified her as white. These examples show flexibility, but they also highlight the power of the intertwined values of legitimacy, virtue, honour and whiteness that the elite, above all, wanted to protect and preserve for themselves. The mixed and lower classes, by default, could not aspire to such values, even if they prided themselves on behaving with honour. As just one example, marriage was not common and although informal unions – concubinage – might be accepted as normal practice among the mixed classes, Vainfas (1989) argues that, for Brazil at least, people still recognised the value difference between concubinage and formal marriage.

The key point here is that a system of racial domination operated through patriarchal norms governing sex and gender that maintained elite privilege and concentrated values of whiteness and material resources, passed on through legitimate inheritance, in the hands of the elite. At the same time, men of the dominant class could, with relative impunity, have sexual (but rarely marital) relationships with women of the subordinate classes. The regulation of racialised sexuality thus intertwined with patterns of sexual conquest. Elite men kept their families' position by controlling who married whom, ensuring legitimate succession and thus keeping control of private property and power in confined circles. This meant control over women's sexuality. Such control and elite positioning also linked powerfully to ideas of purity of blood:

genealogical connections were known, elites married within their class. And because social position in the hierarchy was defined in part by purity of blood, the sexual behaviour of women was crucial and subject to control, as they were considered the agents who could bring contamination into the family and into the elite. If men's semen, and thus symbolically their blood, moved outside these circles, this was not thought to cause internal harm to family or class. Although arguably prefigured in Iberia in relation to Jews and Moors, in the Americas, this articulation of ideas of blood and sex/gender took on more clearly racial form, in which racialised lower classes were dominated. The combination of defending elite families in terms of female honour and virtue and legitimate marriage, alongside informal sexual relationships between elite men and lower-class women is the key to the articulation of race and sex as a form of dominance and regulation.

The articulation of race and sex shows a dynamic process of mutual constitution: sexual virtue (sex) was important to status; blood connections and purity of blood (race) also defined status; what connected sex and race was the process of regulating sexual exchanges through marriage (while sexual exchanges outside marriage enacted the dominant position of white men). This dynamic of mutual constitution is shown further by the way that sex/gender norms changed as the racial order also changed over time. As the class of mixed people grew – becoming numerically dominant in some cases – and as some of them became wealthy and aspired to higher status, the white elite began to feel threatened and to pay more attention to racial status.[17]

Gutiérrez (1991: 193) shows that in a series of matrimonial investigations between 1693 and 1846 in New Mexico, racial labels were infrequently recorded before 1760, but became the main way of recording a person's social status thereafter.[18] In the 1770s, legal reforms were introduced in Spanish America which controlled marital choice in much more direct ways. Previously, the Church had overseen marriage and dealt with disputes that arose when, for example, parents objected to their child's choice of marriage partner on the grounds of social or racial inferiority. The Church generally privileged the sanctity of marriage and the free choice of the individual and tended to find in favour of the couple, against the parents' wishes. (It is worth noting that this qualifies in some respects Silverblatt's implication that the Church and the state formed a coherent front in their race thinking.) In 1776, as part of the Bourbon reforms, new legislation was enacted directed at making sure people chose 'an appropriate partner': this put the control of marriage into the civil courts and allowed parental priorities much greater scope. The 1778 extension of the law from Spain to the Americas explicitly excluded non-whites from its operation (although they were included in an 1805 modification of the law). In 1805 a new decree required the permission of the civil authorities for a racially mixed marriage (Martinez-Alier [Stolcke] 1989 [1974]: 92, 12). This effectively restricted even more the possibility of interracial marriage. In late colonial Buenos Aires, racial inequality accounted for one third of the reasons for parental opposition to marriages and the judge sided with the parents in about half the cases (Shumway 2001: 202). For Brazil, there were similar legislative changes in 1772 and 1775 (Nazzari 1991: 131) and, in late eighteenth-century Brazil, the Church dealt with cases of interracial concubinage by separating the partners rather than making them marry, although it had the power to do so and thus enforce Church ideals of virtue (Nazzari 1996).

There is some debate about the changing nature of patriarchal control at this time. Seed (1988) contends that a shift can be detected from an earlier colonial emphasis on honour as virtue, in which the key idea was to marry virtuously, towards an eighteenth-century notion of honour as status, in which the key idea was to marry a social equal. This shift, driven by increasing economic growth and dynamism – in a word, early forms of capitalism – led to patriarchal control of women. Twinam (1999) counters that the shift is not so evident and that status and virtue were always intertwined, thus implying that patriarchy already structured sex/gender relations. But there is no disputing the fact that, by the middle of the eighteenth century, the elite had become more concerned with questions of racial stratification, that marriage choices became more restricted after the 1770s, and that parental opposition and the authorities limited interracial marriages in ways which implied increased control over women in elite or aspiring elite families. The concern with racial control thus shaped the way sex/gender norms operated.

Resisting Governance through Race and Sex

The regulation of race and sexuality was by no means a straight-forward process. Of course, the history of colonial Latin America is full of instances and processes of resistance to domination. This could take the form of outright contestation in the form of insurrection – slave revolts, indigenous rebellions, popular uprisings. There were practices that directly challenged colonial rule: slave flight and the setting up of refugee slave communities known as *palenques* (Spanish) or *quilombos* (Portuguese); nativist movements in the Andes that sought to re-establish indigenous ways of life, particularly religious ones; and African-derived religious practices.[19] Sometimes people lived largely outside the control of colonial authorities: the freed black ex-slaves of the Chocó province of New Granada (Colombia), who made up 61 per cent of the local population by 1808, had minimal contact with the tiny nuclei of colonial rule in the isolated province (Sharp 1976). Sometimes, people struggled for land and other rights within the structure of colonial rule (Rappaport 1998).

This variety points towards the highly complex issue of the extent to which, within societies dominated by hegemonic values, subordinate people actively resist domination through confrontation; or develop truly alternative values and cultures of resistance, or undermine dominant structures by using 'weapons of the weak' such as recalcitrance, foot-dragging and insubor-dination (Scott 1985); or accept dominant values in principle but live according to divergent everyday realities, the simple existence of which challenges dominant norms; or strive to achieve dominant values in myriad ways that themselves constitute a form of resistance to subordinate status. All these things occur, but it is an empirical question – and a matter of historical interpretation – as to the balance between them. We are interested, specifically, in how governing articulations of race and sex – particularly those around honour – were resisted or undermined. As honour was such a gendered concept, it is evident that the sorts of resistance or undermining that I describe below also operated in strongly gendered ways.

For a start, elite people continued to marry interracially in some cases. The data for Buenos Aires, cited above, indicate that in half the cases where parents opposed marriage because of racial inequality, the judge found against them (Shumway 2001). In 1790 in New Mexico, also mentioned above, even after the 1776 law, 13 per cent of white men married a non-white (Gutiérrez 1991). In the Cuban archives for the period 1807–82, of 199 applications for marriages that involved partners of distinct racial categories, about a quarter had been opposed by the parents, which means three-quarters had not. Only two-thirds of the applications recorded the outcome, but of these about two-thirds were granted permission. Some of these would have been marriages among the non-white classes, as racialised and other status distinctions were made within these strata and parents might object to the marriage of, say, their mulatto son to a darker-skinned woman. Genealogical distance from slave origins was also a concern (Martinez-Alier [Stolcke] 1989 [1974]: 14, 63, 93–4). But some – if only a few – were between elite people (usually men) and others, partly because men outnumbered women among whites, while the reverse was true among non-whites. Some of these marriages formalised an existing relationship of concubinage, probably ones which had resulted in children. Such intermarriage indicates a process of social mobility for mixed-race people (usually women), who were able to contract formal marriages with white people of the elite (usually men), presumably partly because they had the economic status to sustain their ambitions. These interracial marriages challenged strict racial hierarchy and gave non-white women and their children access to some honour, via their white husbands, but the challenge was in the end strongly gendered and ultimately reinforced the symbolic value of white maleness.

Second, non-white women's honour was often at risk from white men, who could seduce them or have extramarital relationships with them. Yet such relationships might also mean access to valuable economic and social resources for her and her children, not least of which would be a lighter skin colour for her offspring. White men were reinforcing dominant values of race and sex, by seducing yet very rarely marrying non-white women, but their actions were also complicating the racial aspect of those values by contributing to the expanding population of mixed-race people who might in due course articulate some claims to whiteness. Men's extramarital sex was not thought to impugn their personal honour, but in the longer term, it could begin to destabilise the security of elite status as a whole by helping create a mixed class from which would emerge individuals who aspired to the honour these men claimed as a birthright. Elite men's illegitimate offspring by non-white women could benefit from some attenuated form of paternal recognition which could help them to progress. Again, the undermining of racial hierarchy obeyed a gendered pattern and reinforced white male dominance; and while the mixed class that emerged would generate both men and women who aspired to upwards mobility, this too would be mediated by gender patterns that gave non-white women better access, via white men, to some forms of social climbing.

Third, notions of honour were often very important to the non-white classes, even if honour was presumed to accrue to high status. For coloured Cubans, ex-slaves in Brazil and plebeian sectors in Buenos Aires and Mexico, the ideals of honourable behaviour were very important, even if these people did not publicly claim the term *honor* (Boyer 1998; Johnson 1998; Lauderdale Graham 1998; Martinez-Alier [Stolcke] 1989 [1974]). While this attests to the hegemonic status of the idea of honour, in that many people agreed on the importance of this cultural value, it also indicates that the white elite had difficulty monopolising honour for themselves. Non-white people also claimed honour, albeit in tacit ways. In doing so, they might subtly alter these values or express them in a certain form. In colonial Buenos Aires, working-class men and women defended their personal and family honour, but the men in particular did so by resorting to violence much more readily than elite men (Johnson 1998). Fights were often with other men, but violence could also be directed against a man's 'own' women if he felt they were threatening his honour. In colonial Mexico, women attempted to limit such absolute assertions of male authority, partly by pressuring men to live up to the image of the good patriarch who provided for and defended his family (Stern 1995: 299–302).

Fourth, although dominant values of honour and morality held great sway, the difficulty of fully realising these values for the majority of the population meant that, in practice, life based on different practices became the norm for large sectors of the population. Informal unions not ratified by marriage, successive consensual unions, illegitimacy, single motherhood, abandonment by male spouses, female-headed households (which formed about one-third of all households in places such as Lima and Mexico City (Powers 2005: 130)), negligible or small properties to inherit or be given in dowries, a highly mixed racial milieu in which questions of racial and class status were more fluid than for the elite, a religious life often shaped by African and indigenous as well as popular Christian ritual practices – all these things were a common aspect of life for much of the plebeian population in colonial society. There were also frequent transgressions of sexual norms: premarital sex, fornication, elopement, concubinage, adultery, incest and rape (although these also occurred in the upper classes and included many whites) (Lavrin 1989b). Sometimes, plebeian people seem to have developed distinctive cultural values. Consensual unions were very common among plebeian Mexico city-dwellers, for example, and they seem to have been accepted as a cultural norm. Having children out of wedlock did not necessarily bar a woman from later marriage: 'plebeians apparently had less regard for female chastity than the elite' (Cope 1994: 69). It may be, however, that this apparent acceptance was *faute de mieux*, making a virtue out of necessity, as it were, and certainly marriage remained a culturally valued form. Cross-cutting the existence of different values and codes between classes was gender itself: as indicated above, women and men took different perspectives on codes of honour: for a man, honour might depend strongly on the power of his authority; for women, it might depend more on providing for the family.

In other cases, plebeians used the very values of colonial society in relation to sex/gender to protect themselves from colonial oppression and achieve some status. Plebeians, and especially women, might actively rebel – in riots, for example – when they felt that colonial authorities had seriously reneged on their unwritten duty to act as a kind of benevolent patriarch towards the poorer classes (Stern 1995: 302–8). In the case of an indigenous woman abused and beaten by a hacienda foreman in 1785 Mexico, her husband complained and testified that 'Although she is an Indian, she is a married woman' (Boyer 1998: 165). Some seventeenth-century Mexican female slaves demanded the right to marry and labelled a refusal of this by a given owner as mistreatment (ibid.: 162). Another late colonial Mexican case involved a man who first denounced his slave wife for adultery and then closed ranks with her, denouncing instead the hacienda bosses who had mistreated and whipped her (Stern 1995: 129). Notions surrounding the protected status of married women and their claim to respect (and thus implicitly some kind of honour) were being deployed to contest mistreatment.

The case of a freed slave woman who petitioned the courts for a divorce from her husband in 1850s Rio de Janeiro shows how an African ex-slave was using the courts and norms about marriage and proper treatment of wives to protect her position in an oppressive slave society. Her complaint was mostly about him, his abuse and his domineering ways – as such she was contesting dominant gender norms which expected her acquiescence – but it was also about the expectation that she help to buy his freedom in ways expected by colonial slave society. Her economic position was of particular concern: although she emphasised the physical harm she suffered, she spoke 'most often and always hotly about money' (Lauderdale Graham 1998: 225). A rather different case, mentioned earlier in this chapter, is that of the 'Andean virgins' (Silverblatt 1987: 197–210, 1994), who adopted values of chastity linked to religious images of devout virginity that derived both from Incan models of virginal servants of the sun god and Christian models of virginal nuns. The Andean virgins, however, dedicated themselves to nativist movements that sought to reinstate Inca traditions. Silverblatt argues that their virginal status not only made them pure and thus fit to minister to native gods, but also protected them from colonial interference, whether in the form of male lust or the vigilance of the authorities (1994: 270).

A clearer instance of a subculture that challenged dominant norms of sex and gender was the existence of 'communities of sodomites' in colonial cities. Mott (2003: 191) argues for 'hints of an embryonic gay sub-culture' in Brazil and, while others question his approach as 'essentialist' or driven by his political gay agenda (Nesvig 2001; Sigal 2003b), it seems clear that networks of homosexual men existed which allowed them to find partners for sex on a regular basis – Mott gives the example of one notorious sodomite who had sex with a man on average every ten days. However, while the active partner in male same-sex practices might not be stigmatised as much as the passive, and while male homosexuals might be recognised figures in local areas, all forms of male homosexual practice were despised and liable to persecution. (Lesbianism was rarely a cause for concern for most of the colonial period.[20]) If sodomites clearly contested sex and gender norms – albeit the active/passive distinction tended to reinforce gendered ideas of dominance – the racial aspect of homosexual practice is much less clear. As we have seen, it can be argued that white men used their position to dominate non-white men: overall, 'sexual obsession, homo or hetero, was a seigniorial privilege' (Mott 2003: 187). But the data are too scant to be certain about the extent to which homosexual practices reinforced or undermined racial hierarchy: sometimes non-white men were the passives, but sometimes white men were.

Ambivalence, Anxiety and Othering in Race and Sex

In Chapter 2, I argued that approaches to understanding the articulation of race and sex that focused on domination and regulation had some difficulty in grasping the widespread presence of ambivalence in this articulation – that is, the coexistence of hate, loathing and fear with love, desire and fascination. I linked this to processes of self formation in relation to others, which tended to give rise, in different ways according to cultural and historical contexts, to ambivalent feelings in relation to others (and self). Since self and other formation processes are strongly gendered, when clear male/female gender differences exist, and even more so when these are deeply hierarchical, ambivalence is likely to be pronounced. It is really a matter of speculation as to whether pre-colonial and colonial Iberian processes of self and other formation led to particular forms of ambivalence, but there is little doubt that there were powerful conceptual distinctions made between males and females and that women were seen as highly ambivalent figures, lustful and sinful on the one hand, but venerated as mothers and virgins on the other (Bellini 1989: 51–61). People identified as others, such as Moors, were also sexually ambivalent: desirable, yet feared. It is also clear that such ambivalences existed in colonial Latin America towards those identified as other. Of course, ambivalence can derive in part from the colonial situation itself: it is partly a consequence of the quandary of colonial rule, which is 'the paradoxical need to enculture the colonised and encourage mimesis while, at the same time, upholding and maintaining the difference that legitimises colonisation' (Carolyn Dean, cited in Lewis 2003: 8). This quandary leads to tactics that create both distance and proximity. But I believe that the ambivalence also has deeper roots and this is indicated by the fact that it tends to focus on realms of sexuality and fantasy; and that it frequently involves a desire for the very thing that is seen as most different and threatening, rather than something that is 'encultured'.

Earlier in this chapter, I referred to the sexualised images that Iberian men had of native American and African people, especially women. This attitude, which had roots in pre-colonial European conceptions of others, was strongly tinged with ambivalence: such sexuality was both disgusting in its perceived lack of control, its inclinations towards sodomy and the dangers it posed to Iberian men (who might fall prey to it) and also fascinating in its licentious-ness and promise of delights. In Latin America, this ambivalence was most strongly seen in the areas of witchcraft, magic and inquisitorial and Church incursions into sexual transgression, in which non-white people, especially women, figured large. On the one hand, magic and sexual deviation – which, as we have seen, were closely linked in the popular and religious imagination – were persecuted and stigmatised. On the other hand, there is evidence that both religious and lay people had a fascination for black, indigenous and mixed-race sexuality and magical powers. For modern Colombia, Taussig (1980b; 1987) has described this fascination and especially the attribution of strong magical and healing powers to black and indigenous people, above all the *indios* who were seen as most wild and savage. For colonial New Granada, he notes that 'female slaves served as healers to such exalted personages as the bishop of Cartagena and the inquisitors themselves' (1980a: 42): the very black women whom the religious authorities might easily persecute as witches and sexual deviants were also recognised for their healing powers. The slave Paula de Eguiluz, whose case I mentioned earlier in this chapter, had a clientele of 'European women and free *mulatas*' for her love magic: she continued to sell her services even while serving out her sentence for witchcraft in the hospital of Cartagena (Maya Restrepo 2005: 602). For Mexico, 'well-off white women ... had close contacts, even friendships, with Indian women, often cast in the role of magical specialists in the colony' and in general, 'Paradoxically, the powerless and conquered ... were viewed as having the most dangerous occult powers' (Behar 1989: 192, 94). In New Mexico, women often sought out mixed-race and indigenous love magic specialists, whom they thought could help control their husbands (Gutiérrez 2007). Just as the Church offered both persecution and restitution, the 'witches' offered both diabolical, destructive magic and healing powers (Lewis 2003: 8). And the fact that the Church clearly believed strongly in the reality and efficacy of witches and the devil lent great weight to their powers.

It is one thing to make use of the healing or love magic powers of black, indigenous and mixed-race witches and another to want to have sex with them or with non-white women in general. The evidence is that many white men did have sex with such women – and generally avoided marrying them – but it is difficult to know from the evidence available whether this was merely as a result of their accessibility for these men in the colonial social order or also because their ambivalent quality lent them a special sexual fascination for these men. I would argue that the mystique surrounding non-white women's (and men's) sexuality and the associated ideas of magical powers, both of which derived in part from the way ideas of the other are formed in the development of the self and then linked to real others in a colonial context, must have played a significant role. The evidence I cited earlier of the way the early conquerors saw indigenous women points in this direction. Concrete evidence from the main colonial period is harder to come by, as data are generally drawn from Church, Inquisition and legal records, which do not generally furnish direct evidence of sexual obsession.

A further area of interest is the sexual behaviour of the clergy. Inquisitors may have been fascinated with the sexuality of the non-white women they investigated, but they were unlikely to say so explicitly or do anything publicly about it. Even if records do attest to their use of female slave healers, I have not come across reports of inquisitors having sex with witches or other women accused of misdeeds, although Tortorici (2007: 317) speculates about the 'rape' effected by the inquisitorial male gaze. There are, however, plenty of records of other clergy having sexual relationships, often of a coercive nature, with women and (usually young) men. This was something that the Andean indigenous chronicler Felipe Guaman Poma railed against in his text *Nueva corónica y buen gobierno* (1615), which detailed all the abuses suffered by the native population of the Andes. These sexual relations are usually described in terms of a simple and hypocritical abuse of power and undoubtedly this is key aspect. Priests were able to 'solicit' in the context of the confessional, at the same time as they were able to quiz confessees about their sexual behaviour and thoughts (Lavrin 1989b: 38, n. 34; Wiesner-Hanks 1999: 119). Priests were powerful figures who had the ability to punish subordinates and shape their lives in important ways.

But it is also interesting to look into the dynamics of religious sexual desire. Piccini (1992) takes a standard Freudian line in analysing the inquisitors. She argues that their religious vows obliged them to repress their own sexuality, which, however, constantly threatened them with temptation, incarnated in the bodies of women, creating a deep-seated anxiety around sex and women. This was then projected onto the scapegoat figure of the witch as a super-sexed female who threatened their chastity and menaced men in general. Piccini notes that witches were thought to castrate men, collecting their penises and keeping them in a box. Witches were accused of making men impotent and the records of the Inquisition in Spain recorded cases of witches who kept castrated male members (Behar 1989: 185). The Freudian argument is undeniably persuasive in some respects and it certainly underwrites a notion of ambivalence, but it suffers from the weakness that male desire is assumed simply to exist automatically, in a 'hydraulic' model of sexuality (see Chapter 2) in which desire just wells up and, if blocked in one place, emerges in another. Even if we may never fully know how inquisitors' desires were shaped, we must assume that they were influenced by social processes and cultural symbols and did not just exist, pre-culturally, only to be repressed and displaced.

Gutiérrez has some interesting thoughts about the Franciscan friars charged with the spiritual conversion and welfare of the colonised Pueblo in New Mexico. He notes their asceticism, which abhorred lust above all, but he also describes the eroticised symbolism of the discourse of union with Jesus, talked of as a marriage between the female soul and the bridegroom Christ in which the former entreated the latter to 'kiss me' and 'enflame me and embrace me totally with the fire of your love'. This, leavened with masochistic descriptions of Christ's agony on the cross and the need to purge sexual desire by self-flagellation, added up to a heady brew, which can be seen as a specific, religiously inflected configuration of male (and, in other contexts, female) desire.[21] The Franciscans despised Pueblo sexuality, which seemed to them sinful and corrupt, yet Gutiérrez argues that their own religious beliefs had some parallels in linking sacredness and sex (although, for the Franciscans, in self-consciously repressed ways). However much the Franciscans were shocked by indigenous sexuality, it is clear that many of the friars also desired Pueblo women, and by the 1660s it was reported that 'all the pueblos are full of friars' children' and that many friars had indigenous concubines (Gutiérrez 1991: 123) – a practice that was common in Europe too, at least among secular clergy (Wiesner-Hanks 1999: 118).[22] I would argue, albeit speculatively, that the combination of religiously inflected sexual desire with already ambivalent ideas around the sexuality of Pueblo people as other must have created a particularly powerful emotional structure of ambivalence in which the tensions between religious chastity and sexual desire were manifested through relationships of colonial dominance which gave privileged access to women who were seen as both depraved and beguiling. Men who already experienced a strong tension between sexual repression and a sexual expression sublimated into religious channels may have encountered a deep affective charge in the ambivalence surrounding women (and men) who were defined as sexually debased but also sexually liberated and who were moreover in a situation of subordination that made them into potential objects for sexual expression. This, I would say, helped construct the idea of indigenous people as a repository of power – power that was both destructive and healing.

For the New Mexican context, Gutiérrez also provides information on the realm of the 'intimate', where what Stoler calls the 'tense and tender ties' of colonial ambivalence operated (Stoler 2001, 2002). He describes the *genízaros* (indigenous slaves) taken in war, Hispanicised and urban-dwelling, many of them females working as servants in respectable households, where they were subject to abuse and ill-treatment, including sexual abuse. These people were, in the eighteenth century, increasingly the target of racial hatred, and seen as particularly child-like, bestial, depraved, licentious and speaking mangled Spanish. They were the 'enemy within', who defined the boundaries between Spanish/white and Pueblo/indigenous (Gutiérrez 1991: 179). The most reviled people were also those on whom the respectable citizens depended, including for intimate services such as wet-nursing, and their owners often referred to them as sons and daughters. Indigenous in origin but uprooted by slavery from their communities, living in towns and speaking Spanish, yet still seen as bestial in nature, these interstitial figures were highly ambivalent, needed yet hated at the same time. They were also the target of many of the witchcraft accusations made by Spanish New Mexicans (Gutiérrez 2007).

The contradictory emotions invested in these relationships between Spanish men and non-white women are well illustrated in the case of Fray Diego Núñez, who was the prior of a monastery near Mexico City (Behar 1989: 195–9). In 1733 he accused his *mulata* slave of bewitching him. Her motive was, he said, because he had caught her in the act of having sex with a young painter who lived in the monastery, and had scolded her severely. Her sorcery targeted his body, especially everything to do with urination and defecation, which had become very painful and afflicted by all sorts of strange symptoms. She relied on her proximity to him in the domestic realm to collect his hair and other bodily substances and then introduce all manner of magical items into his food. The prior suspected her magical involvement in his ailments, had her beaten and sent to work in a sweatshop. There was no suggestion in the records that he had sexual contact with her (he was after all bound by an oath of chastity and we only have his account of the matter), but Behar notes that their relationship was 'almost like that of husband and wife' in its domesticity and intimacy and, of course, it was a sexual transgression that started the whole business. Tellingly, the prior reported that one of the effects of the sorcery was the appearance around his anus of lesions or growths that had '"transmuted the lower posterior to look like that of the female sex"': his slave had literally feminised him (Behar 1989: 197, 98). The prior went to a *mulata* healer, but was dismayed when he found out from another Spanish woman, who was using her services, that this healer too dealt in sexual witchcraft.

What is striking about this story is the tense and intimate coexistence of the prior's mastery with his dependence and of the female slave's subordination with her powers, which drew on images of non-white, female abilities and knowledge. The master's power is riven with anxiety about his own control, his health, his masculinity; his relationship with his slave is highly ambivalent, both intimate and dependent and yet domineering, fearful and antagonistic. The reaction of the female slave we know nothing about, but Behar says of women more generally that they were also very ambivalent about the powers they manipulated. On the one hand, they made use of them to try to control men and protect themselves; on the other, they would often throw away the magical items they used and run to the priests and inquisitors to confess and seek absolution (1989: 186).

A final example which speaks to this theme of ambivalence is Silverblatt's account of non-indigenous women in the seventeenth-century Andes who were accused as witches, but who compounded their heresy by going to rural areas to learn indigenous knowledge and techniques, based on the use of coca leaves and other plants, acquire some Quechua language, learn exhortations to the Inca queen and seek the assistance of the Inca himself. This was one instance of a more general tendency, perceived by the inquisitors, of local people to be 'fascinated by native ways' (2004: 163). Silverblatt argues that these witches may have been contesting colonial rule, but in a way that depended on invoking racialised colonial categories – such as the miraculous *indio*. The women accused were of the white elite and the mixed-race classes and very often their crimes centred on love magic. One Spanish woman was accused of raiding indigenous graves to find the bones of indigenous people who had never been baptised: she was helped by indigenous, black and mixed-race accomplices and teachers, who were in fact directing her activities: 'when it came to the subterranean powers of shamans and witches ... it [the colonial racial hierarchy] put authority in the hands of Peru's subordinates' (ibid.: 172). This same woman was later accused of working with a *mulata* woman, María Martínez, born in Portugal to an African mother and a Portuguese priest, who had a fearsome reputation as a witch and who was accused of having a pact with the devil – evidence for which included the fact that she had not had sex with a man for seven years. María Martínez defended herself as a baptised Christian who confessed regularly, but she admitted trying to find an *indio hechicero* to help her kill a man who had accused her. Although 'revelatory powers [were] ascribed to the viceroyalty's "negros"' (2004: 173), indigenous people had greater magical knowledge and ability, then as now (Taussig 1987). The women themselves – perhaps not surprisingly in formal testimony to the Inquisition – often insisted that they were good Christians. Silverblatt's account is paralleled by two cases in eighteenth-century northern Brazil, in which white women invoked indigenous gods or used indigenous assistants in their love magic (Sommer 2003: 428–9).

   To sum up: the articulation of race and sex in colonial projects of domination and regulation presented a highly ambivalent aspect. Indigenous, black and mixed-race people were seen as subordinate inferiors, yet they – and particularly the women among them – were also attributed significant powers in the realms of sex and magic. This reinforced their status as other, but also gave them the upper hand in some contexts, creating anxiety for the elites who depended on these people in every way, including in the intimate and domestic realms, but also saw them as potentially dangerous and unstable. In some cases, the powers attributed to subordinates were such that elite people took to imitating their social inferiors in an attempt to partake of these abilities. The women who stood accused of possession of these powers might deny them when under investigation and might, as Behar argues, have an anxious and ambivalent relationship to them, but they clearly also used them to create a measure of control and protection, not to mention as a source of revenue for those who could sell such services. Black and indigenous sorcerers reproduced the mythology that gave them special powers in healing and sexual magic.

Conclusion

In this chapter, I have traced the articulation of race and sex, of racial hierarchy and sex/gender hierarchies for colonial Latin America. I started by describing briefly Iberian, indigenous America and African sex/gender arrangements: the key point emerged that Iberian cultures put a huge emphasis on controlling women's sexual and marital behaviour, with premarital virginity being an important value, especially for elite families, and a whole cultural complex built around honour and shame in which the maintenance of female sexual 'purity' was a key theme. At the same time, more or less racialised notions of 'blood' also evoked the theme of purity and the danger of contamination. Indigenous and African systems, while very varied, generally set less store by premarital virginity and female purity – which did not mean that they did not control women's sexuality in other ways. In all three regions, homosexuality existed in practice, but there are indications that it was stigmatised more strongly in Iberia and that it was accepted in certain contexts, especially religious ones, in native America and Africa.

This set the context for the way Iberians used sex in strategies of domination and regulation. First, I explored how sex was deployed as a means of direct racial domination, subordinating colonised peoples by using them sexually, often coercively; conquest and oppression were also legitimated in part by images of native and African sexual practices as sinful and immoral. In this context, there was a difficult, perhaps impossible, line to draw between coercion and consent (especially as any consent by subordinate peoples happened within highly unequal power structures). I argued that the emphasis on sex as conquest tended to ignore the way the sexual desires and motives of the conquerors did not simply emerge from the context of domination itself, but were already shaped by pre-existing ideas about others as sexualised beings.

I then analysed how the colonial project involved not just direct conquest but also the construction and governance of a new social order, based ideally on Iberian principles, but having to adapt to New World realities. Here again, sex was a key concern in the attempt to create a gendered moral order and sex was closely linked to religion, especially through female witchcraft, but also through the persecution of sexual transgressions such as sodomy. Although white people were also accused of witchcraft and sexual misdemeanours, indigenous, black and mixed-race subordinate people were seen as particularly liable to religious heterodoxy and sexual transgression (although not, it seems, to sodomy, for which more white people were investigated). At the same time, ideas of purity of blood and female sexual purity, articulated in the cultural complex around honour and shame, combined to protect white elite interests, while white men also carried on numerous extramarital relationships with non-white women. Sex/gender norms operated in a mutually constituting dynamic with racial domination and a good illustration of this was the way a growing concern with race in the eighteenth century shaped sex/gender norms as marriage choices became more controlled by parents and the state. This system of domination was, of course, not complete and was indeed made inherently unstable partly by the many extramarital (and some marital) relationships between white men and non-white women, which often produced illegitimate offspring. (Domination may also have been destabilised by interracial homosexual relationships in which white men played the passive role.) I explored some of the ways in which subordinate people resisted racial-sexual forms of domination.

Finally, I explored in a more speculative fashion the ambivalence surrounding the sexual and the (often associated) magical powers attributed to, and in some contexts actively claimed by, mixed-race, black and especially indigenous people. My conclusion is that this ambivalence was rooted at some level in gendered processes of the formation of the self in relation to others. I looked briefly at how desire might have manifested itself in priests as a highly ambivalent affective construct of conscious repression of sexuality and sanctified sexual mysticism, which may then have shaped the way they related through sex to others defined as sexually debased and sexually expressive. Whatever the basis of the ambivalence surrounding racial subordinates, it was clearly strongly present in colonial Latin America and led to unexpected, if temporary and limited, reversals of power in which white women might end up imitating indigenous practices.

In the next chapter, I shall look at the articulations of race and sex in the context of postcolonial, independent Latin America, in which the racial-sexual process of *mestizaje* takes on strong ideological dimensions of nation-building and, for a period, eugenics also became an important way of thinking about, nation, race, gender and sex.

4

MAKING NATIONS THROUGH RACE AND SEX

In this chapter, I look at articulations of race and sex in Latin America's postcolonial period, from the time when the region became independent of Spanish and Portuguese metropolitan control – in most cases by the 1830s[1] – until the early decades of the twentieth century. During this period, there are two important processes of change that are particularly important for race–sex articulations. The first is the gradual establishment of what Foucault calls the analytics of sexuality and scientific approaches to both sex and race. The second is the emergence of 'the nation' as the central frame of reference for thinking about social orders in postcolonial Latin America.

I begin by looking at these two sets of processes and then use a number of historical studies to show how honour codes continued to work in the reproduction of gender and racial inequality. I follow this by using a number of studies to examine public campaigns of moral reform that targeted sexual and gender, but also racial differences in the project of building a modern, respectable nation. I then assess how well this historical work deals with the articulation of race and sex/gender. The chapter ends with a consideration of dynamics of ambivalence, focusing on popular music and dance.

Science, Sex and Race

As we saw in the last chapter, the state and the Church were both closely concerned with the investigation and regulation of sexual behaviour in colonial Latin America, but the main lens through which this was viewed was a religious one which defined transgressions as sins, even if non-ecclesiastical courts might also prosecute such practices as concubinage. During the nineteenth century, and especially towards the turn of that century, there was an increasing presence of approaches that rested on the growing scientific disciplines of the day. As outlined in Chapters 1 and 2, sex became a key focus of interest for scientists, especially medics. According to Foucault, in the emergence of what he calls *scientia sexualis*, sex became seen as a principal cause, if an often obscure and elusive one, of all kinds of behaviour. Data were collected from case histories, questionnaires and diagnoses and placed by medics 'under the rule of the normal and the pathological', trans-positions of older categories of virtue and sin:

> a characteristic sexual morbidity was defined for the first time; sex appeared as an extremely unstable pathological field: a surface of repercussion for other ailments, but also the focus of a specific nosography [the systematic description of diseases], that of instincts, tendencies, images, pleasure and conduct. This implied further that sex would derive its meaning and its necessity from medical interventions: it would be required by the doctor, necessary for diagnosis, and effective by nature in the cure. (Foucault 1998 [1979]: 67)

Foucault contends that scientific interest focused on 'four great strategic unities', which first emerged in the eighteenth century, but consolidated in the nineteenth: the woman as a being saturated with sexuality, responsible for the reproduction of children and the social body in general, but who tended towards nervous and hysterical pathologies; the sexually aware and active child, whose sexuality was especially evident in masturbation, who needed guidance and control; the conjugal couple in whose hands lay the biological reproduction of society and whose procreative behaviour needed overseeing; the sexual drives and instincts which could give rise to perversions and pathologies (such as homosexuality) to be corrected by medical and psychiatric intervention.

Foucault's influential analysis has opened up new perspectives, but tends to be short on historical specifics. However, there is little doubt that in the nineteenth century, medical and other sciences of the human, not only expanded, but took a great interest in sexuality, reproduction and latterly what was called social hygiene, a mixture of medical and moral elements seen to be conducive to the health, vigour and propriety of populations.

At the same time, medics, naturalists, biologists and anthropologists, as well as philosophers and scholars of the social, began to study racial difference in more empirical ways, principally through the measurement of bones and especially skulls. The concept of 'race' became elevated to a central place in European and American thought: it was deployed to explain all kinds of differences among humans and to justify hierarchy. Broadly speaking, humans were thought of as divided into several basic 'races' – usually something approximating the familiar categories of African, European, native American, Asian, Aboriginal Australian – which were seen as fairly well-defined biological groups of ancient origin, with stable characteristics that included intellectual and moral qualities. Some thinkers even posited separate, remote origins for these races, a doctrine known as polygenesis. The races were organised in a definite hierarchy, with white people of European descent at the top and black people of African and Australian origin at the bottom. Sexual mixture between races was generally seen as detrimental, leading to degenerate hybrids.[2]

Sex and race were intertwined, as we saw in Chapter 2. The sexual behaviour of the 'lower races' was thought to be immoral, uncontrolled and threatening; their sexual organs were the object of medical investigation. Analogies were drawn between the 'lower races' and women as a gender (Wiegman 1995: ch. 2): 'lower races represented the "female" type of the human species, and females the "lower race" of gender' (Stepan 1986: 264). The vigour and health that were sought in the regulation of sexuality were often placed in a national frame: it was the well-being and reproductive strength of the national population that was the goal – a goal that could be undermined by racial threats both within the nation (Jews often being seen in this way) and beyond, in the colonies. A healthy population also meant a racially pure one.

This type of project had a powerful expression in eugenics, a mixture of scientific theory and moral reform that originated in the 1880s with the Victorian polymath Francis Galton and had widespread influence in the Western world and Latin America until the 1930s (and, under the Nazis, until the 1940s). Eugenics aimed to improve a given population biologically through controlling reproduction. Those considered 'feebleminded' or less 'fit' for reproducing included the mentally and physically abnormal, but also the 'disreputable' working classes and racial categories seen as inferior. Extreme eugenic measures resulted in the sterilisation about 9000 people in some states of the US between 1907 and 1928, not to mention the even more extreme measures under the Nazis; softer eugenic programmes targeted social hygiene and strove to improve education and living conditions in order to improve reproduction. In either case, sex was a key domain in which racial (and class) hierarchies were reproduced (Kevles 1995; Stepan 1991).

As we shall see, these articulations of race and sex in European thought had important influences in Latin America, where they resonated with and developed the articulations already described for the colonial period.

The Nation and *Mestizaje*

With independence came a series of important changes in the social orders of Latin America. The colonial systems of racial discrimination were gradually dismantled as the new republics adopted constitutions strongly influenced by European liberalism in which nation-states ideally were composed of citizens who were equal before the law. The Spanish Inquisition was dissolved in 1834 and the Portuguese one in 1821 and this removed an official source of interest in purity of blood. Statutes relating to *limpieza de sangre* – already abolished in Brazil by 1773 – fell into disuse in Spanish America (although traces remained on the law books in Spain until the 1860s). Even in Cuba, which remained a Spanish colony, the notion of purity of blood ceased to be a formal issue in questions of marriage choice by the 1840s (Martinez-Alier [Stolcke] 1989 [1974]: 18). Legal discrimination against non-white free people – such as that restricting wearing certain articles of clothing – was abolished. Indigenous people's status began to change and many republics tried to integrate *indios* as citizens, for example, replacing indigenous tribute payments with standard taxes and attempting to undermine the landed basis of the indigenous community. Slavery was dismantled and abolished by 1854 everywhere except Puerto Rico (1873), Cuba (1886) and Brazil (1888).

Race by no means disappeared as a social category, however. The emerging class societies of the new republics were still strongly stratified by race and elites were still intent on maintaining their whiteness and privilege. Meanwhile, scientific thought in Europe and North America was giving increasing salience to race as a central organising principle of humanity and society; intellectuals in these regions were linking modernity with whiteness. This emphasis was problematic for Latin American elites, because many of their nations had large populations of black and indigenous people, deemed inferior by scientific racism, and often even larger populations of mixed-race people, considered potentially degenerate by these racial theories. The reaction to this dilemma was varied in Latin America, depending in part on the racial composition of the national population. By the late nineteenth century, Argentina already had large numbers of European immigrants, the Afro-Argentine population was small and the indigenous communities had been decimated by frontier wars. This made is easier for Argentinean elites to claim a Latin American form of whiteness (Helg 1990). In other areas, elites were faced with racial profiles that were much more black, indigenous and mixed.

In mid-nineteenth-century Colombia, for example, José María Samper, a parliamentarian and essayist, described a journey he made from Bogotá to the country's Caribbean coastal region in a barge, poled by black and mixed-race boatmen, known as *bogas* (see Wade 1999). He described them as people of 'savage features, fruit of the crossing of two or three different races, for whom Christianity is a shapeless mixture of impiety and idolatry, the law an incomprehensible confusion, civilization a thick fog and [for whom] the future, like the past and the present are confounded in the same situation of torpor, indolence and brutality' (Samper 1980: 88). He described their dance, the *currulao*, as 'the horrible synthesis of contemporary barbarism', full of 'voluptuousness' and 'shameless lubricity' (ibid.: 93, 94). Yet when Samper was writing a eulogy to the *bambuco* musical style which was being hailed as a musical expression of the national spirit, he took a different tone. In his essay, he lists most of the regions of Colombia, describing variants of the style: 'every race, every mestizo variant, every group of our diverse populations has given it [the *bambuco*] their particular character'. He refers, for example, to the Cauca region, where in the local *bambuco* 'one can feel the groan of the black man, once a slave ... one can perceive the imitative character of the mulatto' (Samper 1868). At the least, these different descriptions hint at some ambivalence in thinking about race and nation: vituperative racism when faced with actual black people; and inclusiveness – albeit heavily tinged with condescension – when thinking about national unity through music.

Already in Samper's writing on the *bambuco* we can see a gesture towards the recognition of Colombia as an essentially mixed and diverse nation which can still find some kind of unity. This kind of approach became a full-blown vision of national identity in various countries by the early decades of the twentieth century. In Colombia, Venezuela, Mexico, Cuba and Brazil – among others – the idea of the nation as essentially formed through *mestizaje* (or *mestiçagem*) and having found unity in the figure of the *mestizo* or *mulato* (I should say *mulata* – see below) became central, albeit in distinctive ways for different nations.[3] In Mexico, José Vasconcelos developed the idea of the *raza cósmica*, a superior blend of all races – prefigured by Latin American populations – which would eventually take over the world (Vasconcelos 1997 [1925]). In 1930s Brazil, Gilberto Freyre hailed mixture as defining national identity and as progressive and democratic. In Bolivia in 1910, Franz Tamayo idealised the *mestizo* as the 'synthesis of indigenous will and *mestizo* intelligence' and the basis of Bolivian national culture (Sanjinés 2004: 58).

As already suggested by Samper's writings, the adoption of a national image of mixedness by no means contradicted the continued existence of racism. First, it was possible to eulogise mixture in the abstract spirit of national unity, while also discriminating against non-white people in everyday practice, especially if they were seen as 'barbaric'. As part of this, it was also very possible to offer at least some acceptance to lighter-skinned mixed people while discriminating strongly against those identified as black or indigenous. Second, mixedness was often seen as a process of progression towards whiteness and 'civilisation', especially through the lens of turn-of-the-century social evolutionist thought, which equated darkness with backwardness and whiteness with modernity, but also envisaged the possibility that the darker races might progress towards modernity. In her study of eugenics in Latin America in the early decades of the twentieth century, Stepan (1991: 138) notes the use of the idea of 'constructive miscegenation' in Latin America, which departed from strict theories of racial determinism that condemned the 'lower races' to permanent inferiority. This resulted in a softer version of eugenics in Latin America, influenced as much by French theory as by more determinist Anglo-Saxon approaches. In Latin American ideologies of whitening, black and indigenous peoples were theoretically candidates to engage in the process of constructive miscegenation, but were also defined as the most backward people who belonged to the past; this could entail fierce discrimination and even annihilation (Gould 1998).

Honour, *Mestizaje* and the Governance of Race and Sex

Latin American societies represented themselves as liberal and democratic and were increasingly representing themselves in terms of race mixture; they were, nevertheless, based on racial and gender hierarchy – sometimes in very explicit ways. The Peruvian constitution of 1823 did not admit either slaves or women to full citizenship, for example, and also excluded servants and day labourers (Chambers 1999: 197–9). The governance of this tension between theoretical equality and actual hierarchy – which is, after all, a tension that affected (and arguably still affects) all liberal democratic societies – found crucial support in the continued power of the codes of honour I described in the previous chapter. Ideas of honour did not persist unchanged: they began to lose their association with simple colonial birthright status and be defined more in terms of acquired characteristics, such as occupation and education and the virtues of hard work (Caulfield et al. 2005). Chambers argues that in early republican Arequipa, Peru, plebeians struggled to link honour – gained through hard work, respectability and civic virtue – to citizenship and thus challenged and altered the colonial meanings of honour. Yet women's sexual virtue continued to play a key role in defining honour, as it had done in the past (Chambers 1999: chs 5, 6).

In the late nineteenth-century city of Ponce, Puerto Rico, honour continued to be a racialised and sexualised assertion of power in relation to others (Findlay 1998).[4] The sugar boom of 1800–45 produced influxes of both black slaves and white immigrants; race and class hierarchies became more defined and honour codes harsher. As usual, women's honour was predicated on their sexual virtue; while men's honour was based not only on the sexual virtue of 'their' women, which they were duty-bound to defend, but also on their personal integrity, honesty and sexual prowess. There was a very clear double standard in relation to male and female sexual behaviour; white men married women of their own class and race, and had informal extramarital relationships, often with darker-skinned women of lower classes. Honour was something claimed most easily by the upper classes, who saw the lower classes as lacking honour because of their low status, their family and sexual practices (many consensual unions, high rates of illegitimacy, etc.), their 'vulgar' behaviour and their blackness. The honour of the elite depended on the relative dishonour of the lower classes, but people of these classes claimed for themselves both honour, albeit understood in different ways, and the associated status of citizenship.

Many plebeian people in Ponce – including a fair number of lower-middle-class whites (shopkeepers, accountants, clerks) – lived in racially mixed neighbourhoods, in consensual unions and with their illegitimate children. Yet racial and social hierarchy and associated ideas of honour and respect were very important to them, even as they defined these things in different ways.[5] Women, for example, often had to work outside the home, 'on the street', a space that by itself threatened the honour of an elite woman. Poorer men could not defend the honour of 'their' women by secluding them in a cult of domesticity; they often lived in consensual, unmarried unions with women who worked outside the home; yet they often claimed the same right to exercise the patriarchal authority over their 'wives' that elite men might exercise over theirs. One stonemason in Ponce beat and raped his 'concubine' when he found her chatting with a male neighbour (Findlay 1998: 50). Women took such men to court, however; they might also denounce upper-class men for attempts on their honour (even if such cases rarely resulted in punishment for these men). Women used honour to claim rights and protection. In 1920s Mexico, for example, a group of prostitutes petitioned the president, declaring themselves nationalists and seeking protection – implicitly for their and the nation's honour – from an ineffective legal system that allowed 'foreign' men to exploit Mexican women in illegal brothels and from public hospitals that were hotbeds of disease and corruption (Bliss 2001: 1–4).

An analysis of court cases spurred by insults in the banana plantation provinces of the Caribbean coast of Costa Rica, between 1880 and the 1930s, shows that 60 per cent of these were brought by women, who were almost always insulted in terms of sexual impropriety, and 49 per cent by black women of West Indian origin (Putnam 2002: ch. 5). The people most likely to bring such suits were those most sensitive about slurs on their respectability and honour – working-class, black women, usually insulted by other black women; and socially aspirant male urban artisans and entrepreneurs, who responded to slurs on their business integrity.[6] (Working-class men did not figure much in these records, as their responses to insults tended to end in criminal proceedings over assault, brawling, etc.) Interestingly, in this context, there were few cases of men defending the honour of 'their' women. Putnam argues that the constant labour migration characteristic of the export-driven economy of the region resulted in the relative lack of strong patriarchal families, the honour of which men felt they had to defend. By the late 1930s, however, with economic depression and the flight of much of the transient West Indian population, the remaining more stable and middle-class black population became increasingly concerned with defining itself as respectable. Faced with intensifying racial dis-crimination in Costa Rica (race-based restrictions on migration into and within the country, racial segregation in some areas), this black middle class tried to emphasise their respectability and honour. This included defending the thing that was often seen by others as least respectable and most defining of lowly social position – black women's sexuality.

The continued power of ideas of honour in gender, class and race hierarchies is revealed in the 450 'deflowering' cases recorded in Rio de Janeiro between 1918 and 1941 (Caulfield 2000; see also Caulfield 2003). These were cases, nearly all of them brought by working-class women and their families, in which men were accused before the police of taking the virginity of a woman under 21 years of age. It was then a case of deciding whether this had been done illegally, which was mainly a question of proving that the man had made a credible promise of marriage which he did not intend to keep or had not in fact kept, or had otherwise lied or committed fraud; and proving that the woman was a virgin and, more generally, 'honest' and virtuous. If the police decided there was a case to answer, it went to court. The defendant generally tried to prove that he had good reason to believe the woman was not a virgin and was in general of dubious moral character, which he could do through many implications and insinuations targeting the woman, her family, friends and neighbourhood to suggest that she was a 'liberated' woman.

A huge amount thus rested on sexual reputation – especially when it was recognised that the state of the hymen was not an infallible guide to virginity – although social status was also important (i.e. it was 'unrealistic' for a domestic maid to believe that her employer would want to marry her, so she must either have been raped or consented to sex without a promise of marriage). Women challenged assessments of their characters in part by asserting their virtue, but also by trying to redefine the criteria by which that was judged: 'modern' women could step out alone and be independent without being 'dishonest' (Caulfield 2000: ch. 4). In some cases, working-class women had very different standards of behaviour: they socialised and courted in public places, 'on the street', and might be unaware that going out unaccompanied was behaviour that, in a law court, could be seen as disreputable (2000: 57).

Caulfield found that there was very little explicit mention of race in the records of these cases (2000: ch. 5). In that sense, people were not readily making overt use of racial labelling in order to establish or imply status and virtue. Rather 'the association between dark skin and moral laxity was not immediate but had to be qualified ... A woman's behaviour, attire or multiple boyfriends ... combined with colour to define social position and moral character' (ibid.: 169). Caulfield concludes that colour prejudice was disseminated among Rio's working class and that whiteness was positively valued, especially in choosing a marriage partner, but that there was also a lot of interracial social mixing within the working class and shared values of honour and respectability – as well as a reluctance to talk openly about race (ibid.: 171).

Many of these deflowering cases recorded the race or colour of the woman and the accused. The data show that in 60 per cent of cases a woman accused a man of the same racial category as herself (white, *parda* or black), but this intra-racial pattern was strongest for white women (19 per cent of whom accused non-white men). Among non-whites, 40 per cent of *pardas* and 31 per cent of black women accused white men. This indicates the familiar pattern in which white men had sexual relations with women of equal and of lower status class/colour, while they tended to marry women of equal class and colour. When Caulfield analyses the cases by race and outcome, she is able to show that the darker a man's skin the more likely he was to be indicted after an initial investigation, while the darker a woman's skin the less likely the accused male was to be indicted or convicted. Again, this shows that white men could deflower darker-skinned women with relative impunity, because these women were more likely to be judged to be of lax moral character, while dark-skinned men were liable to be taken to court. All men were twice as likely to be convicted when accused by a white woman as when accused by a black woman (ibid.: 161–76).

These examples from Puerto Rico, Costa Rica and Brazil indicate the workings of social orders in which racial and gender hierarchy were simultaneously maintained by ideas and practices around female (and male) sexuality. Elite men defended racialised class dominance through patriarchal control of elite women's sexuality, combined with sexual access to lower-class, darker-skinned women. At the same time, patriarchy was strengthened in the context of the need to maintain race–class dominance. Plebeian people participated in the value system of honour that structured the system and this made sense because they themselves were divided by gender and by race and class. But they also resisted by claiming honour for themselves, by using it as a means to claim citizenship rights and by defining it in alternative ways more suited to their lifestyles.

This balance between sharing common values with elites and resisting them is not a simple one. A series of cases from Colombia, Nicaragua and Guatemala shows that *mestizo* men often aligned themselves with patriarchal values that elite men also held, which saw women as both objects of (sexual) conquest and as male property to be defended against other men (Smith 1997). Smith interprets this not as a posture of ideological subordination, but a claim to equality and an act of resistance. *Mestizo* women, when economic circumstances permitted, as they did during the expansion of small-scale coffee production in highland Colombia in the late nineteenth and early twentieth centuries, would often seek to increase their autonomy. This led in the Colombian case to increased consensual unions, more female-headed households and higher rates of illegitimacy – and to increased friction between *mestizo* men and women (evidenced in rape and fights). But *mestizo* men and women might also cooperate to form smallholder households in which they could together resist both economic oppression (e.g. pressures to become wage labourers) and sexual predation by elite men. It might be the case that women in these households were forced into domestic roles, but Smith contends that choices for men and women could also be increased, while their honour was also defended. Men could be united through patriarchy, but as the operation of patriarchy was classed and racialised in ways that divided elite from plebeian men (and women), the lower classes could also resist elite domination. That resistance, however, was often based on claiming the right to the same patriarchal notions of honour that the elites lived by.

Building a 'Proper' Nation

The examples above focus on the detailed operation of race and sex in marital and sexual relationships and everyday interactions. They show how honour worked as an articulation of race and sex/gender (I shall return to how well the studies deal with this process of articulation). These relationships and interactions took place within broader projects of nation-building in which elites, but also other sets of actors, tried to implement projects that would create a proper moral order for their nations as they grew and established themselves in a global arena in which all the ideas about race and sexuality outlined at the start of this chapter were circulating. These moral projects had sexuality as a key focus, but not only was sexuality always mediated through ideas about class and race, but race itself could also form the basis of nation-building projects, centred on representing the nation as racially mixed (or sometimes, rather white) and, in any case, racially democratic. That is, the aim was to create a nation that was morally sound in terms of sexual propriety, and also racially inclusive and tolerant. The same ideas of honour that, as I showed in the previous section, regulated gender and racial hierarchy could be used in a different way to produce the image of a racially democratic society, or rather a racial *fraternity* of men. Meanwhile, moral reform targeted lower-class, dark-skinned women in anti-prostitution campaigns.

A Racial Fraternity

Chamber's study of Arequipa, Peru, noted briefly above, provides an interesting example of a project of moral and civic construction, although it was a region, rather than nation, that was being built (Chambers 1999). This early republican case is rather different from the moral campaigns of social hygiene one can find at the end of the nineteenth and beginning of the twentieth centuries, but it is a moral project nonetheless. Chambers argues that Arequipa forged a reputation of itself as a rather 'white' city, democratic and hard-working, where the class and racial hierarchies characteristic of other regions of Peru are much less marked. (She notes that the city is not alone in this respect: the regions of Antioquia in Colombia and Chihuahua in Mexico have similar reputations.[7])

Her argument is that, although slaves and indigenous communities did form a lesser presence than in places such as Lima or Cuzco, also crucial was that plebeians pushed to be accepted as citizens by redefining honour away from inherited birthright and towards civic virtue and hard work – and respectability. Local elites were prepared to accept this and to take a relatively assimilationist stance towards the local deracinated indigenous people in the interests of containing racialised class conflict; there was a consensus around the images of whiteness, democracy and civic virtue. But there were limits to democracy (1999: ch. 6). First, slaves, servants, labourers and women were not full citizens. The claims of plebeian men to virtue were built in part on their patriarchal control of women's sexuality, a right they shared with elite men. Second, judges retained a certain privilege for the elite by raising the bar of respectability and honour: plebeian men could be judged honourable in a court of law, but they had to try very hard to be as honourable as the elite.

The point is that the construction of a certain racial identity (as white) and class identity (as democratic, linked to the supposed lack of racial hierarchy) was in an important sense the driver for the key role played by sex/gender norms of honour. These, of course, already existed, but they became the means by which this race/class project could be realised: plebeian men could be incorporated into the body politic, defined as (quite) white, as long as they were virtuous patriarchs, controlling and defending the honour of their families and the sexuality of their women.

Meanwhile, a hierarchy of honour, in which elite men were superior to plebeian men, was still enforced.

The project of building a reputation for Rio de Janeiro was likewise beleaguered by contradictions between inclusion and exclusion and what 'modernity' implied in that respect in relation to both race and sex. Caulfield gives an account of the public debates surrounding a 1920 visit to Rio of the Belgian king and queen (2000: ch. 2). There was much discussion of what it was suitable for them to see and what kind of a place Rio (and Brazil) would be when seen through European eyes. Rather than outlining a hegemonic viewpoint, Caulfield traces the conflicting stances people took. On the one hand, there was fairly general agreement that 'honest' and 'decent' people should be spatially segregated from disreputable people – and some of that class-race zoning, phrased in terms of respectability and honour, had already been accomplished in urban renewal programmes enacted in 1902–10. On the other hand, overt racial discrimination was being seen as anti-democratic and un-Brazilian, something that plagued the US, not Brazil. And some intellectuals were discovering grass-roots cultural forms, such as the Afro-Brazilian samba, which could stand for an 'authentic' Brazilian culture. On the one hand, many among the city's elite favoured programmes of social hygiene and moral reform, influenced by European and North American thinking and eugenics (albeit in its softer Latin American version); this would target the darker-skinned lower classes. On the other, 'modernity', European and US-style, was feared as a descent into moral chaos, symbolised most clearly by the independent, 'modern' woman who was thought to defy sexual and gender norms (2000: ch. 3).

In short, the challenge was to define a modern, democratic and racially tolerant society, which was nevertheless based on respectability, sexual virtue and traditional family values. This was difficult because non-racism implied an embrace of lower-class blacks and *pardos* whose sexual virtue was considered lacking and inadequate to prepare them for modernity (which would simply exacerbate their moral defects). One way round the problem was to define modernity as suitable for men, but not for women; and as appropriate for the (whiter) upper classes, but not for the (blacker) working classes (2000: ch. 3). This evasion was articulated primarily through ideas about honour, as a set of gendered and racialised norms of sexual behaviour, which could discipline both women and the racialised masses. Only white men could be both modern and honourable.

In practice, ideas about honour were defined and refined in the legal codes that Caulfield analyses, which sought to protect women's honour, as well as in campaigns against prostitution (seen as tarnishing the city's respectability and its public health) and crimes of passion (which, to some contemporary observers, betrayed a 'medieval' and almost 'pathological' preoccupation with honour among those men who killed women in 'love murders').

Interestingly, Caulfield describes how, under the Estado Novo dictatorship of Getúlio Vargas, from 1937, legal and other reforms put in place more patriarchal and conservative norms regarding gender and sexuality (2000: 183–94). Vargas promoted traditional family values – and male dominance – as part of his corporatist and paternalistic inclusion of different social classes into the political and economic order. Working-class men too could head traditional patriarchal families and defend and promote the nation's honour. At the same time, as Caulfield notes rather in passing, the Vargas regime vigorously promoted ideas of racial democracy and worked hard to incorporate sanitised versions of popular culture – often Afro-Brazilian forms such as samba – into nationalist campaigns for moral improvement. Combining affirmations of national fraternity and racial democracy in this way was not particular to the Vargas era. Seigel (2009: 208) shows that it was already under way in the 1920s. It indicates that honour was once again working as the means of articulation of race with sex/gender: the definition of Brazilian society as a racial democracy was part of the drive towards a more traditional notion of honour. Honour acted as a code that could unite men of different racial and class positions – and possibly women too, even if they came into conflict with men about it. The idea of unity around family and national honour expressed a sense of racial democracy. Meanwhile, honour codes could still act as the means by which racial hierarchy was enforced in practice, as it was in the deflowering cases of the 1920s and 1930s. This case bears strong similarities to that of Arequipa.

Moral Reform, Prostitution and Blackness

The history of Ponce offers telling examples of the campaigns of moral reform that many Latin American elites undertook in this period, in their efforts to build a healthy and morally sound nation (Findlay 1998). Between 1873 (when slavery was abolished) and 1898 (when the US invaded Puerto Rico) male liberals in Ponce mounted campaigns to combat sexual licence, seen as a form moral degeneracy rooted in slavery and blackness, but affecting the whole population, for example, though the popularity of the Afro-Puerto Rican *danza* music and dance style. Sexual looseness was linked to idleness and lack of discipline and all of these to blackness. The aim was to de-Africanise Puerto Rican culture. Women were targeted for moral uplift – and they would then change men – but black women were deemed unsuitable material for reform as slavery had left them, in the words of one commentator, 'reduced to a purely vegetative state' (Findlay 1998: 60). Even when, in the 1890s, feminist movements began to emerge, endorsing female education and economic autonomy, black women were again excluded by the white, 'respectable' women leading the movements.

A good deal of Findlay's material focuses on the campaigns and debates around prostitution in Ponce. Campaigns between 1890 and 1900 sought to enclose and regulate the activities of prostitutes, making them register, pay a hygiene tax, work in licensed brothels and submit to medical examinations. The tone of moral uplift and education became decidedly more repressive when elites were faced with growing numbers of working-class women migrating to the city. Not all these women were black by any means, but Findlay argues – without adducing much evidence – that they were all blackened by association. There was little explicit naming of race in the discussions but 'all "scandalous" or "disreputable" women became discursively darkened' (1998: 90), partly by opposition to white elite women. Similar to the Brazilian case, Puerto Rican elites were developing an official discourse of racial democracy, based on the notion of *la gran familia puertor-riqueña* (the great Puerto Rican family) and plans for 'universal' (actually only male) suffrage, while still discriminating against black women, in terms of their assumed sexual 'dishonesty' and immorality. During a later campaign, led by US authorities during the First World War and now aiming at the complete elimination of prostitution on health grounds, 'promiscuous women' were again targeted, once more in racially neutral language, although Findlay asserts that the discourse 'probably carried racialized class connotations' (1998: 168).

The shortage of concrete data on how working-class and 'promiscuous' women were racialised and discursively darkened is a weakness in Findlay's arguments – and it is a widespread problem when studying race in Latin American countries where race is often left implicit – but in the larger picture it does not matter too much. Prostitution was a major concern in many Latin American countries during this period.[8] Discussions about it were generally framed in terms of social hygiene, the state of the nation's morality and health, the threats posed to these by 'dangerous' women (rather than by the men who made use of their services) and the question of class. Men who used prostitutes came from all social classes, but the prostitutes themselves were always considered lower class. These sex-workers were racially very mixed and many of them – for example, in Rio, Lima and Buenos Aires – were European immigrants enmeshed in the so-called 'white slave trade'. Caulfield (1997) shows that, *among* prostitutes in Rio, there was a race and class hierarchy, with higher-class, whiter and 'French' prostitutes working in the Lapa area of the city centre, while darker-skinned *pretas* but also *polacas* ('Polish' women brought in by Eastern European white slave trading rings) worked in the more peripheral working-class Mangue area.

Yet prostitution was often 'discursively darkened' by association with the lower classes – the term *los negros* can still be used by middle- and upper-class speakers to refer to the lower classes in general, even when they are not particularly black, from Colombia to Brazil and Argentina – and by association with ideas about the sexual licentiousness of black women (and men). Briggs (2002: 59–65) argues that for Puerto Rico, under US rule, most Puerto Ricans were classed as blacks, except the white elite, so it seems plausible that much of the discourse on working-class prostitutes there which Findlay describes for the US-led campaign post-1917 would implicitly take them to be dark-skinned. Briggs shows that US medics also made strong connections between venereal disease and blackness and associated both with Puerto Ricans. Putnam notes that for Puerto Limón, prostitutes were both black women from the West Indies and Hispanic women from Central America – and they catered for racially segregated clienteles. Yet in 1913, the port doctor attributed the spread of venereal disease to clandestine prostitutes who, he said, 'belong in their majority to the Negro race' (Putnam 2002: 91) and in 1925 the governor of Limón shut down a dance hall which, he said, hosted 'scandalous dances of the people of bronze', attended by prostitutes and working-class men (ibid.: 83).

The associations between working-class status, dark skin, unregulated sexuality and venereal diseases were very strong – even more so when many of the working classes were actually dark-skinned. Moral reform programmes aimed to correct 'faults' in the national profile that were associated with both class and race, and particularly with women. Race connoted sex, and vice versa: blackness implied dishonour just as dishonour implied blackness; and the same reciprocal relation held whiteness in relation to honour. The promise of racial democracy held out to non-white men who became honourable patriarchs was belied by these moral campaigns which so clearly reproduced the association between whiteness and honour.

National Honour, Race, Masculinity and Queerness

Questions of honour and social hygiene were linked to female, but also to male sexuality and, more generally, masculinity. The nation's honour had to be protected by properly masculine men. One area in which questions of honour, protection and masculinity surfaced explicitly was the armed forces. In Brazil in the late nineteenth century, the army was widely seen as a very low-status, dishonourable institution (Beattie 2001). At least half of all recruitment depended on impressment (forced recruitment, often of vagrants, criminals, orphans, the unemployed) and 'only extreme circumstances could impel most Brazilians to volunteer as enlisted men' (ibid.: 4). Freed slaves, seen as a threat to public morality, including to the honour of women, were a target for impressment and these men sometimes pretended to be slaves or cross-dressed as women to evade it (Beattie 2003: 240). The division between the *praças* (enlisted men) and the officers was a strongly racialised one, as most of the former were black and mixed-race and most of the latter were white. The ranks were implicitly feminised, referred to with the feminine noun *a praça* (until the early 1900s, at least), subject to physical beatings like slaves and without masculine honour, although career soldiers tended to claim a tough, unruly masculinity for themselves.

Linked to this, the barracks also had the reputation of being a den of sexual perversion, mainly sodomy, and moral degeneracy, partly because known or suspected sodomites were often sent to the army, but also because of contemporary 'bigoted medical assertions that Africans and Indians brought sodomy to the *bagaceira* (the sugar plantation's lax moral environment) and "contaminated" the Portuguese with this "perversion"' (Beattie 2001: 199). Beattie argues that, among the ranks, the stigma attached to homosexuality was mediated by the active/passive divide, with the active penetrator claiming honourable masculinity. The officers, on the other hand, saw both partners as morally degenerate and likely to undermine discipline (Beattie 1997). In his novel *Bom Crioulo* (1895), Adolfo Camhina depicted a strong black sailor in a homosexual relationship with a white cabin boy, causing a scandal at the time. Although some white men were portrayed as homosexuals, Camhina implied that homosexuality was linked to racial degeneration, even if this was in part caused by slavery itself (1997: 70–1).[9] In any case, blackness, sexual perversion and dishonour were closely linked and this persisted into the twentieth century, when medics who formed part of eugenics and social hygiene movements talked about homosexuality, criminality and racial degeneration in the same breath. Although these doctors might not explicitly link blackness and homosexuality, they implicitly did by focusing disproportionately on black, criminal homosexuals (Green 1999: 122–6, 2006: 187, 203).

There was a moral campaign to reform the military in the early decades of the twentieth century, inspired in part by Germanic theories and military practice (Beattie 2001). As a national institution, the army had to defend the nation's honour, as men defended the honour of 'their' women. National honour was deeply sexualised and could be threatened by the same kind of contaminations as women's honour. Homosexuality was also a threat to the nation's honour, a longstanding perception in Europe (Mosse 1985). The honourable, respectable heterosexual family was the necessary building block of national reputation and pride. The armed forces thus had to move away from images of degeneracy, perversion, feminisation and dishonour towards greater moral upstanding and masculinity, in which the barracks could be seen as a home and a family for decent young men.[10] The army instigated conscription instead of impressment and shifted away from recruiting criminals and vagrants towards including more poor whites and 'respectable poor' men. The discourse surrounding the implementation of the draft maintained that it would integrate men of different racial and class backgrounds and this helped 'alleviate the fears expressed by many that Brazil's diverse racial composition and climate would prevent it from becoming a truly modern united and "civilized" nation-state' (Beattie 2001: 281). An integral aspect of the challenge was to recast the sodomitic reputation of the barracks and this was attempted in part by reinforcing the notion that both active and passive partners were equally guilty. This was in line with emerging international trends to see 'homosexual', first, as a person with a medical condition[11] and, second, as a social identity that defined a man, by way of his sexual orientation, rather than seeing sodomy as an act in which men might engage in very different ways.[12]

In short, national projects of racial integration and of moral uplift towards respectability and sexual 'normality' were closely articulated: as in Ponce, moral reform implied de-Africanisation, both in the sense of eradicating sexual practices associated with blacks and by creating racial assimilation and integration.

The connection of national identity with masculinity, as well as femininity, is taken up by Irwin for Mexico, through the lens of literature (Irwin 2003). Building on Sommer's notion that romantic literature in nineteenth-century Latin America focused on heterosexual and often interclass and interracial romances as the symbol of nation formation (Sommer 1991), Irwin argues that national identities were also built around homosocial bonds or the concept of fraternity: 'male homosocial bonding is the key allegory of national integration in literature' (Irwin 2003: xxx). National identity implied a robust virility: male togetherness had to be aggressively masculine. Like Sedgwick (1985), however, Irwin also argues that homosociality merges into homosexuality (see also Bejel 2001).[13] In disavowing this, homosociality brings with it homophobia and, more generally, a preoccupation with masculinity. 'Being a man' is a state in constant need of reinforcement: it is created performatively by acting as a man, but it is also relational, such that a man's masculinity can be put into question by another's more virile performance or by any suggestion that homosociality is nearing the terrain of homoeroticism.

Male bonding was, nevertheless, seen as a good basis for national unity, as heterosexual desire, involving women, although necessary for reproduction, also ran the risk of contaminations, undermining class boundaries, threatening the honour of the family, and so on. Bonds between men were, in some ways, a more robust basis for national unity. In the nineteenth century, the national literature of Mexico glorified close, often intimate, relationships between young, well-off men, although eroticism and homosexuality were never mentioned. The equally virile sexuality of unruly working-class men and criminals was seen as too barbaric and potentially destructive.

After the Mexican Revolution, there was more preoccupation with the nation and its class and sexual aspects – homosexuality had by now become a part of public discourse about men, spurred by a widely publicised police raid in 1901 on a party in which half the men present were dressed in drag. Irwin notes that although the men were of all social classes and must have been both of whiter and darker appearance, the issue of race was not mentioned: the scandal of homosexuality was the key preoccupation (Irwin 2003: 172). However, the question of race emerged in a different way, with the post-revolutionary literary 'vindication of turn-of-the-century notions of barbarous lower-class masculinity' (ibid.: 185) – lower-class and thus implicitly dark-skinned, but virile and the essence of *lo mexicano*. Effeminacy in men, which had always been deplored but not seen as homosexual, was now linked directly to homosexuality, and the virility of upper-class men was seen as more and more suspect, while homosexuality was also linked to foreign influences and the pretentious imitation of European mores (Irwin 2000: 370). In the 1950s, Octavio Paz psychoanalysed the Mexican male as defined by the pressing need to assert his masculinity against the implicit feminisation of his subordination (Irwin 2003: 194).

The consolidation of the image of Mexico as built on *mestizaje* reinforced the role given to a more plebeian, darker-skinned masculinity, seen as quintessentially Mexican. There is an interesting contrast here with Beattie's material, in which lower-class, non-white sexuality was seen as degenerate, quite possibly homosexual and hardly a resource for the nation. But both versions actually built on the same idea of a lower-class, racialised (and especially black) sexuality that was *excessive*, both powerful and dangerous. If tamed in the appropriate way, this sexual energy could be directed towards the building of the nation. Whereas the classic narrative of *mestizaje* tells of white men having sex with non-white women, seemingly displacing non-white men and either effeminising them or seeing them as sexual threats, in fact the narrative could also make room for these men as participants in the nation by way of their properly ordered masculinity.

In Mexico, the emphasis on masculinity masked direct reference to race and invited all men to identify with a common version of manhood. As we have seen for Brazil and Peru, although subordinate men could be defined as dishonoured and thus lacking in masculinity, nationalist projects held out the promise that men of different classes and racial categories would agree on what it meant to be a man (especially in relation to women). De la Cadena also notes that for a time in the 1940s Peruvian highlands, local intellectuals produced a populist valorisation of the tough masculine *cholo* (plebeian *mestizo*): 'as race was rhetorically dismissed, gender became the conceptual sphere that aided intellectual efforts to ... produce the authenticity that their regionalist-cum-nationalist ideologies required' (2000: 148). But the 'dismissal' of race was by no means complete: whatever else the *mestizo* or *cholo* was, he was not white. In Peru as in Mexico, the whole idea of *mestizaje* is a national-*racial* project in which the racialised masculinity of subordinate men, if suitably tamed, could be used as a virile resource, although untamed it could be a threat due to its perceived barbarism or degeneracy.

Homosexuality as a foil to nationalist definitions of masculinity and heterosexuality is also brought out suggestively, but in a different way, in Fiol-Matta's study of the Chilean educator and literary Nobel Prize winner, Gabriela Mistral (Fiol-Matta 2000, 2002). Mistral (1889–1957) was born in Chile and worked there as a schoolteacher, publishing poetry from about 1904. In 1922, the Mexican educationalist José Vasconcelos, the author of *La raza cósmica*, invited her to work with him in educational reform. She became an international figure, living in France, touring the world, acting as Chilean consul in Brazil during the Second World War and winning the Nobel Prize in 1945. She championed the project of *mestizaje* in Mexico and Chile and, although accepted as white, began to self-identify as a *mestiza*, setting herself up as a defender of indigenous people too. She was also influential in Latin American thinking about educational reform and was known as the 'schoolteacher of America'. Fiol-Matta presents her as a 'queer' figure, probably a 'closet lesbian' who became a patriotic 'mother for the nation' and backed state policies that promoted the home and heterosexual family. It was her queerness – her masculine appearance and attire, her lack of a male partner, her place in a male world of government and diplomacy – which suited her to take this apparently traditional female role:

> Mistral made use of a straightforward posing, as mother, as mestiza, but her posing abetted – instead of destabilising – the national discourse. Indeed, posing is part of nationalism's effectiveness, for it engages the complicated question of identification.... Mistral's figure enabled citizens to take part in the productive nature of power, specifically in the pleasures of identification – pleasures that underwrote both liberationist and repressive actions, to be sure.... Mistral's example provides a model for the incorporation of queerness into the state's project and makes the case that Latin American queerness was not as invisible as one may have thought.... The state ... was attracted to her queerness, to what she and only she could accomplish in a biopolitical realm of power. So the union was consummated: Mistral would perform in the public sphere as the state's star attraction, posing as so married to the national cause that she had sacrificed her most personal fulfilment for the good of her and the state's 'national children,' the citizens. (Fiol-Matta 2002: 5–6)

Fiol-Matta is unsure whether the state consciously deployed Mistral's queerness or used her 'straightforward maternal presence' (ibid.: 217), although it is hard to see much 'straightforward' about Mistral's maternity, but her argument is that Mistral was attractive to the state as an ideal vessel for promoting ideas about family, home and *mestizaje*. Part of the attraction lay in the Chilean state's effort to make itself responsible for the proper reproduction of the nation's children, taking over from actual mothers, deemed inadequate – without of course being able to remove 'the despised mother' from the affective landscape. Mistral's non-reproductive maternal and schoolteacherly figure suited this state-led, educationalist agenda (ibid.: 94). Fiol-Matta argues further that Mistral's queerness as a mother figure gave her a kind of 'iconicity' or 'super-personhood' that could 'speak directly to the deployment of desire by the supposedly neutral and nondesiring liberal state', the state that treated everyone equally and did not prefer one citizen to another (ibid.: 215).

The overall idea is that Mistral's indeterminacy and out-of-the-ordinariness gave her a special appeal and power. In a letter to a friend, Mistral reported that when Vasconcelos met Chile's best-known feminist of the time, he dismissed her, saying, 'Of *these*, we have lots in Mexico; in fact, too many', whereas he said of Mistral, 'But the one I took with me [meaning Mistral] is different and queer [odd, strange]' (the Spanish word was *rara*) (ibid.: 9, Fiol-Matta's translation).

Her position as a mother of the nation gave her an authoritative voice on issues of *mestizaje*, which involved precisely the nation as it was being (re)produced by the collective mothers of the nation (Mexican, Chilean or Latin American in general). Fiol-Matta clearly shows that Mistral had a strongly integrationist view of *mestizaje*, similar to Vasconcelos' own: women had a special role to play in guiding the direction of mixture, but these had to be 'state-approved' mothers (ibid.: 80, citing Donna Guy). At times, however, Mistral gave whiteness a privileged place in guiding mixture and she certainly had fairly racist views about black people, seeing them as unworthy contributors to the national mix – although also sexualising them in a slightly fetishistic way during her sojourn in Brazil (ibid.: ch. 1). It is not clear in Fiol-Matta's account how Mistral's queerness added to or mediated the way she expressed what were, after all, fairly common ideas about race in many regions of Latin America at the time: the championing of mixture, the speaking out on behalf of indigenous people (especially women) but with integration as the ultimate goal, the marginalisation of blackness in the national project – all these things could be found in the thinking of other intellectuals. But it was unusual to find a woman in such a prominent position, and one idealised as a mother of the nation, expressing these views in a way directed at an area that was both at the heart of *mestizaje* as a national-racial project and her own privileged area of expertise and authority – that is, social reproduction as enacted through the heterosexual family, the raising of children and the school.

The work of Beattie, Irwin and Fiol-Matta discussed here suggests that the articulation of race and sex in Latin American *mestizaje*, while reproducing images of racial democracy and sexual heteronormativity, depended crucially on reference to racial and sexual difference. Black and indigenous people had to be mentioned in discourses of *mestizaje*, if only to deny or patronise them; homosexuality – or more generally queerness in the sense of non-heteronormative sexuality – was always the possible referent behind discourses of heterosexuality. These absent presences were not just negations, but were productive: the discourse of *mestizaje* could not exist without blackness and indigenousness, as well as whiteness; heterosexuality depended on its masked other.

More generally, this work shows that in the governance of race and sex in a nation-building context, men and masculinity were as important as women and femininity. With male sexuality, there was not the concern with the possible racialised 'contamination' of reproductive processes that surrounded women's sexuality; indeed, Green and Irwin remark that homosexual interactions occurred between men of different racial categories in Brazil and Mexico without an apparent concern for 'contamination', although Green observes that these interactions were strongly structured by race and class (Green 1999: 11, 61, 283; Irwin 2003: 172). But the nation required masculine men for its well-being and honour, so male sexuality remained an important concern. Men linked to blackness and indigenousness, by their physical appearance and class status, had a dual role here. On the one hand, they were seen as a threat: as heterosexuals, their sexuality, often seen as barbaric and uncontrolled, threatened white women and the qualities of a mixing or whitening nation; as homosexuals, their depraved sexuality (which they shared with white homosexuals) was linked to criminality. In both cases, their forms of masculine sexuality had to be regulated and improved. On the other hand, their sexuality could, in appropriate form, be the basis of a powerful, virile masculinity that set a better basis for the nation than that of effete, upper-class white men.

Articulating Race and Sex

The question I address now is the extent to which the literature discussed above really manages to tackle the articulation or intersection of race and sex/gender. What seems to stand out in many of these studies is that they are primarily about sex and gender and secondarily about race. This is self-consciously so in most cases and most of the studies do not headline 'race' in their titles, even if it is an important topic in the text, as it is for Caulfield and Putman. Others – Stepan, Findlay, Briggs, Beattie – do include 'race' in their titles, although in Beattie's case at least, the theme does not occupy much of the main text. If, theoretically speaking, race and sex articulate together to form a new functional structure in which they mutually constitute each other, then how well are we able to appreciate this in these studies?

Briggs gives substantial theoretical room to race in her study of US imperialism in Puerto Rico (2002). She demonstrates with convincing detail and analysis the way a racialised imperial project governed through the channels of sex, gender and the family, mainly targeting prostitution, sexually transmitted diseases and women's 'uncontrolled' fertility, while also categorising Puerto Ricans as black and seeing these sex/gender matters as linked to Puerto Rican blackness. This is useful material, but there is rather little about how race and sex/gender articulate with and shape each other. Sex is a field on which racial domination is enacted.

Putnam argues that race and gender operate at different social levels. Gender is made in personal, intimate family relations between people who live together and know each other well; race is made at a distance, through national politics, workplace encounters, contact and conflict 'at the fringes of social networks' (2002: 16). This may work for Limón, but I think it is not a helpful theoretical approach, because it denies precisely the intersections of race and gender, some of which come across in Putnam's own data: gender is also subject to distant, national politics (e.g. programmes of social hygiene, although these were minimal in Limón), while race is also reproduced in intimate circles (e.g. in marriage choices, family honour and the insults aimed at a person's private sexual life).

Although only alluded to briefly above, Stepan's study of eugenics has an elegant and concise approach to the articulation of race and gender. Stepan's main interest is in the way eugenic thought was adopted and adapted in Latin America in the 1920s and 1930s.

She argues that elites tended to avoid extreme eugenics based on sterilisation and strict racial determinism; and favoured social hygiene programmes, influencing matrimonial and reproductive practice and thinking in terms of 'constructive miscegenation'.

Gender was crucial to eugenics because sexual reproduction was the channel for hereditary transmission; race was also crucial because 'it was through sexual unions that the boundaries between races were believed to be either maintained or transgressed'. Sex was the terrain on which race and gender overlapped. Both race and gender became, in the 1920s and 1930s, increasingly linked to nationalism, since this was a discourse of racial improvement and reproductive vigour (1991: 103–5). The main chapters of the book, however, do not entirely carry through this explicit description of the intersection. One chapter focuses on gender and how elites tried to control marriage in Argentina, Mexico and Brazil. Only for Argentina is this 'matrimonial eugenics' explicitly linked by Stepan to ideas about improving the racial profile of the population 'through matrimonial selection based on principles of heredity and adaptation' (1991: 118). Otherwise the emphasis is on sexual education, sexual health and birth control as means to improve 'the race' in a very general sense, although Stepan does point out that poorer non-white women were often the main targets for this kind of policy (1991: 110). In another chapter, the focus is on race and the emergence of ideas of constructive miscegenation, but there is little mention of marriage, sex and gender and more of social hygiene and immigration control.

Stepan, of course, makes no claim to analyse the mutual constitution or articulation of race and sex/gender, but it is interesting to pursue this question in light of her material. In one sense, eugenics itself *is* the historically specific articulation of race and gender: it is the discursive space within which race and sex/gender operate; it is the new functional structure of ideas and practices which is more than the sum of the race and sex/gender parts that constitute it (although one would have to add nationalism as a third part). Within this, we can see how race and sex/gender operated and shaped each other.

The racial project of improvement, whitening and constructive miscegenation was deeply shaped by the nature of gender and sex relations in the region, based on the defence of white women's sexuality and honour, together with the privileged access of white men, via informal unions, deflowerings and rapes, to lower-class, darker-skinned women. This already racialised sex/gender structure – which does not come within Stepan's purview – had generated a type of socially sanctioned mixture with which Latin American eugenicists had to contend: they had to confront the large *mestizo* population which was partly a product of white men's informal unions with darker-skinned women. The nation-builders' racial projects could hardly hope to emulate those of North America or Europe in terms of racial purity (or segregation) and had to adapt, using more positive ideas of mixture.

At the same time, gender relations were shaped by the racial project of improving 'the (national) race': women were targeted, not only in terms of honour, but now also as medicalised objects, biological reproducers, whose health was at issue. Stepan notes that prenuptial examinations and certificates were introduced in some countries, albeit mainly in terms of controlling health rather than interracial marriage (1991: 122–8). The sexual health of lower-class women was, in this context, more of a concern than that of elite women, in marked contrast to questions of honour. The racial project of improvement underwrote a rebalancing of gender norms away from honour towards health, and away from upper-class towards lower-class women.

It is this mutual constitution of race and sex/gender, in an ongoing process that produces mutating articulations and intersections, that is quite hard to capture. Caulfield, for example, while paying detailed attention to race in her book, clearly privileges sexuality and honour. Her book, she says, 'is about gender, honour and nation-building'; in her analysis, 'sexual honour stood for a set of gender norms that, with their apparent basis in nature, provided the logic for unequal power relations in private and public life'; thus 'sexual honour was frequently used to reinforce hierarchical relations based not only on gender, but on race and class as well' (2000: 3–4). Sex and gender come first and help legitimate class and race. The last two are effectively conflated here, whereas one could argue that race has an elective affinity with gender due to a discourse that is more powerfully naturalising than that of class. However, the richness of Caulfield's data and the incisive account of the racial aspects of deflowering cases allow us to gain insight into the way race and sex/gender shaped each other.

Specifically, although race is implied to be theoretically secondary, it is clear that the racialised project of Brazilian elites and jurists – the construction of a racially democratic nation (which nevertheless retained racial hierarchies) – shaped sex/gender norms. Caulfield states that in the deflowering cases, 'notwithstanding the absence of racism in Brazilian law, judges, prosecutors and the police could use their "interpretive power" in judgements of sexual honour in ways that allowed them to espouse, and perhaps even believe in, racial democracy while practising racial discrimination' (2000: 147–8). It was this interpretive power that made sex and gender norms apply differently to women of different classes and racial categories and that produced the race and gender patterns that Caulfield found (described above). The project of enacting racial democracy, while maintaining racial hierarchy, shaped sex/gender norms. Meanwhile, sex/gender norms that enshrined a sexual double standard for men and women had already helped to generate the racially mixed society that was part of the basis for the very claims of racial democracy in the first place. In that sense, as we have seen for the colonial period, honour was the mode of articulation of race and sex/gender; it was the functional complex within which they shaped each other. As such, it necessarily had a close underlying relationship with eugenics and its related programmes of social and moral hygiene: in effect, eugenics and hygiene were medicalised and scientific versions of honour, which consciously linked individual and family sexual behaviour to the level of population and nation, and grounded them both in racial biology.

Findlay explicitly aims at a concept of race, class and sex as 'mutually constitutive' and sees 'racially charged attempts at moral reform, conflicts over the legitimacy of various sexual norms and practices, racialised discourses about sexual respectability and honor, as well as the strategic silencing of racial differences' as all key to state governance, social movements and everyday identities (1998: 6, 3). Honour as a mode of control of female sexuality is 'rooted' in the desire to preserve in equal measure racial precedence, material patrimony and patriarchy (1998: 25). In a way, Findlay's constant awareness of race and how honour functioned to maintain racial hierarchy, through everyday interactions and campaigns of moral and social hygiene, leads her into the difficulty (noted above) that race was actually not talked about very much and that sexuality became a way of implicitly referencing race, while maintaining an image of 'the great Puerto Rican family' – that is, an image of racial democracy – despite popular and some political insistence on the presence of racism.

At the end of her book, Findlay highlights this issue with the argument that gender and sexual relations may be a key to understanding how racial democracy coexists with racial dis-crimination. She cites Kutzinski's work on the figure of the *mulata* in nineteenth- and twentieth-century Cuban visual and literary representations of the nation, which argues that Cuba's evolving national cultural ideologies both 'engendered and deracialised Cuba, thus further entrenching racially and sexually determined social hierarchies'. The figure of the *mulata*, the mixed-race, brown-skinned, eroticised woman became, especially from the 1920s, '*the* site where men of European and of African ancestry rhetorically reconcile their differences and, in the process, give birth to the paternalistic political fiction of a national multiculture in the face of a social system that resisted any real structural pluralism' (Kutzinski 1993: 10, 12–13). Like others analysed in this chapter, Kutzinski highlights the homosocial bonding that gives an appearance of racial democracy, a shared masculinity underwritten by the *mulata* or other figurings of the woman, such as the prostitute (and implicitly by the homosexual man). Findlay's analysis, however, goes beyond visual and literary representations to show how a focus on (implicitly non-white) female sexuality – centrally but not only in the figure of the prostitute – shaped marriage patterns, hygiene campaigns and feminist and other political movements.

The overall point is that a racial hierarchy can be reproduced by deploying sex/gender norms in a racially unequal way, focusing particularly on women's sexuality, respectability and honour, while apparently not talking about race at all and projecting an image of racial democracy, based in part on a cross-racial homosociality or fraternity, itself underwritten by a common masculinity, defined in reference to women – perhaps reinforced in the worship of a mixed-race figure such as the *mulata* – and the absent presence of homosexuality.

Mestizaje, Othering, Desire and Mimesis

A key aspect of the dynamics of race and sex during this period, as during the colonial period, but one that receives rather little attention in the histories I have been discussing, is the evident ambivalence of attitudes towards those identified as others in the mixing, modernising nation: the black, indigenous and mixed-race working classes, the unruly and dishonourable classes who were the target of the campaigns of social and moral hygiene, from which came the prostitutes and the single mothers, the drunkards and criminals. The ambivalence goes much deeper than the tension between, on one side, the evident contempt and fear felt for these people by the middle- and upper-class nation-builders and, on the other, their inclusion in the project of becoming a racially democratic, modern (and hopefully 'whitened') nation. Because it is clear that people from these classes, or perhaps at times just their imagined figures, generated powerful desires in the minds of their self-declared social superiors.

As I have outlined in Chapter 2, I think this deep-seated ambivalence has its roots in processes of gendered and sexualised self formation that happen in relation to others, during but also after childhood, such that the self carries the other within it, in an ambivalent relation of repulsion and attraction. In a context of the class and racial hierarchies of Latin America of this period, working-class and non-white people would easily take on the role of other for middle- and upper-class people, but in complicated ways that reinforce ambivalence. Racial-class others, for middle-

and upper-class people, were in many ways spatially segregated, especially in urban settings; but they would also be encountered at close quarters, through the provision and consumption of goods and services and especially through domestic service. One need only recall that the middle and upper classes of the period under discussion in this chapter, like their colonial counterparts, would all have had servants, some of them living in the house in intimate contact and some of them nannies and wet nurses who did a great deal of the day-to-day childcare, and most of them women and men of the working classes, black, indigenous and mixed-race. Racial dynamics operated and were constituted not only in the public realm of hygiene campaigns, but also in these intimate domains where people clearly identified as subordinate others were nevertheless entwined in close and often emotional relationships and were perhaps spoken of then, as they are now, as 'part of the family' (Gill 1994; cf. Stoler 2002: ch. 7). There does not seem to be a great deal of direct evidence that men in these families routinely had sexual relationships with their female domestic servants, but this doesn't mean that such relationships did not take place, just that they did not show up in the legal records (Caulfield 2000: 166–8). For Bolivian Aymara servants, sexual abuse was 'an ever-present threat' in the 1930s, as it was in the 1980s (Gill 1994: 25, 74).[14] But this does not undermine the fact that white people grew up and lived at close quarters with subordinate, racialised others.

In Chapter 3, I used the case of witchcraft and magic to delve into the murky waters of ambivalence. In this chapter, a fruitful area in which to explore the same theme is that of music and dance. A key dynamic that stands out for this period is the enjoyment and often appropriation by the middle and upper classes of music and dance forms associated with the lower classes and often explicitly with black people; these styles frequently became nationalised as emblems of the cultural essence of the people. Examples abound: *danza* became the main dance style of Puerto Rico between the 1890s and the 1920s; *danzón* dominated Cuba around the same period, followed by *son*, which became a national institution in the 1920s; tango emerged in Buenos Aries in the 1880s and became the very soul of the Argentinean nation; *maxixe* from the 1880s and then, more famously, samba from the 1910s became the central Brazilian styles known at home and abroad; *cumbia* and *porro* swept Colombia in the 1940s; *merengue* became the national music of the Dominican Republic; Afro-Peruvian styles became popular in Lima from the 1950s.[15] Musical styles associated with indigenous people fared rather differently: although middle-class intellectuals took an interest in them as a source of authenticity and cultural identity from the early decades of the twentieth century, they remained defined as 'folklore' and did not become commercialised popular genres or national icons in the same way (at least until the more recent popularisation of Andean pan-pipe music and perhaps the success of *chicha* music in Peru).[16]

The processes behind the nationalisation of these black, working-class styles are complex: after 1900 they had a lot to do with the burgeoning international record and media industries; they were linked to currents of cultural nationalism that, in line with ideologies of racial democracy, incorporated plebeian cultural forms (often in a 'sanitised' form) as part of the national culture; and transnational currents of primitivism that valorised a 'primitive', especially 'black', sensuality were also influential (for a discussion, see Wade 2000; see also Seigel 2009: ch. 4). One important, but more subterranean, factor was the interaction of middle- and upper-class men with lower-class men and women, often in contexts of leisure, music and dance – in brothels, bars, dancehalls, beer gardens and other public venues associated with 'the street', which represented a threat to the reputation of respectable women. Caulfield describes this for 1920s Rio's bohemian zone of Lapa where 'men gathered to drink, eat, listen to samba, rub elbows with *malandros* [rogues or conmen], enjoy the paid company of waitresses and prostitutes, or purchase sex' (2000: 69). The increasing entry of 'liberated' and 'modern' women of the middle and upper classes into new, city centre spaces of hotels, casinos and 'jazz-clubs', apart from scandalising conservatives, began to break this exclusion of women from spaces of public leisure, but did not end the association of such spaces with a transgressive sensuality. Green notes that Lapa's adjacent area of public squares and parks served as the main place for homosexual encounters for men of all social classes and racial backgrounds (1999: 64).

Samba was consecrated in the 1920s in similar encounters between white intellectuals and black and mixed-race *sambistas* from Rio's poorest classes, a pattern linked to the longstanding tendency of the Brazilian elite to patronise music of the blacker lower classes (Vianna 1999: chs 1, 3). An account from 1805 describes elite families in Bahia who, at their parties, would start with 'elegant entertainment'; after drinking copious wine, however, 'the song would soon give way to the enticing *Negro dance* ... which is a mixture of the dances of Africa and the fandangos of Spain and Portugal' (Vianna 1999: 17).

Likewise in urban Cuba in the 1920s–1940s, there were *encerronas* (literally, shut-ins, or private parties hosted by powerful men), the *academias* (dancing 'academies', where men could meet dance partners, often paying them for their services) and the beer gardens where, again, men of all classes would consort with women and men of lower, darker classes, listening and dancing to music played largely by black and mixed-race men (Moore 1997: ch. 4). Very similar patterns were found in Colombia in the 1930s and 1940s and these had longstanding roots. Accounts of dances in Cartagena in the 1830s described how men in the high-class dances 'furtively deserted' their own women in search of women at less prestigious celebrations. President Juan José Nieto (1804–66) had children by a lower-class *cuarterona* (quatroon) whom he met during a fiesta. In his description of Barranquilla around the 1940s, one local composer of popular music remembered that

> when the dances in the Country Club or the Club Riomar [elite social clubs] had finished, the men went to *echar colita* [euphemism for 'have some fun'] and they would go to the Carioca [a popular venue], but in disguise, and they used to say that was the real fun; and they'd stay there until dawn, but in their masks – during carnival. They couldn't go without a mask; that would be criticised. (Wade 2000: 70)

It is interesting that this composer recalls that men would have been criticised for what was by all accounts a common activity. It suggests an ambiguous line between public and private behaviour for respectable men.

Chasteen (2004), focusing on Cuba (*danzón*), Brazil (*maxixe* and samba) and Argentina (*milonga* and tango), elaborates a general argument that touches on this theme. For him, these dances, which became national icons and international crazes, all represent the enduring and endlessly repeated encounter between African hip-swinging and European couple dancing which fused in the New World to produce a series of dances that were seen as erotic and socially transgressive, in large part because they involved hip-swinging at close quarters between men and women. Key contexts for this in the nineteenth and early twentieth centuries were the theatres, carnivals, brothels, dancehalls, parties and salons in which cross-class, cross-racial encounters took place, in a specifically gendered way.

The middle and upper classes initially deplored these rhythms, associating them with blackness, the 'uncivilised' lower classes and licentiousness, but then adopted them, often in a stylised form that masked but retained some elements of the excitement that made them attractive in the first place. In late nineteenth-century Puerto Rico, where the *danza* was so popular, there was silence surrounding the relationships with Afro-Puerto Rican women that 'were so integral a part of moneyed men's lives' (Findlay 1998: 56). In contrast, many commentators voiced loud dismay at the influence on polite society of the *danza*, played by mulatto musicians. According to them, elite youth had succumbed to the 'seductive murmur' of the *danza* and 'beauty's magic attraction' and to 'intoxication with soft luxuriousness ... and moral decay'. If this type of language were not enough to suggest a subliminal excitement, one Liberal noted explicitly that the *danza*'s 'melodies rocked me to sleep in the cradle and excited me in my adolescence; they evoke all my lovely memories of youth. I have still not learned to curse that which I love' (cited in Findlay 1998: 56–7).

Other contemporary commentaries reiterated this sexualising and erotic discourse. One 1885 essay by a prominent intellectual advised readers to appreciate *danza* outside the dancehall because within it, the lights, the perfumes and 'everything producing physical excitement will lead us to psychological disturbance', above all because the woman clasped in one's arms, the 'contact with the expressive softness of her form' and the promise of 'ineffable delights' would distract the attention of the listener. Even outside the dancehall, the music would be 'sensual' and 'intoxicating', 'taking control of your organism'. Another, more lip-smacking observer wrote in 1882 of the 'lewd and happy pairs of dancers' that gave themselves up 'with the voluptuousness of satyrs to an orgiastic dance' in which one could watch 'the brazen and sensual mulatta … her lips pursed in a paroxysm of pleasure' (cited in Quintero Rivera 1996: 171–2).

There was a clear fascination with black sexuality linked to music and dance. Take, for example, this description of the *mapalé*, a black dance usually associated with the Caribbean coastal region of Colombia, penned by Tomás Carrasquilla in the 1920s and presumably drawing on his own experience (and imagination), although set by him in the mid-eighteenth century in the town of Yolombó:

The *mapalé* is delicious. There are twelve dancers: they form up in rows, negroes on one side and negresses on the other; they raise their candles to an equal height with a single movement; they cross, they alternate, arms interlace, the flames unite. Face to face, eyes rolling, lips vibrating, they magnetize each other. They mark the rhythm with expert feet, now forwards, now backwards. They embroider and trace without drawing apart an inch. They rise up, they shake, they bend, they crouch…. The little windmill spins and spins in a whirl of flames. They break apart suddenly and continue as before in pairs. The culmination is supreme. They shake their hips in convulsive agitation; their breasts tremble as if they were jelly. Those mouths pant, those bodies twist and turn, gleaming with sweat, eyes, earrings and necklaces shine. Their bodies embrace in a frenzy, they turn to bend, they turn to straighten; they support themselves with their arms, throw their breasts backwards; they hurl away their candles and they are finished. It is the apparition of distant Africa, which they carry in their blood and which their eyes have never seen; it is a rite performed before a cruel and grieving Eros. (cited in Wade 1993a: 90)

There was a complex interplay of denigration and imitation in the way white and elite people related to these music and dance styles. In the case of tango, although its origins are contested, there is agreement that it emerged from the working-class neighbourhoods of 1880s Buenos Aires, based on African-influenced *milonga* (itself influenced by Cuban *habanera* and European dances) and very possibly the dances performed by the black Afro-Argentine *candombé* clubs. One version suggests that tango emerged as non-black working-class urbanites copied, indeed parodied, the *candombé* dance styles of their black neighbours – just as the Afro-Argentines were also dancing European polkas and mazurkas – and introduced these elements into the *milonga*. From there the new dance spread across Buenos Aires and into the higher social classes, with help from the young men of polite society, who learned 'the scandalous dance on their trips to the houses of ill-fame' (Taylor 1976: 282).[17] Interestingly, the argument contends that, in the Afro-Argentine *candombé*, men and women danced apart; the elements that were introduced to the *milonga* were the dynamic *quebradas* (breaks) and *cortes* (cuts) – improvised, dramatic, sudden moves – which then became part of the *milonga* style in which men and women held each other in European, couple-dancing style (Collier 1995). In any event, the dance was strongly associated with Afro-Argentines, as contemporary illustrations clearly show (Collier 1995; Savigliano 1995). Chasteen (2004) adds another level to this game of mimesis and parody when he describes Afro-Argentinean groups who 'blacked up' in imitation of white men who 'blacked up' to imitate them.

In 1940s Colombia, when *cumbia* and *porro* were making their entry into Bogotá's social scene, from the Caribbean coastal region of the country – with the musical styles and the region both associated with blackness – one newspaper columnist also worried about imitation. Noting that modern music had been 'infiltrated by black art', he lamented that whites, less 'invulnerable' than they had seemed, had taken it into their heads to 'imitate the blacks and obey them': 'the culture best received these days, especially in the swanky clubs, is that which has the acrid smell of jungle and of sex'. In short, 'modernism requires this: that we should dance like blacks in order to be in fashion'.[18]

All this material indicates a powerful fascination with working-class and particularly black cultural forms, linked strongly to sexuality. It indicates a desire to appropriate such sexuality through direct contact and also through mimesis which, as Taussig (1993) has argued, is thought to capture something of the sensual concreteness of the original. Black music represented a powerfully attractive and sexualised realm, one of leisure, pleasure and quite possibly escape: Radano argues that for North America the idea of 'hot' black rhythms was based in part on a myth which 'cast black music as the primordial cure for the ills of a civilised and increasingly mechanised modern society' (2000: 460). A key mechanism by which this fascination operated was the interactions of white or light-skinned middle- and upper-class men with darker-skinned women and men of the lower classes, often in contexts in which music, dance and quite often sex were central activities. While lower-class, black cultural forms might be decried and subject to various kinds of campaigns aimed at reform and improvement, they also exercised a powerful attraction. This most obviously exerted its effect on men, who had the freedom to enter the social milieux in which they could indulge their interests; but given the popularity of these dance forms with men and women of the middle and upper classes, once the music had been suitably stylised and was being played in fashionable clubs (especially if international audiences had given their stamp of approval to it), it seems very likely that women also found a strong attraction in these cultural forms.

I believe that grasping this ambivalence is necessary to seeing how race and sex articulated at this time. Well-off white men did not maintain relationships with darker-skinned working-class women just because the sexual double standard allowed them to, or because this expressed their racial and class dominance; they did so because such relationships responded to dynamics of desire that also had roots in deep-seated processes of self formation and relationships with 'others'. These processes were powerfully shaped by these men's experience of gender and race hierarchies, both in their childhood and later in life. Dark-skinned women represented to these men an other that was inferior but also powerfully sexually attractive, and music and dance provided the context in which such desires could be both expressed and generated. Although white women are less visible in this whole process, there are indications that similar dynamics also operated. However, their rather different experience in relation to gender and race hierarchies must have given such dynamics a different form.

Ambivalence from Below

Tracing ambivalence from the perspective of the dominant class inevitably raises the question of whether the 'others' experienced ambivalence and, if so, how. What about the non-white women involved in relationships with white men? What about the black and mixed-race musicians catering to white tastes? Ambivalence of some kind seems a likely reaction to the experience of subordination in a society that claims to be inclusive. After all, it was in 1897 that the North American black intellectual W. E. B. Du Bois coined the term 'double consciousness', which he described as 'this sense of always looking at one's self through the eyes of others, of measuring one's soul by the tape of a world that looks on in amused contempt and pity', and as being 'an American, a Negro; two warring ideals in one dark body, whose dogged strength alone keeps it from being torn asunder' (Du Bois 1897). Writing several decades later, Frantz Fanon (1925–61) clearly also felt this powerful tension, as we saw in Chapter 2. Seeing oneself through the eyes of others is, from a psychoanalytic point of view, part of the human (or perhaps only Western) condition, but feeling that others view one always with contempt and pity is clearly specific to the experience of a subordinated class.

Although sources do not allow us easily to uncover feelings of ambivalence among the dominated, specifically related to race and sex, for this period – and this is especially true for women – it is clear that a powerful underlying ambivalence existed in relation to the sense of being a citizen in the new nation and of being black, indigenous or mixed-race. Helg's study of the Cuban independence wars and their aftermath show clearly that Afro-Cuban leaders aimed above all at being included in the nation: their demands were that liberal, democratic ideals be made real, that racial difference be irrelevant in the public realm. To accomplish this, however, some of them saw the need to create an autonomous black political party in 1908, provoking a white backlash that ended in the notorious 1912 massacre of Afro-Cubans (Helg 1995). In a similar vein, the Afro-Cuban mutual aid societies or *cabildos* that had existed from early colonial times had a dual role in late nineteenth-century Cuba (Howard 1998). On the one hand, they were organisations that promoted assimilation, encouraging blacks to educate themselves and adapt to white, European norms. On the other hand, the *cabildos* were organisations of resistance, which fomented Afro-Cuban cultural forms (religious, musical) seen as dangerous and immoral by many whites and yet also fascinating and powerful to the extent that some whites purchased Afro-Cuban 'secrets' and formed their own societies. Fernando Ortiz noted that Catholic priests in Cuba reinforced the powers of the black *brujos* (sorcerers, who were not necessarily connected to *cabildos*) because they thought them to be in league with the devil (1917 [1906]: 257). Moreover, 'rich women of elevated lineage' participated in ceremonies conducted by *brujos* 'at the altar of fanatical belief' (1917 [1906]: 147). It seems likely that Afro-Cubans were well aware of the fascination for whites of some of their activities around secret religion, witchcraft and healing and played to this strength in a way that gave them more power, but of a circumscribed kind.

The work of black writers of the period is a useful way into questions of ambivalence. A good deal of the critical literature on these writers traces the extent to which they expressed a black identity and a racial consciousness and there is no doubt that many of them wrote about racial and social inequality, racism and the experience of being black in a country such as Cuba or Colombia. But many also adhered to a wider, more humanist agenda, espousing broad principles of social equality and decrying poverty and injustice in general.[19] And several of them also reinforced images of blackness that were being purveyed in *negrista* literary currents led by white writers. The Afro-Cuban poet Nicolás Guillén, for example, offended the (light-skinned) black middle-class intelligentsia of Havana in the 1930s by his use of working-class Afro-Cuban vernacular and questioning of racial inequality; but he also deployed fairly stereotypical images of black dancing and drinking in poems such as 'Canto Negro' or 'Secuestro de la Mujer de Antonio'. More generally, Kutzinski argues that *poesía negra/mulata* in Cuba did not humanise racial stereotypes as much as 'define an ideological space that all Cubans, regardless of colour and caste, could presumably inhabit on equal terms' (1993: 155). The Afro-Colombian poet Jorge Artel, who published *Tambores en la noche* in 1940, also attributed sensuous rhythm to black people in Colombia's Caribbean coastal region as part of his project to recognise and valorise African ancestry in the nation. Prescott argues that he was interested in integration and the creation of 'an authentic and whole national identity', while at the same time he 'laid bare the spiritual void and perennial paradox of a nation whose citizens lived relatively free from political oppression and racial persecution but were heavily burdened by shame and fear of the "colored" roots of their reputedly proud mestizo identity' (2000: 221, 19).

Something parallel seems to have characterised indigenous intellectuals of the 1920s–1940s in the Peruvian Andes. These men were intent on defining a version of *indigenismo* that protected indigenous history and culture and did not promote its melding, through *mestizaje*, into a national culture. Yet they also associated *indios* with illiteracy and poverty and allied themselves with *mestizo* values of education and propriety (De la Cadena 2000: chs 1–3). Going into the 1950s–1970s, beyond the main period covered in this chapter, this ambivalence is also evident among the female market vendors in Cuzco, who identified themselves as *mestizas*, not because they thought of themselves as non-indigenous, but because they were hard-working and economically successful and thus merited *respeto* (a working-class value of interpersonal respect) and because they were also *decente* (a middle-class value of decency and propriety). *Indios*, on the other hand, tended, in their view, to be not only poor, but also lazy, dirty and stupid. Market women were often portrayed as sexually provocative, exciting and available: they, however, actively resisted such imagery in their account of themselves as decent and meriting respect (De la Cadena 2000: chs 4–6). It is an open question, but in De la Cadena's account, these women do not seem particularly ambivalent about being indigenous and yet discriminating against *indios*. Perhaps their sense of their own accomplishments weighed against a sense of double consciousness, yet the way middle-class values of decency had seeped into working-class values of respect does suggest a possible basis for such a sense.

None of this gets us very close to ambivalence around the sexual aspects of race (and even less so for women), but it suggests that black and mixed-race men certainly felt a powerful ambivalence in a general sense – at once part of the nation and yet marginalised within it, at once proud of their black heritage and yet committed to an integrated national culture. Some of them may well have actively promoted a certain sexualisation and sensualisation of blackness or, more accurately, of black and mixed-race *women* and this itself was an ambivalent act, since it both valorised blackness (albeit in a stereotyped way) and also fed into a sense of nationalism built on male bonding around the figure of the eroticised *mulata*. Black musicians may also have actively reinforced stereotypical images of innate black musicality and sexy, 'hot' rhythms, but the economic power they managed to conquer by doing so was often circumscribed, as white bands monopolised the best commercial opportunities, leaving black musicians to the percussion section or the non-public recording sessions.[20]

Conclusion

The material in this chapter demonstrates once more how closely intertwined are mechanisms of domination and regulation in the articulation of race and sex. In Chapter 3, we saw how direct, domineering sexual conquest by more powerful, white men of the bodies of less powerful, non-white women (and some men) was a key tool of power. Alongside this, the protection of elite white women's sexuality was a central mechanism in the defence of the social status of the dominant class. The whole cultural complex around honour combined sexual conquest with sexual regulation. The evidence from the late nineteenth and early twentieth centuries suggests that these basic patterns persisted, despite the dismantling of formal concerns with *limpieza de sangre* in contracting marriage and in other public domains. Lower-class and especially darker-skinned women were assumed to be less honourable; whiter, more upper-class men continued to be able to have informal sexual relationships with these women and, if the latter protested that their honour had been compromised, the men concerned were likely to be better protected by the law than darker-skinned men of lower-class status.

The key difference from the colonial period was that the sexuality of the racialised lower classes was now set in a nation-building project. This had two aspects. First, there were sustained attempts to create a socially and morally 'hygienic' nation, based on the scientific ideas of the period about race and class. This underwrote a series of social and medical campaigns, often targeting prostitutes, which sought to better the nation by improving its biological and racial composition. Second, Latin American nations were defining themselves to a greater or lesser extent as liberal and democratic and thus, by implication or in some cases by explicit affirmation, as racially democratic and inclusive, the more so because of the extensive mix that characterised many national populations and was often becoming the basis for national identities. This coexisted with continuing racial hierarchy and racism which included racialised sexual exploitation and the targeting of non-white sexuality as immoral. The image of racial harmony could be promoted by the idea of a fraternal, homosocial masculinity, which bound men together in national honour – even if, in practice, honour codes actually functioned to defend elite family status and undermine dark-skinned women's reputations and thus placed darker-skinned men at odds with whiter men. In some cases (notably, Cuba and

Brazil) the idealisation of the brown-skinned, mixed-race woman, the *mulata*, crystallised these ideas of racial mixture and harmony, male consensus about masculinity and, of course, the supposed sexual promiscuity and desirability of non-white women.

Finally, we saw that, as before, there was intense ambivalence surrounding race and sex, with disgust at and fear of lower-class sexual morality combined with a fascination and desire. This was articulated in large part through the relationships of middle- and upper-class white men with lower-class, non-white women, mediated by urban leisure, music and dance. In this, blackness seems to have played a special role as the locus of sensuality and excitement. It seems likely that the ambivalence attached to otherness was expressed in an especially powerful way for well-off white men in the figure of the non-white woman (and to a lesser extent the non-white man); this may have been reinforced by the racialised patterns of domestic service that placed race in the sphere of the intimate. Ambivalence was also a characteristic of those categorised as others, but here it had a different form and was similar to what Du Bois defined as double consciousness, that sense of being both part of a nation and yet excluded from it; of being both part of a minority culture and a national culture at the same time. The sexualised aspects of that ambivalence, however, remain to be uncovered.

5

THE POLITICAL ECONOMY OF RACE AND SEX IN CONTEMPORARY LATIN AMERICA

In this chapter I examine three areas relating to race and sex: interracial sex and *mestizaje*, beauty and eroticism, and sex tourism and sex worker migration. All of these are loosely linked to the notion of political economy in the sense that they all operate within a kind of 'market' of erotic, affective, economic and status values, in which people make choices about whom to marry or have sex with, what is beautiful and desirable, and how to make a living and improve their lives. These choices shape and are shaped by hierarchies of race, gender and class and they enact the simultaneous presence of both racism and racial democracy. Both the markets and the hierarchies have national and transnational dimensions.

In the next chapter, I shall explore how race and sex intersect in the fields of identity, citizenship, the state and social movements, looking at public policy on sexual and reproductive health, the way gender and sexuality influence ethnic and racial movements, and the politics of identity and *mestizaje* among Latinos in the US.

Racism, Racial Democracy and *Mestizaje*

The realm of race in contemporary Latin America is characterised by a fundamental tension between racial democracy and racism. On the one hand, nation-states in the region generally claim – or have claimed until very recently – that racism is not a serious problem for them. This claim is legitimated in several ways: by implicit or explicit comparison with the US or South Africa, where racial segregation and racial violence have been very obvious; by claiming that the key social divide is class, not race, because the lower classes, and to a greater or lesser extent the middle classes, are often racially heterogeneous; by arguing that race is not a central factor in the way people treat and classify each other in daily life; and, above all, by characterising Latin American societies as shaped by race mixture (*mestizaje* or *mestiçagem*). This process, it is claimed, has blurred racial boundaries, made racial categories unimportant and turned the majority of the population into *mestizos*, sharing a common national culture and identity. In addition, race mixture shows that people of different racial categories are willing to have sex with – and even marry – each other, a trait taken to indicate the unimportance of racial factors. Such claims have been made by intellectuals and political leaders in many Latin American countries and have also been underwritten by some social scientists: other studies have also claimed that, if not completely free of racism, Latin American nations are characterised by such ambiguity of racial identity, caused by extensive and prolonged race mixture, that it is impossible for systematic racial discrimination to take place.

On the other hand, racism has been shown to be alive and in robust health in the region. The weight of academic evidence now indicates quite clearly that, although class is a major factor in social inequality, not only does it often overlap with racial inequality quite closely, but race has a strong independent impact on a person's life-chances; that racial identities, although often shifting, fluid and unclear, are not so ambiguous as to make racial discrimination impossible, even if it is not as weirdly 'systematic' as the segregation practised in the US under Jim Crow legislation or in South Africa under apartheid; and that the existence of a large, even majority mixed-race population is no barrier to the persistence of racism against certain categories of people and also within the *mestizo* majority itself, within which racialised hierarchies (e.g. of skin colour) assign some people more value than others.[1] In the 1990s and 2000s, many Latin American governments have given official recognition to ethnic and cultural diversity – although less often to 'racial' difference – within their nations and, linked to this, some have recognised the continuing existence of racism (Htun 2004; Wade 2002a: 12).

The coexistence of claims to racial democracy with the existence of racism is not a unique paradox. In 1944, Gunnar Myrdal called the conflict between the US's ideology of liberty and its blatantly racist system of segregation 'an American dilemma' (Myrdal 1944). Although the paradox was particularly acute in that case, Myrdal could have expanded the scope of his analysis. In some sense, all societies founded on an ideological basis of liberalism encounter the same dilemma: on the one hand, an ideology of equality; on the other, the persistence of inequalities of class, race and gender. There is a central tension between universalism and particularism, between equality and hierarchy and between sameness and difference (Balibar 1991; Baumeister 2000; Cottrol 2001; Modood 2007).

In Latin America, the racialised aspect of this conundrum has a specific character. The coexistence of racism and racial democracy has a very *simultaneous* and very *coterminous* character: the very things that underwrite the idea of racial democracy are the ones in which racism operates; racial democracy and racism happen at the same time and in the same space. The fact that within a single family there can be individuals of different racial identities or given different racialised labels is both proof of racial democracy (racial heterogeneity crosses class, community and even family boundaries) and a site for the reproduction of racism (racial difference and discrimination enter into even the most intimate domains of kinship). The fact that race mixture creates a large category of *mestizos*, whose racial identity is shifting and fluid, is both evidence of racial democracy (society is not segregated into clear racialised groups) and a location of racism (*mestizo* national identities privilege whiteness and marginalise blackness and indig-enousness; *mestizos* may also discriminate and be subject to discrimination). The fact that people of different racial categories or identities marry one another, perhaps not as often as nationalist myths of *mestizaje* would imply, but still with a greater frequency than in, say, the US (on Brazil, see Telles 2004: ch. 7) is both an indication of racial democracy (intermarriage is often seen as the acid test of racial tolerance) and a place where racism is made manifest (people's marriage choices are guided by ideas about race, even as they cross boundaries). The fact that, in Guatemala, the *ladinos* (the non-indigenous class) increasingly repudiate racism, acknowledge cultural diversity in the nation and fervently defend equality is both evidence of racial democracy and, at the same time, the very discursive space in which racism is reproduced (the 'cultural' difference attributed to Mayans becomes a mode of cultural racism in which Mayans are seen as culturally threatening or inferior; the discourse of cultural equality is a means to ignore the structural privileges enjoyed by the *ladinos*): this is what Hale (2006) calls the 'racial ambivalence' of the ladinos.

In seeing this simultaneity of racism and racial democracy, it is important to grasp that racial democracy is not *just* a rhetorical discourse, a cynical mask behind which lies the hard reality of racist acts. While it certainly can act in that way, it is vital to the maintenance of Latin American styles of race relations that it is also more than that: it is a lived reality as well. The existence of *mestizos*, of racial ambiguity, of interracial marriages, of the absence of clearly defined racialised groups in many contexts – all these things are real aspects of people's lived experience, alongside the experience of both practising and being the target of racism (Fry 1995–96, 2000; Wade 2005b).

Mestizaje and its associated imagery and practice of interracial sex are central to the simultaneity of racism and racial democracy. As we saw in the previous chapter, it was in the realm of sex and gender that it was possible both to valorise a racially democratic brotherhood of men and, at the same time, to practise the sexual conquest of darker-skinned women by lighter-skinned men and, more generally, to practise an honour-based discrimination against darker-skinned men and, especially, women. The simultaneity of racism and racial democracy are lodged deep in discourses and practices of *mestizaje* and this makes it difficult to construct alternative discourses of *mestizaje* 'from below', contestatory and subaltern versions of the ideology that have been identified by various scholars who contrast these plebeian views of mixture with dominant elite versions (Hale 2005; Klor de Alva 1995; Mallon 1996). Because the dominant discourse of *mestizaje* already contains *within it* the possibility of racial democracy, it tends to defuse and co-opt alternative visions that pursue that goal more thoroughly.

In this chapter, we shall see how sex is a key arena for the simultaneous existence of both racism and racial democracy as aspects of lived experience. In this arena, domination and regulation are, as before, closely intertwined: power is both repressive and productive. Racism reproduces racial domination and oppression, while at the same time the essentially *moral* project of creating a racially democratic nation is also under way, not only as a state-driven endeavour but also as a personal ethic of everyday behaviour. As in previous chapters, we shall also see how race and sex shape each other and articulate together to form a mutable armature of power relations: the whole racial order is, in an important sense, thought and enacted through sexual relations (especially of *mestizaje*), while the discourses and practices around sex and gender are shaped by the racial order (crucially, in the realm of sexual and marital partner choice, but also in the aesthetics of beauty and, arguably, in the formation of sexual identity). Also as in previous chapters, we shall find these domains of social practice criss-crossed by patterns of ambivalence and anxiety in which love and fear interweave with each other.

In the sections that follow, I shall look first at processes involving interracial sex and marriage, before exploring the racialised aesthetics of beauty, sex tourism and sex migration and, finally, the ambivalences and anxieties of desire.

Interracial Sex

Cholas and *Mestizaje*

In Weismantel's rich and fascinating study of 'stories of race and sex in the Andes', interracial sex is seen principally in terms of abuse and domination (Weismantel 2001). One of Weismantel's key figures is that of the *pishtaco*, a mythical bogeyman usually described as a large white man who attacks indigenous people and steals their body fat; he may also be a rapist. This figure represents the exploitation and abuse practised by (white) capitalists, and Weismantel equates him with a dominating, emasculating, Freudian father figure (ibid.: 220). The *pishtaco* occupies a structural position of whiteness and dominance: the term can be used to accuse anyone, including indigenous people and women, seen to be exploitative and domineering; the word can be used as a verb, *pishtar*, generally meaning to abuse sexually or rape (ibid.: 169).

The *pishtaco* figure speaks of coercion, oppression and domination in which sex is a key realm of meaning. In Weismantel's account, racial democracy figures only as a myth, as does the ideology of *mestizaje* (ibid.: xxviii, 89, 96). Race is a 'fundamentally binary' construct: white versus non-white (ibid.: xxxii). Yet processes of race mixture and, especially, people understood as racially mixed are at the centre of Weismantel's stories of race and sex. The other key figure in her book is the *chola*, a term with multiple meanings, but which usually connotes a mixed-race woman (typically a daughter of a white father and indigenous mother). In nationalist ideology, the *chola* may be the rather whitened, sexually desirable and accessible woman located at the heart of *mestizaje* understood as the process underlying the emergence of the (Ecuadorean) nation. She may also be a more indigenous-looking woman, dressed in traditional clothing. She has a typical, indeed iconic, image, reproduced in postcards and photographs. The *chola* represents a long history of white male sexual predation on non-white women: 'A nativity scene deformed by racism, the story of the white man, the Indian woman and their *mestizo* child is written into every epoch of Latin American history' (ibid.: 155) and 'attitudes and practices that assume white male access to nonwhite bodies for sexual gratification remain strongly entrenched' (ibid.: 156). Weismantel traces the pervasiveness of these ideas in elite discourses – even those tinged with left-wing ideals – in literary depictions and even in some intellectuals currents of *indigenismo* that defended indigenous culture and history. These ideas explain why there is such an iconic image of the *chola*, but not one of the male *cholo*.[2]

Weismantel shows that the term *chola* is also applied to urban market vendors, women who may or may not be mixed-race, are physically large and strong, assertive, usually fairly well-off and often seen as somewhat masculine or, rather, sexually ambivalent, combining aspects of masculinity and femininity in their dress and behaviour. These women represent a challenge to masculinist and nationalist ideas about *mestizaje* and *cholas*. As I mentioned in Chapter 4, De la Cadena (2000: ch. 4) also shows how Peruvian market women reject the image of the *chola* that emerges from Peruvian regionalist and nationalist discourses which cast them as desirable, but also impure and immoral (i.e. lacking sexual honour). Instead, they define themselves as respectable and hard-working.

If we want to look for the simultaneity of racism and racial democracy in Andean conjunctures of race and sex, Weismantel's account does not appear at first sight to be a supportive source of data: her emphasis is strongly on racism as expressed in sexual conquest and the (always flawed) project of producing a democratic nation through *mestizaje* comes across, if at all, as a lie and an ideological myth. Yet the simultaneity is there if we look more closely.

To start with, Weismantel shows clearly the unstable character of the *chola* identity: she emphasises its performative nature and how it is specific actions, rather than a phenotype or ideas about genealogy, that define it: just as someone who abuses and exploits can be labelled a *pishtaco*, so being a *chola* is a matter of becoming rather than simply being; of being a market vendor and dressing and behaving in the appropriate assertive, sexually ambivalent ways. Although she does not present it in this way, this is typical of how Latin American racial orders manifest aspects of democracy: racial identities are not fixed, and part of their flexibility is produced through gendered and sexualised performances. In urban Ecuador, for example, in the San Marcos district of Quito, men and women identify in ethnic and racial terms in varied and flexible ways: women have a greater tendency to identify as white, while most men identify as *mestizo* (Radcliffe 1999). If racial identity is flexible and performed in this way, then systematic racial discrimination and segregation are hard to enforce.

On the other hand, Weismantel shows that this performance of race takes place within a field of action powerfully charged by structures of race, gender and class that are much more stable. Actions seen as abusive lead the abuser to become in effect whitened and masculinised; just as racial whiteness gives sexual and economic advantages, so economic power or sexual dominance whitens and masculinises (2001: 173, 247–8). The women market vendors' economic power and control of money is part and parcel of their masculinisation and of their distance, as *cholas*, from a straightforward indigenousness. Dominance is strongly associated with maleness and whiteness, or at least distance from indigenousness. Boesten's work on rape and military violence in Peru reinforces this: she shows that, during the military persecution of Shining Path insurgents, indigenous women were called *cholas* by soldiers and policemen while they raped them, both evoking and reproducing the supposed sexual availability and desirability of this figure (Boesten 2008: 210).[3] Such behaviour was doubtless facilitated by the fact that military forces in the Andes tend to instil 'hyperaggressive notions of masculinity' in their recruits, as well as concepts of citizenship that distance the men from their indigenous background (Gill 1997: 528). The flexibility of racial identification in San Marcos, Quito, is likewise shaped by national-racial hierarchies: Radcliffe (1999) argues that women tend to avoid identifying as indigenous and prefer to see themselves as white because of the negative images of sexuality and immorality attached to indigenous women and because, as (potential) mothers of the nation's citizens, they are expected to shape the overall process of *mestizaje* towards a whiter endpoint. In short, national hierarchies of race and sex structure the flexibility of identifications.

The stabilisation of performative flexibility also takes place, Weismantel argues, through the repetition of exchanges (economic, sexual) that cause the body to accumulate certain traits in a more stable way: identities may be fluid, but if you enact them continuously, they begin to stick. Indigenous people's feet are physically shaped by their lifestyle (going barefoot or wearing rough rubber sandals leading to wide, splayed, calloused feet) in ways that are read by them and others as signalling indigenousness (2001: 189). Thus the very thing that constitutes a possibility for racial democracy (unfixed racial identities) is simultaneously a means through which racism works.

Second, juxtaposing De la Cadena's work on Peruvian market women with Weismantel's reading of Andean (mostly Ecuadorean) market women suggests, as we saw in Chapter 4, that these women define themselves as *mestizas* in a way that distances them from indigenous people without creating a rupture. They are 'indigenous *mestizas*' (De la Cadena 2000: ch. 4). They do not deny their indigenous heritage and roots, but their economic success and the *respeto* (respect) they have earned through honourable hard work (*trabajo honrado*) define them as *mestizas* at the same time. This breaks with elite notions of *mestizaje* insofar as these imply that one cannot be indigenous and *mestizo* at the same time, but it also buys into the racially democratic ideal that one can become a *mestizo* by working hard and acting honourably: it is a matter of class not race. Indeed, one can become a *mestizo* while remaining indigenous – a radical claim of racial democracy. And the claim is being made via sex in the sense that the place of the *mestiza* as a victim of white male sexual predation is being contested: the equality is racial and sexual at the same time.

Yet De la Cadena also argues that these women reproduce the racism lodged deep in ideologies of *mestizaje* by discriminating against people identified simply as *indio* – sometimes abusively so. Typically, they abuse them for being 'lazy' and 'dirty' people, who have not earned respect through honourable hard work. The link to notions of honour here is vital because *cholas* are subject to stereotyping as sexually immoral and lacking in sexual honour. These market vendors are thus claiming honour in ways familiar from Chapters 3 and 4; this includes not only hard work, but a 'proper', well-organised family life, even if this does not meet the local elite's standards of 'decency' (e.g. being officially married, women ideally staying at home). Although plebeian values of *respeto* are thus different from elite values of 'decency', the latter 'leak in' to the former by way of shared beliefs about the value of 'urbanity and education' – and, I would add, honour. These *mestizas* begin to invoke the values of 'decency' that are wielded by the local elites against the market women themselves in accusations of immorality, indecency and insolence (De la Cadena 2000: 228; cf. Gill 1994: 98).

Third, Weismantel refers to the nation-building discourses of *mestizaje* which frame the more specific ethnography of the *cholas*. De la Cadena gives greater space to such intellectual currents – although they were rather specific in the Peruvian case, in that ideologies of national *mestizaje* were at least balanced by indigenist ideologies of keeping native Andean peoples and cultures separate, pure and unmixed. Of course, the connotations of equality and racial democracy that such discourses can evoke have to be seen in their simultaneous relation to the racism they also carry, but it seems plausible to argue that the instability of categories such as *chola* and *mestizo* – which help open them to assertions of racial equality – derive in part precisely from these nation-building discourses of mixture which deploy such categories in changing and semantically unstable ways.

If we turn to Guatemala, we find basic patterns, which are by now familiar and bear witness to their geographical ubiquity and persistence in Latin America. today. Nelson (1999: ch. 6) focuses on discourses about *mestizaje* and indigenous people as deployed by *ladinos* (the dominant elite class, identified as white). She argues that *mestizaje* reproduces differences of race, but also of gender. She draws on the famous account of elite racism in Guatemala by Casaus Arvú (1992), which highlighted the preoccupation of elite families with bodily appearance and genealogy and the way these function as mechanisms of racist exclusion, but she points out that Casaus Arvú was not alive to the gendered and sexualised nature of this racism. A white man can have sex with a non-white woman without this constituting a problem for his lineage; indeed, his act 'improves the race' of any resulting children. White women who have sex with non-white men, however, stain the lineage and damage 'the race'. *Ladinas* are therefore continuously produced as sexually pure, to be defended and controlled. White men, on the contrary, are sexually privileged, with access to all women, and Nelson shows how non-white women are sexualised as both desirable and available for sex (albeit coerced) – but not for marriage.

Hale confirms this basic pattern, noting that 'sexual predation is ubiquitous, if rarely talked about openly', although he managed to collect enough 'descriptions of cross-racial sex to be sure that in Chimaltenango it has been commonplace' (2006: 159). This sexualisation of non-white women is worked into his analysis of 'racial ambivalence' – the adherence by *ladinos* to ideals of equality and rights to cultural difference, alongside the retention of structures of racial domination – in terms of the *ladinos*' fear that their racial dominion may actually be compromised by indigenous claims to equality which 'go too far' and become insurrectionary. Part of the fear is that indigenous men would wreak sexual revenge on *ladinos* for all the sexual violence and predation visited by white men on indigenous women. *Ladino* men become particularly incensed by indigenous leaders and congressmen who date white women (Nelson 1999: 219) and they tend to make 'self-evident connections between interracial romance and violent (racial) revolution' (Hale 2006: 159). Hale's analysis could perhaps be pushed a bit further by considering that the realm of sex/gender, rather than being simply an aspect of racial ambivalence, is fundamentally constitutive of it; that racial ambivalence is founded on the notion of *mestizaje* as a gendered, sexualised and racialised process in which white men defend their position by defending the gendered sexuality of white women and sexually conquering non-white women.

For her part, Nelson focuses on the racism inherent in *mestizaje*, but she also notes that the bodies that are produced by *mestizaje*'s discourse of race, sex and desire are complex and contradictory: they are unstable and unpredictable. In her phrase, punning on Butler (1993), they are 'bodies that splatter': they 'break apart wetly under the weight of the signification they are meant to carry ... messing up any clean, unified categories' (1999: 209).

Nelson gives the example of a young *ladino* man (in her eyes, quite light-skinned) who told her that his mother always instructed him never to sit next to an indigenous woman on the bus: the danger was that people would assume he was the woman's son. The mother clearly saw something in his appearance that signalled *indio* to her and might to others too (ibid.: 231). Yet categories such as *indio* and *ladino* are also popularly (and academically) supposed to be cultural ones. So, on the one hand, such identities are constituted through dress and language; and, on the other, they are signalled in phenotype. And even then, the phenotypical signals are profoundly unstable and might indicate both *ladino* and *indio*. Many *ladinos* say they can always tell if someone is indigenous by certain physical markers; but 'everyday *ladino* practice suggests the terror of not being able to tell' (ibid.). As in the case of the *chola* category described by Weismantel, this instability of racial categorisation is, in one sense, potentially racially democratic: people are not fixed into racial categories. In another, simultaneous sense, the same instability is driven by a deeply lodged racism in which being mistaken for an *indio* is a threat.

Nelson also recognises this duality: she is very aware of the racism inherent in *mestizaje*, but also says: 'Although I am suspicious of its liberatory claims, *mestizaje* discourse may be a tool in fluidary politics – as long as we examine the regulatory norms and erasures that structure it' (ibid.: 238). 'Fluidary politics' goes beyond simple fixed categories and acknowledges complex and contradictory subjective and ethical positions. Nelson is, in effect, proposing the possibility of a *mestizaje* 'from below' which is contestatory – a proposal put forward by others who have also recognised the existence and possible potential of such a discourse (Anzaldúa 1987; Hale 2005; Klor de Alva 1995; Mallon 1996); indeed, de la Cadena's 'indigenous *mestizos*' are also articulating a vision of *mestizaje* 'from below'.

There is no doubt that *mestizaje* has different meanings and can be read both with and against the grain. The problem I see with formulations that counterpoise *mestizaje* 'from above' to that 'from below' is that they tend to misrecognise the overlap or even complicity between the two versions. I argue that *mestizaje* from above has within it the simultaneous existence of racism and racial democracy, which means that versions from below that enshrine racial democracy as a goal always run the risk of being co-opted and subverted by dominant readings which can also claim such goals – which does not, of course, mean that alternative readings and practices of *mestizaje* are not worth pursuing as a political goal. This overlap and complicity operate in great part in the domain of sex/gender. As we saw in the case of De la Cadena's market women, subaltern values of *respeto* and elite ones of decency 'leak' into each other via the notion of honour. Or again, as we saw in Chapter 4, plebeian claims to citizenship and racial equality can become figured as the inclusion of men into a national brotherhood of patriarchs, united in the protection of female and national honour.

Interracial Marriage Patterns and Racial Hierarchy

Weismantel, De la Cadena, Nelson and Hale approach interracial sex from the vantage points of *mestizaje* and, for the Andes, the figure of the mixed-race *chola*. We can also look at interracial sex by exploring data on actual marital (and sexual) relationships and their offspring. The consensus of scholars is that interracial marriages and partner selection are strongly shaped by racism, even as they also seem to challenge racial boundaries. To start with, statistical data show that marriage patterns in Latin America are generally racially endogamous and thus confound the superficial image of Latin America as a region where there is generalised racial mixing. Census data for Cuba in 1981 show that only 14 per cent of marriages were 'interracial' (according to the self-declared racial categories of white, black and mixed). Rates of in-marriage varied by racial category, being highest among whites at 93 per cent with blacks at 70 per cent and *mestizos* at 69 per cent (Fernandez 1996: 114 n. 5). Specific cases of interracial union in Havana could also meet with opprobrium (ibid.). In a survey of three neighbourhoods in Havana, a clear majority of 'white' respondents said they thought interracial marriage was inadvisable, while a large majority of those classed as black and *mestizo* were in favour (Alvarado 1998; Sawyer 2005).

Brazilian 1991 census data, in which people self-classify mainly as white, brown and black, show that 77 per cent of marriages were racially endogamous (compared to 87 per cent in the 1960 census). Again, white people were more endogamous than either black or brown people: 80 per cent of white women married a white man, while 75 per cent of brown and 60 per cent of black women married their racial equal (Telles 2004: 176). White out-marriage varied a good deal by region, but this was related mainly to the size of the non-white population in different areas and thus the chances of encountering non-whites in daily life. White out-marriage also varied by class, with lower-class whites (who were more likely to live in highly racially mixed neighbourhoods) out-marrying more than middle- and upper-class whites. For the city of Cali, Colombia, 1999 survey data (using racial self-categorisations) show that household heads generally made a racially endogamous choice: 88 per cent of whites did so, as did 88 per cent of blacks, 82 per cent of *mestizos* and 76 per cent of mulattoes (Urrea Giraldo et al. 2006: 134). For Cali, white endogamy did not vary by class.

When we look at the interracial marriages themselves, patterns emerge that are easily interpreted as indicating the pressures of racial and gendered hierarchies. There is a notable trend towards whitening, in which racially mixed individuals tend to marry whiter rather than blacker – this applies to men and women, but with different patterns in each case. Thus in Brazil in 1991, while 49 per cent of black men married a black woman, 32 per cent of them married a brown woman and 20 per cent married a white woman. In contrast, 60 per cent of black women married a black man, 24 per cent married a brown man and 16 per cent a white man. (Not surprisingly, black women spent more time single than white and brown women.) Brown men, however, only 'married down' racially in 3 per cent of cases, while they married 'up' 26 per cent of the time; brown women married darker in 4 per cent of cases and lighter in 20 per cent of cases (Telles 2004: 176, 91).

These gendered patterns of whitening may be linked to gendered trajectories of upward social mobility in which individuals try to 'marry up' as part of an overall strategy of social ascent: they may be able to marry lighter because they have moved up in class terms (education, employment, income) or because they have other resources that they can trade on the 'marriage market' (good looks, sex appeal). The classic story here – narrated in Brazilian literature, sociology and much popular opinion (Moutinho 2004) – is that of the socially aspirant black or brown male who marries a white, or at least whiter, woman. The obverse side of the story is the black or brown female who can marry lighter because of her good looks or sex appeal, rooted in the sexualised image of the non-white woman, especially the *mulata*. In fact the picture is more complex.

For the Brazilian census, Telles (2004: 190) tested for 'status exchange', in which one partner 'compensates' for low racial status with higher status in other areas, although he could only use educational level as an indicator of class. He found that status exchange was present for black men and women: they tended to be better educated than their brown and white partners. This was not the case, however, for brown men and women, though this does not mean that other forms of value, not measured in censuses, were not operating (Moutinho 2004: 39). The situation in Cali can be interpreted in a similar way: 'black, mulatto and even *mestizo* people develop strategies of social ascent in their unions, which, because of the racialised hierarchy of Colombian society, are expressed as forms of "whitening"' (Urrea Giraldo et al. 2006: 135): for black and mulatto people, interracial marriage is more frequent the higher their income. What isn't clear from the Cali data is whether the better-off non-whites are actually marrying whiter and whether these are men more than women. For the Colombian city of Medellín, I found clear patterns linking upward social mobility to racial exogamy for black individuals, among whom there were as many females as males (Wade 1993a: 309–10).

Goldstein (1999; 2003: ch. 3) describes a related but distinct pattern for female dwellers in the *favelas* of Rio de Janeiro. They dream of finding and seducing a *coroa* (literally, a crown) – a wealthy man, usually white and also considerably older than they are – who will at least help them out financially and, if their dream really comes true, lift them out of their lives of poverty and transport them to a middle-class lifestyle of plenty and leisure. The darker-skinned woman trades in her (black) sexuality for material rewards. The man she gets, if she is lucky, may be rich, but he is old and, so the women's jokes say, unlikely to make a satisfactory lover.[4] The image that exists of Brazil, including among many of these Brazilian women, is of a 'colour-blind erotic democracy', where sex conquers racism, but the reality is one of highly skewed and unequal relationships in an 'erotic market' to which (white) men and (non-white) women bring different and unequal forms of 'capital'. Black female sexuality is 'valorized and considered erotic because it is suspended in a web of power relations that make it available in a particular way', i.e. as a sexual commodity (Goldstein 2003: 110, 25).

The racial–gender structuring of interracial marriages is evident in the prevalence of the assumption that social aspiration motivates the darker partner in interracial unions (Moutinho 2004; Viveros Vigoya 2008). Moutinho argues that the idea is especially powerful in relation to successful darker men, while darker women are more likely to be seen as trading on their erotic capital. These assumptions are clearly based on people's perceptions of marriage-choice patterns, but they also carry a pejorative moral charge in which base materialism is accused of triumphing over love. Moutinho argues that the reality is much more complex. To start with, she shows that the pairing of a black man with a white woman tends to be ignored in Brazilian narratives, whether literary, sociological or popular, about interracial sex. When it does appear, it is usually in terms of tragedy or in relation to the man as a social climber. In fact, the statistics show that, in terms of actual marriages, there are more unions between non-white men and white women than between white men and non-white women, despite the classic story being one of white men sexually conquering non-white women (Moutinho 2004: ch. 1). (It is important, however, that while Moutinho does not limit herself to formal marriage and is interested more widely in 'heterochromatic' relationships, she does not pay much attention at all to informal unions between white men and non-white women, which are, after all, the key element in the 'classic story'.) I also found for Medellín that 'the classic pattern of white men having sex with black or mulatto women is not always the case': there were also many formal marriages and proportionally more black men married non-black women than non-black men married black women (Wade 1993a: 313).

Moutinho shows that, while social aspiration may be part of the story, there is a whole dimension of affectivity and eroticism that is being missed. White women's motivations in forming a union with a non-white man are rarely addressed. She shows that non-white men are generally considered superior to white men in erotic and physical terms and this is often a strong motivation for white women engaging in interracial unions. White men, rather than being seen as highly sexed predators, are sexually 'opaque', marked by a lack of attributes, although they are often seen as more romantic (2004: 345, 58). Blackness, rather than being something that has to be compensated for in status exchange, has its own value (ibid.: ch. 5). Moutinho gives useful nuances to the picture of interracial sexual relationships, but the basic picture of an erotic market – or a 'market of pleasures' (ibid.: 27) – in which people have different sorts of resources that can be traded against each other remains the same. Also Moutinho does not consider that black men may be marrying whiter women who are lacking in some other value seen as desirable in the 'market' (youth, beauty, etc.), as apparently happens to some black men in Colombia (Viveros Vigoya 2008: 263). Black men who marry whiter may have erotic value as well as or instead of monetary value, but the mechanism is the same and, above all, the market still works on a racist logic in which blackness is sexualised and eroticised. And while 18 per cent of white married women in Brazil had a brown husband, only 2 per cent of them had a black one (Telles 2004: 176), which suggests that, as for the *mulata*, brownness is seen as more attractive than blackness.

A similar picture exists for interracial unions in Bogotá, Colombia, which are mainly between local women and black migrants from the country's Pacific coastal region (Viveros Vigoya 2008). Black women are often seen as sexually available and become objects of sexual harassment, while black men tend to be stereotyped as sexually virile and good dancers, traits which may also link into a personal project of sexual liberation for some white women. When black women marry white men, they often find they have to desexualise themselves and become very 'respectable' in their behaviour in order to avoid stereotypes of black female sexuality; white women, on the other hand, run the risk of marking themselves as sexually 'loose' by marrying a black man.

Afro-Colombian men's relation to the stereotypes of them as highly sexual is ambivalent: either they tend to accept the images, inverting their value and using them to claim a certain masculine status, but also reproducing the sexualisation that constrains them; or they reject the images and seek to integrate as 'normal' Colombians, distancing themselves from blackness and, in effect, legitimating the low value attached to it (Viveros Vigoya 2002a: ch. 6, 2002b).[5] Overall, Viveros shows how powerfully racial hierarchies and imagery shape the 'erotic-affective market': even people in stable conjugal relationships 'find themselves obliged to position themselves continuously in relation to [sexual stereotypes]' (2008: 275, 72). Likewise, I concluded for Colombia that a racial hierarchy 'pervades the realm of race mixture and ... motives stemming from *blanqueamiento* [whitening], conscious or inferred, are pervasive' (Wade 1993a: 313).

I would note at this juncture that the image of the 'market' in which people trade different elements of status – wealth, colour, beauty, age, desirability – is useful, but needs nuance. The whole point of traits such as race, age and beauty is that they are not fully commodified and thus cannot be completely 'sold off' or alienated. A black man who uses his economic success to 'compensate' for his colour and 'buy' a whiter wife does not erase his blackness, he simply relocates it in a different context. In this sense, the economic exchanges at work here have as much in common with a gift economy as a marketplace. The 'items' or qualities which are being exchanged remain corporeally attached to the giver and his/her social context and create ongoing social relationships between the giver and the recipient.

A second reason to be cautious with the market model of tradable personal resources is that it leads to a rather additive model of race, class and gender (see Chapter 2). The model implies that all these qualities can be measured on a single scale of value and that a given person's total capital can be calculated by adding their various statuses. What this misses is precisely the articulation or intersection of different qualities, in which they mutually shape each other. Thus money in the hands of a black man may be 'worth more' than the same money in the hands of a black woman, which is to say that blackness for a woman is 'more costly' than for a man. This is similar to the way that the money that women earn can be devalued as 'pin money' or 'lipstick money' *because* it is being earned by a woman, and the jobs that they do may be classed as semi- or unskilled, *because* they are being done by a woman (Humphrey 1987; Joekes 1985). This can be captured in a reduced way by saying that being female carries a 'cost', which a woman brings to the marketplace, but such a formulation misses how the marketplace itself is shaped by gender.

Likewise, people do not simply come to a marriage market with a portfolio of qualities that define their value; the market itself is structured by the same forces that give those qualities their value. The act of marriage itself is, in a sense, 'worth more' when performed by richer, whiter people. So the process of getting a partner whiter than oneself is costly not only in terms of his/ her whiteness, but also because *marrying* a white person means performing a costly act. Much of this cost derives from the first caveat about the market model noted above: that the blackness of the upwardly mobile partner is not 'bought off' by his/her wealth or education; the embodied nature of blackness gives it the ongoing power to devalue not only the marriage itself but also the whiter partner in the eyes of others. The fact that, as Viveros shows, a white woman who marries a black man may be seen as sexually 'loose' is a clear instance of how the institution of marriage itself can be devalued by blackness: the very thing that would usually protect a woman against accusations of sexual promiscuity – marriage – loses some of its power when contracted between a white woman and a black man.

Interracial Marriage Patterns and the Simultaneity of Racism and Racial Democracy

In assessing the evidence for how racism and sexism structure interracial marriage, however, we need to be alive to the *simultaneity* of racism and racial democracy. As Goldstein says, 'In Brazil, it is widely believed that miscegenation and racism are contradictory, yet it is precisely their superficially uncomplicated coexistence that is part of Brazil's uniqueness' (2003: 127). In slightly contradictory fashion, Goldstein (ibid.: 135) also distances herself from the 'Brazilian exceptionalism' – the idea that Brazil is somehow unique or exceptional in terms of race (Hanchard 1994; 1999b) – which she associates with Peter Fry, who in fact also argues that 'the myth of racial democracy coexists with the myth of the inferiority of the black' (Fry 2002: 304). It is by no means a case of arguing that Brazil is exceptional by virtue of an absence of racism – something that Fry never affirms – but instead of finding the specificity of Brazil (and other Latin American countries) in the simultaneous coexistence of racism and racial democracy, a coexistence which, as I argued earlier, is a version of the tension between universalism and particularism that is constitutive of political orders based on liberal principles. Indeed, I would contend that it is something more than a matter of 'coexistence' – as if racism and miscegenation (or racial democracy) were two separate phenomena that happen to operate side by side. In using the idea of simultaneity, I am suggesting that racism and racial democracy operate, in time and space, through the very same sets of phenomena – in fact, the key mechanism is the sexual process of race mixture (or miscegenation) itself. In that sense, Goldstein has it slightly wrong when she says racism and miscegenation coexist, as it is principally in miscegenation that racism and racial democracy coexist.

If we look back at the statistics on intermarriage, it is clear that most commentators emphasise the degree of racial endogamy, especially among whites. But just how racially endogamous are Brazil, Cuba and Colombia if we compare them to, say, the US or the UK? Telles is one of the few who takes up the challenge and shows that endogamy rates in the US in 1991 were over 99 per cent for whites and over 95 per cent for blacks, compared to overall rates of about 77 per cent in Brazil (2004: 175).[6] Data from England and Wales show that 'same ethnic group marriages' were 98 per cent of the total in 2001.[7] Intermarriage data are complex and depend to some extent on demographic proportions: if a given group is a very small one embedded in a much larger population, then out-marriage is likely to be high. But, all things considered, it is evident that interracial marriage – and we are talking mostly here about formal marriage – is much higher in Brazil, Colombia and Cuba than it is in the US or the UK. Even taking into account that endogamy tends to be higher for whites in these Latin American countries and that a good deal of intermarriage takes place between 'black' and 'brown', it is still the case that interracial marriage is relatively common. White out-marriage was 7 per cent in Cuba (1981), 12 per cent in Cali (1999), 20 per cent for Brazilian wives and 16 per cent for Brazilian husbands (1991). For a small frontier town in north-western Colombia in 1982, I found that the most exclusive ethnic group, self-identified as non-black and occupying a dominant economic position in the town, had 14 per cent exogamic unions (marriage and 'free union') (Wade 1993a: 362). There is very significant variation here, which should alert us to the risks of generalising about Latin America; but even for Cuba in 1981, white out-marriage was over three times the rate for the UK in 2001. And, as we have seen, rates of 'interracial' marriage for non-white people are even higher, as 'browns', '*mestizos*' and 'blacks' intermarry with each other.

There is no doubt that some of this intermarriage corresponds to strategies of social mobility, as non-white men and women 'trade in' their economic or other forms of capital for a whiter partner, but it is also important to put this in demographic and social perspective. Motivation is only part of the story. For Medellín, I argued that in many cases, choosing a whiter partner may be a result of the fact that upwardly mobile non-white people often find themselves, at university, at work and in the neighbourhood, surrounded mainly by white people (Wade 1993a: 302). Telles also notes that non-white Brazilians with higher education tend to marry whites, because their peers are very likely to be whites (2004: 184). This is part of a structural link between whiteness and higher-class status in these societies and the selection of whiter partners by non-white individuals tends to reproduce the link by ensuring that blackness is 'diluted' in the middle classes (even if those classes become more mixed in the process). But it may be that many individuals are choosing someone they like and who shares their values and aspirations in a general sense, with little conscious attention to matters of race. Viveros notes that for some people in long-term marital relationships in Colombia, questions of race, while they may be inferred and imagined by other people, become unimportant as everyday routines take over (Viveros Vigoya 2008: 264).

To point out these features is *not*, by any means, to argue that these Latin American societies are racial democracies or that race is insignificant there because, as we have also seen, it is precisely in the realm of intermarriage and mixed unions that racist assumptions continue to operate and racial hierarchies are reproduced. This raises the question of how racism and racial democracy coexist in this simultaneous manner. Interracial unions are part of the fabric of lived personal experience for an important number of Brazilians, Colombians and Cubans; they are part of the observed fabric of society for many more. Yet these same unions are the terrain on which racism is reproduced. In her article, Goldstein (1999) argues against false consciousness – the idea that the *favela* women she worked with are simply duped by the dream of finding a nice rich white man and are thus blinded to the realities of racism; she argues that people are not dupes and can see – because they experience – the racism that disadvantages them. Yet the question arises of the difference between false consciousness and her conclusion that the *coroa* phenomenon, as dream and lived reality, 'helps to mask and normalize everyday racism and internalized racism in Brazil' (Goldstein 1993: 573). In her later book, the same issue arises as she presents her work as a 'fine-tuning' of Hanchard's analysis of the operation of racial hegemony in Brazil (Goldstein 2003: 131), according to which myths about the nonexistence of racial discrimination coexist with the enactment of racism, continuous symbolic denigration of blackness and valorisation of whiteness and coercive and pre-emptive action against those who challenge the system (Hanchard 1994: 56–67).

The point, in my view, is that *both* racism *and* racial democracy are lived realities. The *nonexistence* of racial discrimination is indeed a myth, but the presence of aspects of racial democracy is not. They exist alongside, or rather *within*, racism, so that the very same practices can be racist and non-racist at the same time and in the same space. It is precisely this simultaneity that makes racial hegemony work; hegemony in general works most effectively by creating overlapping but *partial realities*, rather than by duping people with simple ideology. One effect of simultaneity in Brazil is to push some people's reactions to racism into a realm of silence or jokes and indirect comments (Goldstein 2003: 131). Likewise in Guatemala, race becomes a realm of anxiety and ambivalence, which is dealt with through humour, often mordant and morbid in tone (Nelson 1999: ch. 5). It is, I think, very important that a key field for the simultaneity of racism and racial democracy is sexual relationships. This roots the simultaneity in vital arenas of life which are at once very familial and personal and very public; it also roots the simultaneity in profound processes of the formation of self and other. On both counts, it lends to racism and racial democracy a powerful naturalisation of lived experience and a powerful and very personal ambivalence.

In this sense, race and sex are mutually constitutive: the fact that it is through sex that a large part of the simultaneity of racism and racial democracy operates shapes the field of race, helping to naturalise and silence or deflect it. The fact that sex is expressed through race shapes the meanings and possibilities of sex: rather than a field ordered by masculine and feminine, it is given shape by, among other figures, black and white masculinities, and white and indigenous femininities. Together, race and sex form an articulation that is more than the sum of its parts.

Interracial Homosexuality and the Figure of the Black Male

While there is an increasing literature on homosexuality in Latin America (López-Vicuña 2004), there is not a lot of attention in this to the intersection of race with homosexuality.[8] This is in contrast to the US, where there is a burgeoning literature on black queer, gay and lesbian studies, which points out how queer, gay and lesbian studies have tended to work from a tacit assumption of whiteness and how a consideration of race fractures and complicates non-heterosexual identities and political solidarities (Boggs 2000; Ferguson 2003, 2007; Somerville 2000; Wright and Schuhmann 2007).

Homosexual relationships – and most of the material that there is focuses on male homosexuality[9] – are generally considered deviant in a Latin American context, although as we have seen, there is debate about whether it is only the passive-receiver role that is stigmatised, while the active-penetrator role is not, or whether both roles are in some sense regarded as deviant (linked in part to the idea that the dualism is not as clear-cut as it sometimes appears) (Girman 2004: 41–60; Murray 1995a; Nesvig 2001). The challenge homosexuality presents to heteronormativity might make it appear a field in which ideas about race could also be challenged, given how deeply these are rooted in ideas about *mestizaje*, with its heterosexist assumptions of sexually active males pursuing more passive females, whether for conquest or for social climbing.

For example, one of the interviewees for Parker's study of homosexuality in Brazil, an upper-middle-class Rio resident, said, 'At some level, of course, homosexual desire cuts across these kinds of [class and race] distinctions, creating possibilities for interaction. Sexual relations that cut across class [and thus often race] lines are common' (Parker 1999: 117). On the basis of interviews with three black homosexual men who lived in the suburbs and *favelas* of Rio, Moutinho also argues that they had a wider 'field of opportunities' than heterosexual people from the same areas (2006: 106). These men could contract sexual relations with white men (usually foreign tourists) and they would visit Zona Sul and Copacabana (middle- and upper-class districts). She argues that the men did not talk about their relationships as either melancholic (destined to fail) or Machiavellian (directed at social climbing), but rather as giving them a 'better chance of living and accumulating new and diverse experiences, as well as increasing their cultural, economic and social capital' (ibid.: 114). In the field of literary studies, a number of Latin American autobiographical writers 'envision utopian spaces crossed by homoerotic desire and male-male solidarity' (López-Vicuña 2004: 242). For example, the 1936 poem 'Nocturno de los ángeles', written in Los Angeles by the Mexican Xavier Villaurrutia, evokes the image of homosexual desire and contact as forces that erase (racial) difference: 'any kind of difference is annulled through erotic contact' (Irwin 2003: 178).[10]

Yet it is rather predictable that these domains of sexual relationship are by no means simply ones in which racial barriers are transcended, any more than heterosexual interracial unions can escape racist assumptions and the reproduction of racial hierarchy. Parker's Brazilian informant went on to say:

Class differences can even be part of the erotic game and it is typical for middle-class *bichas* [passive homosexuals] to be infatuated with *garotões pobres* (poor young men) – or for *bichas pobres* to use sexual relations with better-off partners as a way of climbing up the social ladder. But class differences are never forgotten in these relations – class is always present and you can never escape from it, even when you don't acknowledge it openly or talk about it. (Parker 1999: 117)

Interestingly, the thing that this speaker barely talks about is race (which, he says, is 'determined by class'). It is after all very likely that the middle-class *bichas* would be white and quite likely that the poor young men would be non-white. In homosexual circles in Bogotá and Rio, the image of the black man as desirable and sexually potent is very pervasive and makes him attractive to homosexual partners, usually as an active partner. Some black men are said to capitalise on this image as a tool for attracting attention and finding partners (Díaz 2006). On the other hand, some black homosexuals interviewed in Cali felt constrained by the assumption (especially frequent among white men) that they would always take the active role (Urrea Giraldo et al. 2008: 296).

Despite the attractiveness of black men, blackness remains a stigma and a problematic identity for homosexuals in Brazil and Colombia. First, the stereotype of the black man as hypersexual, but in heterosexual mode, means that being *negro* and *marica* (effeminate homosexual) is perceived as a defiling contradiction by many, especially heterosexual black men and particularly in the working classes, where, for example in Cali, there is a strongly developed image of the tough, hypermasculine black male.[11] Being either gay or black is a negative condition and being both is a double stigma (Díaz 2006; Urrea Giraldo et al. 2008). But I would argue that it is more than a simple 'addition' of race and sexuality. Precisely because being a black male is taken to entail being *heterosexually* powerful (which by implication displaces homosexuality onto the nonblack population), the stigma of being a black homosexual is something different from the simple addition of prejudice against blacks plus prejudice against gays. It is especially defiling because it involves a contradiction in the terms of racial stereotyping. As Weismantel says: 'when race intersects with sex it changes the meaning of both' (2001: 241). For a man to be black and gay is seen as a betrayal of a supposedly essential racial identity, while at the same time it does not fit with the normative non-black gay identity. Interestingly, Fry (1995) notes that, in Belém, many men involved in Afro-Brazilian religious groups, such as Candomblé and Umbanda houses, are *bichas* – and one assumes that many of them are black, although he does not mention this. His argument is that the deviancy of these religious groups and of homosexuality, in relation to the mainstream, makes the cult houses an attractive niche for these (black) homosexuals – I would say, a place where the contradiction between being black and being gay can be overridden by religious authority.

Second, blackness is still a low-status condition. For a black homosexual to be successful in the erotic marketplace, he has to be especially good-looking, well-dressed, urbane and polished in his manners: blackness has to be offset by other indictors of value (Díaz 2006: 297). For black gays to have access to the erotic marketplace of Cali they have to have the resources and cultural capital to mix in the homosexual spaces of the city, which are dominated by white middle- and upper-class styles of consumption (Urrea Giraldo et al. 2008: 307). To be black and gay is difficult enough, to be black, gay and vulgar is seen as worse, even among black gay men. Youth also seems to be a critical factor here in allowing access to these spaces for black men. The public spaces frequented by gays in São Paulo, Rio, Cali and Bogotá (not to mention New York and Johannesburg) tend not to have black men over the age of about 30 (Urrea Giraldo, personal communication). Older (wealthier) white men and younger (poorer) black men mix and consort, but middle-aged black men are rare. The reason for this is not very clear, but it seems to be connected to 'status exchange': black men only appear if they suit the market requirements for young, sexually charged males. Following the market model referred to above, one could say that for young black men, youth and sex appeal outweigh their blackness, whereas for older black men they don't. But this fails to capture the articulation of race, sex and age in which the very contours of the market for erotic experiences are defined by the desires of white men: what is to count publicly as an erotic experience is shaped by this articulation.

There are no statistics to show whether interracial homosexual relations are more frequent in Latin American countries than in the US or the UK. It is difficult to argue that these relationships help create a sense of racial democracy, except insofar as it is clear that such interactions do cross racial and class divisions. As with heterosexual relationships, however, the very same encounters are the ground on which such divisions and hierarchies are reproduced.

There are differences between the heterosexual and the homosexual fields of action. Heterosexual interracial sex supports the entire narrative of *mestizaje* and, *in part*, the construction of the racially democratic nation, while also enacting racism. It speaks of generalised mixture of all with all, but actually privileges white men having sex with non-white women. It enlists non-white men as partners in a shared masculinity, but demands that their sexuality is tamed and orderly and does not involve having sex with white women. It creates a space for the attraction of white women to eroticised non-white men, but when these men's expressions of shared masculinity actually include having sex with white women, this is a threatening event and is typically denigrated as social climbing, as their 'getting above themselves'. Homosexual interracial sex, on the other hand, does not feed into narratives of *mestizaje* at all, in the sense that it conflicts with the heterosexist principles that underlie it. Yet in another way, it operates on the same terrain, because it speaks of cross-racial sexual interactions in a racially hierarchical society and, as we have seen, the same simultaneous dynamics of racial harmony and racism work in the fields of both homosexual and heterosexual action. What homosexuality does highlight is the heteronormativity that sustains *mestizaje*: black, white and mixed heterosexuals of all classes agree that a black gay man is a contradiction in terms. It seems that in Latin American social orders based on *mestizaje* (and perhaps other racialised social orders too), despite the fact that the hypersexual black male is often seen as a threat, there is actually a need for such a figure to exist, albeit in disavowed form, as a source of sexual energy for the nation and as a counterpoint to 'civilised' white sexuality.

The hypersexual black man (on which more below) is an important figure that emerges from counterpointing hetero- and homosexualities: he appears in both fields of sexual action and again unites them. The eroticisation of black men becomes part of *mestizaje* in the sense that, at least according to Moutinho, it shapes the choices made by white women (and white men). At the same time, it acts as an important concept in the reproduction of racism in that it presents black men as a threat and as limited to their sexuality.

Beauty and Eroticism

An important arena in which race and sex articulate and in which dramas of *mestizaje* and the simultaneity of racism and racial democracy are played out is that of bodily aesthetics and erotic desirability. Various studies show clearly that the dominant aesthetic is a whitened one: blackness is generally equated with ugliness; African-type hair is called *cabelo ruim* (bad hair) in Brazil and, all over Latin America, black women spend hours straightening their hair. Although this is not straightforwardly a conscious act of whitening and may also be a choice of one style among many, it is hard to dissociate it from the widespread idea that African-type hair has low aesthetic value. As we have seen, blackness in both men and women is often associated with sexual desirability – at least when allied with youth and beauty – but the erotically desirable is not always the same as the aesthetically beautiful, and the aspects of the black body typically marked out as desirable are often quite specific, especially legs and buttocks in women (cf. Hobson 2005); buttocks, upper body and, of course, the penis in men.

Indigenous appearance is also generally equated with ugliness by the dominant aesthetic, while the erotic charge associated with indigenous men and women is much more ambiguous. The sexuality of indigenous women seems to receive different constructions according to country. In Guatemala, it seems *indias* are seen as sexually desirable, but also sometimes as ugly and bad smelling (Hale 2006: 159; Nelson 1999: 224). In Peru and Ecuador, it is the *chola* rather than the *india* who is seen as desirable (De la Cadena 2000: ch. 4; Weismantel 2001: 155–65). Indeed, some intellectual men in 1940s highland Peru believed that 'Indian women became *mestizas* (cholas) just by transforming their racially conditioned sexual xenophobic deportment' (De la Cadena 2000: 202) – that is, by becoming sexually inviting, they became *cholas*. In any event, it seems clear that indigenous women in Ecuador are not figured sexually in the same way as black women: they often 'appear as nonsexual beings who supposedly smell bad ... Their bodies are represented as unattractively small and deprived of the curves that characterise black women's bodies in the popular imaginary' (Rahier 2003: 301).

The figure of the indigenous male seems to carry a low erotic charge, even if it is wrong to say this figure is not sexualised at all. The historical material in Chapters 3 and 4 clearly indicates that in colonial times, indigenous men were seen as sexually degenerate and excessive, and often viewed as sodomites. In the nineteenth and early twentieth centuries, indigenous – or more often *mestizo* – virile masculinity was harnessed to nation-building projects. (This was even more the case in the US, where the sexualisation and masculinisation of the native American male seem to be much clearer (Clark and Nagel 2000).) The comments by Nelson and Hale earlier in this chapter about *ladino* fears of indigenous male sexual predation on white women point to the sexualisation of Latin American indigenous men in the late twentieth century. There is also the case of the alleged rape by the indigenous Brazilian leader Paiakan of a white woman in 1992, which caused a major scandal (the national magazine *Veja* ran a cover photo of Paiakan with the words 'The savage'). Yet these instances do not amount to the pervasive and engrained image of the hypersexual black man. Canessa comments that, in Bolivia, indigenous men are seen as virtually asexual (2008: 53).

The reasons for this difference between black and indigenous sexual images are not immediately clear: both indigenous and black men and women were or are 'other' and subaltern, the men alternately feminised and seen as sexual threats, the women open to sexual abuse, and so on. My view is that black sexuality – both male and female – has historically been differently constructed from indigenous sexuality for a number of reasons. First, the particularly open sexual abuse that slavery permitted made black women especially accessible and black men especially powerless, thus raising the spectre of black male sexual revenge. Second, black (African and African diaspora) sexuality became an international icon/fetish and a capitalist commodity in a complex conjuncture of a) abolitionism, which spoke of the iniquities of rape, sexual abuse and the denial of a proper masculine role to black men; b) racial domination in the US and in European empires in Africa in which the sexuality of black people was a constant concern; and c) currents of artistic and literary primitivism from the late nineteenth century, which mystified and commodified black sexuality. Third, the greater integration of black people in the New World into urban environments in which images of black sexuality were commodified and circulated (with some active participation of black people themselves when they could extract some advantage from this process). This matter will have to await further research. What concerns us now is the power of the dominant, whitened aesthetic, alongside the pervasive images of black and brown men and women, and to a lesser extent, indigenous and *mestizo* women (and men) as erotically desirable, if not beautiful.

The success of the Brazilian model and TV presenter Xuxa shows the striking dominance of whiteness as the norm of female beauty. Xuxa's Aryan blonde looks and her manipulation of her sexual image converted her into a Marilyn Monroe-style sex symbol who, through her pervasive media promotion, both reflected and strongly reinforced the value attached to whiteness. Interestingly, early on in her career, she had a six-year relationship with the black soccer hero Pelé, her lover but also a mentor who helped propel her stellar career. This helped create Xuxa's iconic status, because she was able to 'embody … the myth of racial democracy': the link with Pelé gave her 'a kind of proof of immunity to racism' and represented the whole edifice of Brazilian *mestiçagem* (Simpson 1993: 32, 39). For Simpson, Xuxa's image is simply a mask which hides the reality of racism. Simpson has little to say about the cult of the sexy *mulata*: she admits that *mulatas* are promoted as beautiful and sensual women for tourism, but says they are only 'second class sexual objects' compared to white women (ibid.: 39, citing Sueli Carneiro).

Bolivian beauty pageants also demonstrate the tremendous value attached to whiteness in a predominantly indigenous country. The regional and national contests are dominated by tall, white women – who may, however, dress up in some version of 'indigenous' garb, albeit entirely exoticised. Indigenous women are seen by *mestizo* men as sexually available and desirable, even if they are not seen as physically attractive: 'Sexual desire here appears to be constructed not out of a sensual aesthetic but out of an erotics of power' (Canessa 2008: 43). Indigenous men are seen as barely sexual at all: they have to be masculinised, modernised and urbanised in order to count as proper citizens (cf. Gill 1997).

The insidious power of dominant aesthetics is revealed in the narratives black women in Ecuador told about their sex lives (Rahier 2003). Speaking to four women (two university graduates and two sex workers) Rahier found that they all agreed with dominant images of the black female body as sexually attractive and voluptuous and most of them also said that black women (and men) were sexually 'hotter' than whites or *mestizos*. Yet most of them had troubled relationships with their own feminine blackness. The two university graduates were both so wary of the images of sexual looseness attaching to their bodies and the attention that other people paid to their bodies that they had serious psychological blockages about being sexually penetrated or having a sexual relationship. One of the sex workers also explicitly avoided both black clients and boyfriends, and saw blackness as ugly.

But whiteness is not always dominant in a straightforward way. On two occasions in Ecuador, a black woman has won an important beauty contest: in 1995, when a black Quito-born woman, Mónica Chalá, was elected Miss Ecuador and, in 1997, when a black woman, Jacqueline Hurtado, was elected as the queen of Esmeraldas province – the region of the country with the highest proportion of black population (Rahier 1998; 1999).[12] Rahier argues that the 'election of Mónica Chalá made the edifice of the racial order tremble' (1998: 425) and elicited worried reactions from many commentators. He explains her success in terms of the increasing value being given to a certain internationally fashionable and modern blackness, associated with the US and Europe; the fact that Chalá met the aesthetic requirements of this model of blackness (tall, slim, long hair, etc.); and that she presented herself as representing the nation, avoiding any mention of racism and not identifying herself with Afro-Ecuadorian communities or political currents. When she represented Ecuador at Miss Universe, she straightened her long curly hair and wore light-brown contact lenses. The 'subversive fact' of her election was defused (1998: 428). Hurtado's 1997 election as Miss Esmeraldas already had the precedent of Chalá's victory but even so it was the first time the contest had even been open to black women, as the pageant had been controlled by local elite social clubs, dominated by white and *mestizo* elites. In 1997, the local mayor had wrested control of the contest from the local ruling elites and ruled that the outcome be decided by popular vote, not by a small jury. In effect, the mayor was pursuing a populist political strategy by using blackness as symbolic trope for 'the people'. The day after her victory, Hurtado had her hair straightened and started wearing light-brown contact lenses (Rahier 1999). In the end, then, the racial order of Ecuador reasserted itself.

We have already seen that black men and women may agree with dominant images of their own 'hot' sexuality and, especially among men, some take pride in this, although women and also some men often feel constrained – and even damaged – by constant expectations of sensuality, sexiness and sexual prowess in the bedroom (see also Viveros Vigoya 2002b, discussed above). The emergence in north-east Brazil of the black male figure of the *brau* (which seems to derive from the English 'brown') shows that rearticulations of ideas about black aesthetics and eroticism can constitute a form of resistance to dominant images of beauty, while also reiterating some of those images. A fan of US black soul music (especially James Brown), the *brau* is 'associated with the world of petty crime and linked to an aggressive and hyper-sexualised masculinity' (Pinho 2005: 132). He is part of the re-Africanisation of the city of Salvador and a challenge to dominant aesthetics. Alongside this, a new female image of *beleza negra* (black beauty) has emerged, with the Black Beauty Contest run from 1979 by the local black community organisation Ilê Aiyé and the increasing appearance of braided corn-row hairstyles along with the proliferation of small hairdressing salons specialising in this style (Pinho 2004; see also Sansone 2003). Like the *brau*, this black female aesthetic can purvey an essentialist image: *beleza negra* does not shy away from connotations of black female sensuality, if not sexual availability (Pinho 2004: 118).

Thus far, there is a pretty clear picture of a dominant white aesthetic, which masks a racism that deems blackness and indigenousness ugly, but good for simply sexual purposes. Apparent lapses in this – such as the election of a black beauty queen – end up reaffirming the status quo, while black people themselves may resist the aesthetic by re-signifying existing, or creating new, images of blackness to assert an alternative aesthetic. Such 'resistance', however, may reaffirm elements of the original images of sensuality and hypersexuality. A few studies, however, draw a more nuanced picture, which shows the complex duality and simultaneity at work: beauty can be a terrain for hegemonic oppressions of race and gender, but also of empowerment and pleasure (cf. Craig 2006). Pravaz (2003) argues along these lines in relation to the image of the Brazilian *mulata*, which is both a figure linked to sexist and racist forces in ideologies of *mestizaje* – the brown woman who is the product of and open to white male sexual desire – and a personal ideal for some black women, who may identify themselves as both black and *mulata* in strategies directed at upward mobility and personal empowerment. Pravaz examines the practice of *mulatice*, the performance of the classic *mulata*'s fetishised features of sensuality and samba dancing, but contests the idea that the women she worked with in Rio who perform *mulatice* are just 'blindly taking on the myths of racial democracy and mestiçagem as the truths of national identity' (ibid.: 118). Instead, they dedicate work and embodied effort into the performance of a 'strategic hybridity' which is 'both an emancipatory and a constraining political project' (ibid.: 118, 28). Pravaz does not deny that ideas about mixture and racial democracy can act as myths that hide racism, but she emphasises that these ideas also have productive effects in the everyday lives and identity formation processes of black and brown women. These women are not just duped by these myths, they act with and on them in order to recast their racial identities (e.g. from 'black' to 'brown') and attempt to live out in partial form the promise of racial democracy.[13]

The recent explosion in Brazil of beauty products and services for black people, generally of middle-class status, and the proliferation of advertising that targets this new demographic also reveals this tension. Fry (2002) argues that the beauty and media industries do not just cater to a new social category – the black middle class – but help create and shape it in symbolic terms. This trend, however, has contradictory effects. On the one hand, the liberal capitalist ideology of individual choice in the marketplace beckons black people as equals with all others in the world of consumption – a racial democracy. On the other hand, the inter-pellation of black middle-class people as *blacks*, who are asked to consume beauty products aimed at black skin and black hair and visit beauty salons specialising in dealing with black people, helps create the kind of encompassing black identity that, Fry says, the black political NGOs have barely managed to achieve. This simultaneity of sameness (in consumption) and difference (in race) is worked out through bodily aesthetics. The reality of the (tenuous) emergence of a black middle class, which speaks to the democratisation of race, is accompanied by the simultaneous emergence (also tenuous) of a black identity – or rather, aesthetic – which speaks to the experience of racism and racial solidarity.

Finally, the increasing popularity of plastic surgery in Brazil shows contradictory elements in relation to blackness. Edmonds documents how this industry is driven in part by a female corporeal model that surgeons associate with Rio – pronounced bottom, narrow waist, small breasts – and that has become a national ideal, leading to many operations to enlarge and round the buttocks, while breast augmentations are much less common. One surgeon links this female form with prominent buttocks to the 'mixture with the black race' and Hanchard (1999a) has used it as an example of the spread of an African aesthetic in Brazilian culture (Edmonds 2007: 90). But Edmonds argues that this female form is generally seen as *national*, not *racial*: the product of a process of mixture which has undone racial distinctions and created a national type. When a brief trend for breast enlargement was sparked by the 1999 carnival, it was debated in terms of whether it was a foreign import undermining Brazilian national identity.

On the other hand, a widely practised operation is the 'correction' of the 'Negroid nose'. This is not seen as a means of changing a 'black' into a 'non-black' person, as this facial trait is not seen as linked only to a specific category of 'blacks'; instead the operation is simply seen as a technique of beautification. Yet the trait is clearly linked to blackness and seen as a defect. Edmonds concludes that 'The myth of mestiçagem ... sustains an oscillation between racial identifications and their transcendence, between the embrace of mixture's harmonious beauty and the rejection of the persisting, stigmatized trace of blackness' (2007: 95). On the one hand, a black bodily aesthetic becomes assimilated and nationalised, losing its racial identity; on the other, a black facial trait is stigmatised as a defect. (Edmonds does not comment on this, but it does not seem coincidental that it is the black *body* that is accepted, while the black *face* is stigmatised.) As we might expect, then, within the same arena – the body and its physical enhancement and augmentation – both racism and the transcendence of race are simultaneously played out.

Sex Tourism and Sex Migration

Many of the dynamics we have seen operating in interracial sex are also evident, first, in sex tourism – characterised mainly by white men (and women) from Europe and North America visiting specific sites in Latin America with the more or less explicit idea of having sex with local, non-white women (and men) – and, second, in sex migration, by which I mean the migration of mainly women of varied racial identities, from Latin America to North America and Europe, to work in the sex industry there, but perhaps also to find a husband. What we observe here is a global political economy in which Latin American sexuality, usually non-white and female, is commoditised and exchanged in transnational capitalist circuits (Jeffreys 2008). Scheper-Hughes says that the global trade in human organs 'follows the modern routes of capital: from South to North, from Third World to First

World, from poor to rich, from black to brown to white, from female to male' (2000: 193) and one could say much the same of the global sex trade in relation to Latin America, although, as we shall see, there are nuances and complexities involved.[14]

Sex tourism and sex migration are both arenas in which racism exists in simultaneity with racial democracy, but, especially in the case of sex tourism, the power with which racial hierarchy and racism are reasserted and re-enacted is very clear. Racial democracy appears timidly and very conditionally in three ways: the agency that the women involved have in the control of their own sexuality; the opportunity some women have to improve their economic standing; and the image of romance that often surrounds some aspects of the industry and may lead to more stable relationships. But all these aspects are simultaneously ones in which racism also operates and, as we shall see, gains force from the transnational dimensions of the trade. The articulation of race and sex in Latin America has always had a transnational dimension: colonialism had this aspect, by definition; the Inquisition was, if not global, certainly transatlantic; the nation-building processes that occurred in the nineteenth and twentieth centuries were undoubtedly set on an international stage and in relation to ideas about race, sexuality and morality that operated transnationally. In sex tourism, however, we see the increased power of white men from the global North over non-white Latin American women; we see black Latin American men selling their sexuality in ways already prefigured in the eroticisation of the black male, but now more overtly racialised and commodified. In short, the commodification of sex is intensified by tourism in a way that reinforces global and national racial hierarchies. The fact that some North American male tourists label Dominican women 'Little Brown Fucking Machines' is an example of the kind of extreme objectification and racialisation that sex tourism seems to encourage (O'Connell Davidson and Sanchez Taylor 1999: 45).[15]

One of the findings of Brennan's study of Dominican sex workers in the tourist resort of Sosúa is that those who work the international tourist trade have a good deal of autonomy in their activities. In contrast to the women who work the national market and who have to stay in grim conditions in bars, controlled and exploited (but barely protected) by male bar owners, the 'independent' women who work with foreign tourists live in their own rented rooms or flats, are not controlled by pimps or bar owners, keep their earnings and organise their timetables. They are, however, vulnerable to abuse from clients and harassment by the police. This sex trade is not always about the simple purchase by a client of the services of a prostitute for a short time. Often a man will maintain a relationship with one or more women during his vacation. These Dominican women are often mothers with strong aspirations to improve their lives. Like the Rio *favela* dwellers seeking a *coroa*, they chase the dream of marrying a European or North American man and going to live in his home country. Short of this, not infrequently, they maintain some kind of ongoing relationship with one or more men, who send them money from abroad and return to visit them (Brennan 2004). The tourist men visiting Sosúa, and other locations such as Rio de Janeiro (Ferreira 2005) and Fortaleza in north-eastern Brazil (Piscitelli 2002), apart from wanting sex, often seek something more than the typical tourist package: they tend not to stay in fancy hotels, they stay longer than one week, they avoid the standard tourist cultural sightseeing, they want to have an 'authentic' experience with 'real people'. They may end up having a longer-term relationship with a sex worker, send her money, or even set her up in a flat and visit her regularly. These aims are part of a desire to avoid sexual relationships that seem too blatantly commercial, to avoid being taken just as a source of money.

One of the motives driving male sexual tourists is that sex workers in their home countries are, they say, too profit-oriented, too business-like; in contrast, Latin American and other non-Western women supposedly enjoy the sex they have with these men and make the relationship feel more like a romance. Many male sex tourists also say that women in their home countries are too independent, too controlling and demanding of men, in a word too 'feminist'. They seek Latin American females who 'act like a woman' and make them 'feel like a man'. This is also a motive for North American and European men, who use Internet matchmaking services to find a bride in Colombia (Ford 2004).

O'Connell Davidson and Sanchez Taylor (1999: 40) argue that, in psychoanalytic terms, Western sexuality is characterised by a hostility that derives from an infantile desire for revenge against the other on whom s/he depends for recognition and love (see also Chapter 2). This hostility can find expression in the objectification and control of another person in sex and the prostitute can make an ideal candidate for such objectification. But if the woman becomes nothing but an object, then she cannot show the desire that the male client also wishes to see and that acknowledges him as a subject. Hence there is a contradiction for a man between wanting control over a woman as a sexual object and wanting that object to be autonomous enough to recognise him as desirable. This contradiction is being managed, although not resolved, in the sex tourist trade. Men can feel desired and also powerful. Even if they are not good-looking, not very well-off and find it hard to get female partners at home, their economic position and status in Latin American sites of sex tourism are enough to bring them female attention, flattery and, above all, sex in ways which they can control. This explains the preoccupation these men voice with not being 'ripped off' by the sex workers they have relationships with. Although there is less information on homosexual sexual tourism in Latin America (Allen 2007; De Moya and García 1999; Moutinho 2006), it seems likely that the same play of power and control is at work: the 'other' in the psychoanalytic dynamic outlined above does not have to be a woman. By virtue of their money and status, older male tourists can command the attentions of young, sexually attractive men.

Women visitors also engage in sex tourism in the Dominican Republic, Cuba and other locations and in this case the aura of romance is even more marked, reflecting perhaps that women buy sexual services less frequently and the fact that their partners are men operating with gender codes in which men are supposed to be in control (Allen 2007; Brennan 2004: 91–106; Herold et al. 2001; O'Connell Davidson and Sanchez Taylor 1999: 47–52). The men involved are usually black or brown and are often 'activity directors' in local hotels or work in beach activities (e.g., hiring out jet skis): they go under a variety of labels, which tend to be euphemistic: beach boy, hustler, gigolo, *sanky-panky* (derived from hanky-panky), etc. The women tend to deny that 'prostitution' is involved at all, even though they recognise that they make material contributions towards the man in the form of cash, food, drinks, trips, and so on. As with male sex tourists, longer-term relationships may form, the men may visit the woman's home country and marriages may result. As with male tourists, women express a fear of being 'played', i.e. being used for purely material ends (Brennan 2004: 202–4). Women sex tourists also experience a sense of power and control, including the ability to attract good-looking men much younger than themselves, which they might not have at home (O'Connell Davidson and Sanchez Taylor 1999: 49). In Barbados, these women may paradoxically adopt rather traditionally feminine roles, alongside what they identify as the rather macho stance taken by Caribbean men: the women are experimenting with being both (economically) in control and also (sexually) submissive; they are playing at being both male and female 'in the centre of the Other' (Phillips 1999: 198).

In all this, race is absolutely central (Kempadoo 1999: 21). The white male tourists in Sosúa constantly refer to the darkness of the Dominican women, which they link to the women's supposedly natural enjoyment of and talent for sex (Brennan 2004: 195–6). Dominican women tend to reaffirm those stereotypes, seeing themselves as sexually superior to white women, especially Europeans and North Americans whom they, like their male clients, see as unsympathetic to men. Likewise, male tourists in Fortaleza seem to find the darkness of the Brazilian sex workers a vital part of the exoticism and authenticity that they seek (Piscitelli 2002), while some Brazilian men identify female sex workers in the north-east of the country – many of whom would be dark-skinned – as 'more romantic and less professional' than in other regions (Gilliam 1998: 66).

Female tourists to Caribbean sex tourist sites also tend to have relationships with black men. Sanchez Taylor identifies some women tourists as 'white supremacists' for whom the black male represents 'the essence of an animalistic sexuality that both attracts and repels'; other women adopt a more liberal stance, but may still exoticise black men (O'Connell Davidson and Sanchez Taylor 1999: 50). Racial identity may also shape the perception of relationships formed between locals and tourists: there is a strong link in Cuba between having a *mulata* identity and being a *jinetera* (a woman who consorts with tourists for material gain). Fernandez (1999: 87–8) recounts how a privileged white Cuban woman who had a sexual relationship with a Mexican tourist was seen as conducting a romance, while Afro-Cuban women engaging with tourists are generally seen as *jineteras*.

I have already referred to the image of the hypersexual black male which is ubiquitous in homosexual imaginaries in Latin America and it is plausible to conclude that this is also what helps drive the homosexual sex tourist trade. Foreign homosexual male tourists to Brazil seem to favour dark-skinned young men (Moutinho 2006). There is also a strong eroticisation of Afro-Cuban men in the homosexual market, although it is less clear that foreign tourists especially favour Afro-Cuban *pingueros* (male sex workers) (Allen 2007: 198).

The interesting question of what happens when the tourist him- or herself is black has not been much studied, but black female tourists have sexual relations with local black men in Jamaica and the Dominican Republic (Sanchez Taylor's sample suggests that they do so less frequently than white women) and, although it is not clear how they perceive black male sexuality, they reject the hostile sexual fantasies of the 'white supremacists' (O'Connell Davidson and Sanchez Taylor 1999: 49–51). Black American tourists exoticised and sexualised Latin American women – although it is not clear whether they reproduced notions of a 'hot' black sexuality – but it also seemed that the men's experience of economic power and privilege was important to them (ibid.: 44, 46).

African American male sex tourists to Rio differ markedly from the other main category of African American tourists to Brazil, who overwhelmingly tend to be women on an ethnic roots tourism package (Ferreira 2005: 58–72). Unlike the latter, the sex tourists had little interest in Afro-Brazilian culture and were not particularly critical of the myth of racial democracy or of the mixed nature of society which, to the ethno-tourists, seemed to make blackness rather 'invisible' in Rio by comparison with the US (indeed, the sex tourists liked the freedom that 'invisibility' gave them). Also, they did not particularly wish to interact with Afro-Brazilians – indeed, one African American woman tourist discovered to her surprise that these sex tourists did not necessarily 'prefer coloured women' (Ferreira 2005: 65).

The emigration of women from Latin America to Europe and North America in which sex is a main factor may follow a relationship established through sex tourism, or it may involve the trafficking of women through organised channels that force them into the sex industry abroad, or it may be a more individual move in which a woman migrates with the more or less explicit intention of using her sexuality as a way of making a living.[16] As in sex tourism, the motives and agency of the women involved have been emphasised by a number of authors who seek to avoid characterising these women as always victims (Agustín 2007; Hurtado Saa 2008; Piscitelli 2004). In their studies of black and brown women migrants from Fortaleza, Brazil, and Buenaventura, Colombia, Piscitelli and Hurtado show the varied trajectories of these women: they may work as, among other things, cleaners, domestic servants and sex workers; they may establish long-term relationships with European men and even marry them; they may divorce or separate; they may shuttle between Europe and Latin America, perhaps returning home where their earnings may give them considerable economic standing by local standards.

The question of race in these sexual circuits has not been much studied, but there are indications that it is similar to the field of sexual tourism. Black women in Buenaventura, Colombia, known locally as *italianas*, who have returned to Colombia from Italy (or Spain) narrate that in Europe some men express disenchantment with white European women, who are paradoxically seen as too materialist (Hurtado Saa 2008: 352). These men seek out Latin and other immigrant women whom they see as more feminine and sexually desirable. In Spain, marriages between Spanish men and foreign women have increased markedly in the last 15 years, despite reports in these narratives of opposition by the man's family to marriages with a black woman.[17] For the women, marriage with a white man can represent a real rise in status, especially back home. As one woman put it: 'But the triumph is to bring home a man, number one white, which ought not to be an advantage, but when they arrive here [in Buenaventura] it certainly is' (ibid.: 365).

The emphasis on women's (and men's) autonomy and agency in sexual tourism and sexual migration, plus the possibility that the aura of romance attaching to some of these relationships – more marked among white women with black men – can lead into long-term relationships and marriage, are, in some sense, linked to possibilities of racial democracy: black people can control their own sexuality and have access to significant economic opportunities; racial hierarchies can be overcome in personal relationships. Yet these possibilities are consistently the same ones through which racial oppression and the reaffirmation of racial hierarchy are also enacted. It is very clear how often the Dominican women in relationships with foreign men – even relationships of marriage – end up with almost nothing significant to show for it (Brennan 2004). The marriages frequently do not last – the men are often drunks and philanders who leave them for younger women. The men rarely transfer significant economic assets to their partners. The women are pushed by economic necessity, reinforced by the lack of support from the fathers of their children. Yet they retain an attachment to a fairly traditional gender ideology in which marriage will solve their problems. If some of these women have lived in Europe for a time, they tend to remember this as a good time, glossing over the racism, alienation, loneliness and their husband's inadequacies. In the end, the men call the shots: one minute they are wiring money on a regular basis, the next their attentions have turned elsewhere. They may not be wealthy, but their First World position gives these men the ability to live well in places like Sosúa and they seem to have few qualms about using their position to please themselves. Relations of power equip them 'with an extremely high level of control over themselves and others as sexual beings and, as a result, with the power to realise the fantasy of their choosing' (O'Connell Davidson and Sanchez Taylor 1999: 52).

In addition, much of the entire sex tourist industry and sex migration are based on the relative powerlessness of women (and men) from regions such as Latin America. For every *italiana* who returns to Colombia with plenty of money, many must remain in Europe in much more difficult circumstances. The industry and migration also rely, to an important extent, on the racialisation of the workers and migrants as sexually desirable and available because they are non-white. Brennan shows how Dominican sex workers adhere to a view of black women as sexually attractive and better lovers, which, while it affords them certain opportunities, also reinforces the racial hierarchy in which black people are limited to and by their sexuality.

Ambivalence and Anxiety

The articulation of race and sex in Latin America is a field full of ambivalence and anxiety. Some of this derives from the very basic ambivalence that the self-in-formation feels toward the other on which s/he depends for love and recognition, but which therefore also limits his or her autonomy and control; that other is nearly always gendered and linked to sexuality and when the other is racialised too, the ambivalence expresses itself through an articulation of racial and sexual ideas and practices. Some of the ambivalence and anxiety derives from the simultaneous coexistence of racism and racial democracy, which means that the racialised other is both included and excluded at the same time. The fact that this coexistence operates in large part through *mestizaje* – itself a conjuncture of race and sex – means that the ambivalence is not just an abstraction, but is lived as an intimate question of family, kinship, genealogy, sex and the internal essences and external form of one's own body (even if one sees one's own body as not mixed). In a sense, race is always about such intimate matters (Stoler 2002; 2006) – as well as about public politics and the job market – but *mestizaje* gives the intimate a powerful role. What Bhabha (1986: xiv) calls the Otherness of the Self is peculiarly apposite to the Latin American case, insofar as the racialised other can be (imagined to be) inside the self, part of his/her body (Wade 2005b).

As we have seen in previous chapters, a key form of ambivalence is the notion, originating in dominant ideologies, that blackness and indigenousness are inferior, despicable and even fearful, yet also attractive and desirable, especially sexually. Anxiety is a product not just of the fear or contempt that indigenousness and blackness provoke, but also of the uncertainty provoked by the ambivalence of repulsion and attraction, of exclusion and inclusion. This emerges clearly from Weismantel's (2001) and De la Cadena's (2000) material in which the *chola* is both an insolent, money-grubbing price-hiker, aggressively masculine and/ or sexually licentious; and, at the same time, a sweet, young and desirable emblem of the nation and living embodiment of sexual enticement. The *chola* is other, but also *is* the nation; she is the product of interracial sexual congress, while sex with her will also continue to make the nation, reaffirming women's femininity and men's masculinity in the process.

Nelson's work is also replete with evidence of profound emotional ambivalences and anxiety among *ladino* Guatemalans. Indigenous women are, as usual, both signs of the nation and classed as inferior. *Mestizaje*, says Nelson (1999: 224), 'emerges from a double bind of prohibition and incitement': racism turns men away from indigenous women; while 'the demand to "whiten"' incites them to have sex with these women, added to which the women may be seen as sexually desirable. Anxiety for the men is produced by the fear that they themselves are 'never white enough' to carry out this task properly. This fits into the related fear that Nelson describes (see above) – that of being mistaken for an indigenous person and of not being able to tell when someone is indigenous, because the physical signs are ambiguous. As we have seen, there is also the anxiety of *ladino* men and women linked to the fear that indigenous men will exact sexual revenge by attacking white women during a racial insurrection. Yet the indigenous woman is held up as the embodiment of national identity and her traditional dress (*traje*) is not only displayed in museums but adopted by *ladino* women, who 'wrap themselves in traje and embrace or "become" the Indian as an expression of what it means to be Guatemalan' (Carol Hendrickson, cited in Nelson 1999: 12 n. 16).

The jokes directed at the Mayan activist Rigoberta Menchú indicate the ambivalence she evoked: her 1992 Nobel Prize was a cause for national celebration, but also anxiety at the fear that she and her prize represented the emergence of racial divisiveness in the country and, more importantly, the 'uppiness' of the indigenous population. The jokes – which Nelson (1999: ch. 5) interprets in Freudian style as revealing hidden anxieties – typically had a strong sexual element, implying that Menchú was both aggressively masculine, sexually unattractive and yet sexually available. The most popular joke played on the idea of a Menchú doll acting as Barbie's servant, thus combining images of servitude with a sexual *frisson*.

The images of the sexually desirable black and particularly *mulata* woman and the sexually potent black man need little elaboration at this juncture: they clearly underlie patterns of sexual tourism in which the economically inferior position of non-white black women and men in the sites of tourism combines with the image – cultivated by them – of superior erotic qualities to manage precisely the ambivalence of inferiority and superiority. These eroticised people are obliged to give their sexual powers – and in a way that makes it seem willingly done – to people who wish to 'consume' those powers. The exclusion expressed in their poverty is in tension with the inclusion expressed in their apparent willingness to have sex with the tourists. Anxiety does not seem to be a prominent characteristic of people engaging in sexual tourism – doubtless because the context is carefully set up to avoid it – but it is clearly related to ambivalence in two ways. First, both male and female tourists are anxious about being 'taken advantage of' or being used for their money: this would upset the careful balance that sexual tourism creates between exclusion and inclusion. Second, male tourists at least express anxiety about sexual relationships with white women 'back home': this is resolved by having relationships with black women who are in a relatively powerless position.

For the US context, a good deal has been made of the sexual anxiety of white men confronted with the image of the hyper-sexual black male – an image which, it is argued, has been largely created by white men as a threat against which they can defend white women's honour, for example by lynching black men. Such anxiety was manifest in the frequent castrations and genital mutilations that accompanied lynchings (Di Leonardo 1997; Hall 1984; Hernton 1970; Hodes 1993, 1997). For Latin America, less is said about the possibility that white men feel threatened by the idea that black men are better in bed than they are. White men are generally cast as the sexual predators, who historically had lots of sex with indigenous and black women. Yet as Moutinho shows for Brazil, nowadays white men are generally seen as sexually unexceptional or 'opaque', while black and brown men are described with many adjectives connoting power, force and attractiveness (2004: 348–58; see also Rahier 2003). Moutinho does not explore much white men's perceptions of black male sexuality (nor does Viveros 2002b), but she does show that some white men see black men as 'racist': 'if they can, if they have money, they get hold of a white woman' (Moutinho 2004: 315). This suggests some sense of competition and it seems quite likely that white men may feel threatened by black males' sexual reputation.

From a rather different angle, Ellis (1998; 2002) analyses the relationship between whiteness and masculinity in his work on the Peruvian writer and political Mario Vargas Llosa. Vargas's father imposed the model of a macho, white, dominant patriarch on his son, with repeated violence and threats: the other – the indigenous and racially mixed, the subordinate, but also the homosexual – was implicitly feminised. A real white man had to dominate this other and define his whiteness and masculinity. In his writing, Vargas distanced himself from this sadistic racism and machismo, which he criticised as an integral aspect of Peruvian society, but, argues Ellis, he ended up adopting a heterosexual, masculine and white identity, as he placed his own development as a man against a background of uncivilised nature (the Amazon) and the slightly queer, or less than fully heterosexual, social circles in which he moved as a young man. At the same time, he was reticent about identifying fully as white, as shown by his reluctance to do so when competing with the Japanese-Peruvian Alberto Fujimori who aimed to capture the vote of the non-white majority. While this analysis does not suggest insecurity about white male sexuality suffering in a comparison with a more virile non-white male sexuality, it does indicate uncertainty about white masculinity in general. Vargas was wary of seeming racist and macho, yet wanted to be white and masculine – qualities defined in opposition to indigenousness and homosexuality.

These instances of ambivalence and related anxieties about race and sex speak to the wider question of the dependence of some domains of white cultural experience on the sexual and other energies of non-white men and women. If some white men find non-white women more sexually desirable than white women, while some white women seek out black men for sexual satisfaction, then not only does this cast doubt on the sexual adequacy of white men and women, it also indicates a certain reliance of these white people on non-white people to get what they want. Of course, dominant classes by definition rely on subordinate classes for labour and service, and this generates 'precarious dependencies' (Gill 1994), but I am talking here about dominant classes attributing special powers to their subordinates. We saw something similar at the end of Chapter 4 in the realm of music and dance, where black-inspired cultural forms were appropriated as national icons, in large part because of their perceived energy, sexiness and – linked to the image of sexual liberation – modernity. The nation could be energised and rejuvenated from below, as it were, as long as these forces were appropriately tamed and 'civilised' – a condition that glossed over the fact that these 'forces' were not simply authentic and natural emanations from a traditional, uncivilised substratum of society, but were already a product of long-term and transnational interactions between dominant and subordinate classes and regions (Wade 2006b). This dependence of specific sets of people, and of the image of the nation in general, on their subordinates has a strong sexual element because the mode of domination is deeply implicated with sex, as we have seen throughout this book. But this element changes historically. In the colonial period, whites feared and desired the sexual and healing magical powers of black and indigenous witches. From the nineteenth century onwards there is a more explicit concern with white sexuality as having become alienated from nature – in short, a nostalgic preoccupation with the idea that modernity, while desirable, has as one of its costs the distancing of people from a simple and direct engagement with their 'natural' sexuality and the 'repression' of their sexual drives.[18] Thus black music, at once modern and sexual, becomes the perfect commodity for managing this preoccupation. But, of course, such dependence is necessarily an anxious one, as it implies not only inadequacy, but also lack of control.

The ambivalences and anxieties that affect black, indigenous and mixed people are, not surprisingly, intimately connected with those affecting white people, but they are not identical. As I argued at the end of Chapter 4, they are more linked to the dilemmas of 'double consciousness', of being part of a nation and yet being excluded from it; they concern adhering to and yet rejecting stereotypes of blackness and indigenousness that may empower in certain ways, but also constrain; they concern feeling drawn to values associated with whiteness and yet also feeling anxious that this constitutes a betrayal of self and a stigmatisation of blackness and indigenousness in general. In this chapter, such ambivalences have constantly surfaced. The *chola* market women define themselves as indigenous and also *mestizo*, yet discriminate against people they define as *indios*; they adhere to plebeian values of 'respect', but these are tinged with elite values of 'decency' (which have connotations of moral and sexual propriety). *Chola* domestic servants in La Paz may incur debts to buy or rent fancy versions of the 'typical' Aymara women's *pollera* skirts, shawls and hats, but equally they may eschew these markers of gender and ethnic identity and wear urban, Western-style clothes: they have an ambivalent relationship to dominant aesthetic standards (Gill 1994: 103–6).

Afro-Colombian men may deploy images of their hypersexuality (Urrea Giraldo et al. 2008; Viveros Vigoya 2002a; 2002b) – perhaps as part of their self-image of highly virile conquerors of women, perhaps as capital in the erotic marketplace (see also Pinho 2005). Yet they may also feel constrained by such images, fearful that people, especially women, may only see them in sexual terms or that they are always expected to perform like a stud, or take a dominant active role in homosexual relationships. The literature on sex tourism also shows that black and brown women tend to affirm images of themselves as highly sexed and good lovers: such images attract tourists to them and open opportunities for upward mobility, but they also reinforce the idea that such women are sexual commodities. In what is probably the most intimate and poignant set of narratives, Rahier (2003) shows how these images of black female sexuality are reaffirmed in general terms even by Afro-Ecuadorian women who are desperate to distance themselves as individuals from such images, that is, *not* to be seen above all as a sexy body – to the point where these women have phobias about sexual contact.[19]

Some black men in Brazil admit to feeling sexually attracted to white women – 'I get *tesão* [sexual desire, and also an erection] for white women; it is very difficult to feel sexual desire for a black woman' – yet feel that they have to defend themselves against accusations of betrayal or even racism (Moutinho 2004: 307–12). Black men who are active in the black movement have particular problems in reconciling their political agenda with their sexual desires, and black women criticise them as hypocrites. Moutinho reports of her interview with a black university student who participated in the black movement that, despite his usual articulateness, he tried to avoid differentiating between white and non-white women and 'spent the whole interview balancing on the tightrope which linked desire, his popularity in the Faculty and with young women, and his political commitment' (ibid.).

For Frantz Fanon (1986 [1952]), the dilemmas involved in being black in France, the Caribbean or French North Africa were about wearing a white mask over black skin, about being instilled with a sense of the inferiority of blackness and the value of whiteness, and yet being marked with a black body (see Chapter 2). But we have seen that, while blackness and indigenousness are clearly marked as inferior, there is a powerful ambivalence at work, which also gives them, and especially mixed versions of them, a certain (limited) power and value. Fanon saw the black man as a screen onto which white men could project their own sexual problems and, for all Fanon's black-centred perspective, this constructs black men as rather passive. We have seen that black, indigenous and mixed men and women are active participants in a hall of mirrors in which they look at whites looking at them and shape the images that go round and round. This does not resolve ambivalences and dilemmas, but rather makes them more complex and varied.

Conclusion

My central argument in this chapter has centred on the simultaneous coexistence of racism and racial democracy in Latin America, a coexistence which operates in great part via the ideas and practices of *mestizaje*, understood as an articulation or intersection of race and sex which shapes the way people make constrained choices about whom they will marry and have sex with. In the fields of interracial sex and marriage, beauty and eroticism, and sex tourism and sex migration, racism and sexism are reproduced through the same practices and ideas which simultaneously provide channels that unsettle racism and sexism. This simultaneity and its presence in the articulation of race and sex that constitutes *mestizaje* accounts in great part for the specific character of Latin American racial orders. It also helps us to understand the character of ambivalent emotions about race in Latin America: the constant dynamic of inclusion and exclusion of blackness and indigenousness, which takes place in large part through discourses and practices of sex and which can occur at the level of the nation, but also the family and the body, permits a very fluid movement between cordiality and anxiety that is both profoundly personal and very public.

Before proceeding to the next chapter, it is worth looking back briefly to trace some continuities. In Chapter 4, I started with an account, drawing on Foucault, of how a science of sex and race emerged in the nineteenth century, alongside the emergence of the nation as the key context in which race and sex would articulate. The science of sex has developed and grown, and sexuality remains a key domain of governance and the understanding of self. From about the middle of the twentieth century, the science of race underwent profound changes (actually rooted in the early twentieth century) as the concept of 'culture' became dominant over 'biology' (Smedley 1993), with Latin America arguably being in the vanguard in this process (De la Cadena 2000). Racism did not decline, but changed its form so that racial discourse increasingly became about cultural difference. Yet 'cultural racism' in my view retains an important naturalising element and many people in Western contexts still operate with ideas about blood, inheritance and, nowadays, genes – not to mention the continued central importance of physical bodies (Wade 2002b; 2007b). The material in this chapter indicates that race works absolutely centrally through sex, which includes ideas about the mixing and passing on of blood, the inheritance of physical traits and the production of physical bodies. In this sense, Foucault's 'symbolics of blood' intertwines intimately with the 'analytics of sexuality'.

The nation remains a crucial domain in which race and sex articulate. It was never an isolated entity in the nineteenth century and both race and sexuality were the subject of transnational (especially scientific) discourses and also figured strongly in the globalising practices and discourses of Empire. In the twentieth century, this transnational aspect has changed with the intensification of globalisation, migration and tourism. The 'market' in which people operate in their sexual-racial strategies is now larger and more open, such that women in the small Colombian port city of Buenaventura can migrate to Italy, make money there and return to their home town to build new houses and start businesses, offsetting their reputation as prostitutes with their newfound wealth in what is now a transnational process of 'status exchange'.

6

RACE, SEX AND THE POLITICS OF IDENTITY AND CITIZENSHIP

In this chapter, I shall look at how race and sex articulate in the struggles around the politics of identity and definitions of citizenship in Latin America and beyond, into transnational circuits of migration and diaspora. Particularly since the 1960s, social movements have emerged in the region that vindicate – among a wide array of issues – the rights of ethnic and racial minorities and challenge the dominant concept of *mestizaje*, contesting the image of homogeneously *mestizo* and racially democratic nations. In response to such demands, but also as part of global processes of recognition of minority rights and multiculturalist redefinitions of citizenship, many Latin American states have, from about 1990, adopted constitutional and other political and legal reforms that concede some official recognition to ethnic and cultural diversity in their nations (Assies et al. 2000; Greene 2007; Hale 2006; Sieder 2002; Van Cott 2000; Wade 2006a). Although, prior to this, indigenous populations may already have had some measure of official recognition as distinct groups, they often achieved more rights and recognition – at least on paper – in these reforms. For black or 'Afrodescendant' groups, in contrast, this was often the first official, political recognition of cultural distinctiveness (Hooker 2005; Wade 1997: ch. 6).[1]

In this process, transnational networks have been important: first, for social movement activists, who have drawn inspiration and support from an international community of activists (especially in North America), from instruments such as the International Labour Organisation's 1989 Convention 169 on

Indigenous and Tribal Peoples, and from the recent interest of multilateral agencies such as the World Bank in Afrodescendant and indigenous peoples; and, second, for state legislators, who have been concerned to bring their systems of governance into line with international ideals of modern democracy and the concerns of multilateral funding agencies (Fontaine 1981; Radcliffe 2001; Wade 1995, 2009 (in press)). These networks and connections indicate the importance of thinking about identity politics in a transnational framework, including the diaspora formed by Latin Americans who migrate outside the region. The theme of *mestizaje*, for example, is no longer just a Latin American affair and is debated in the US as well (Nash 1995).

The question that concerns us, in this context, is how issues of sexuality, and related issues of gender, articulate with these racialised processes of political-cultural activism and multicultural governance, both centred on questions of citizenship. I shall start by looking at the regulation of reproductive and sexual health, tracing how a multiculturalist recognition of difference, alongside a denial of hierarchy (ironically very like traditional ideologies of *mestizaje*), is underlain by tacit reaffirmations of racial hierarchy (as in *mestizaje*). I shall then examine sexuality in ethnic-racial social movements, exploring the apparently persistent connection of masculinism and power, which implicitly reinforces some of the basic tenets of male dominance in ideologies of *mestizaje*. As we shall see, the regulation of sexual health is not a domain separate from ethnic-racial social movements – top-down governance versus bottom-up resistance. The two are closely intertwined, as movements may be directly involved in the regulation of sexual health. In the last sections, I examine sex and race among Latinos in the United States. I look first at sexualised images of Latinos – the macho conqueror and the seductive, available woman of the imaginaries of *mestizaje* – and how these are deployed in the construction of the racialised 'Latino' category. I then look at how *mestizaje* – the process of interracial sex – is both challenged by and challenges the US racial landscape.

The Governance of Sexual Health

In previous chapters, we have seen how the regulation of sexual behaviour was often strongly linked to questions of reproduction and fertility. As Foucault's work leads us to expect, the state, along with an array of (especially medical) experts, deploys a science of sexuality in pursuit of the production of a vigorous and healthy national population. In Chapter 4, we saw the concern of the state with the regulation of prostitution and, through eugenics, with the fertility and sexual health of the population, especially its female half. Often, these concerns were strongly racialised, with black and mixed-race women (and men) assumed to be more of a sexual threat than white women to the health and welfare of the nation. The good citizen was one who behaved in a sexually appropriate way, which did not mean being sexually inactive – on the contrary, men and women had a duty to produce plenty of healthy children – but rather meant channelling sexual behaviour in proper, modest and decorous ways. Black sexuality was seen to carry the threat of licentiousness, impropriety and immodesty. Indigenous, or rather *chola*, sexuality was also seen as improper. White males, in contrast, could indulge in seemingly licentious behaviour – having extramarital sex and children with non-white women, for example – with a good deal of impunity.

Studies of the regulation of sexual health in the twenty-first century indicate a good deal of continuity in this picture, although the new multiculturalism provides a different context. Sexuality continues to be a matter for state concern and regulation, mostly through the provision of education and support services, and sexuality is thought about and dealt with in racialised ways. Often that racialisation is implicit, despite the overt possibility of being explicit about difference in a multicultural state: this implicitness obeys a desire to avoid any taint of racism or hint that particular groups are being discriminated against; instead, reference is made to 'cultural' difference, as it has been for many decades. The 'cultural' differences that are seen as relevant, however, relate to black and indigenous categories.

In her study of a maternity clinic in Salvador, Brazil, McCallum (2008) analyses the practice of doctors, nurses and social workers and their attitudes towards their clients, most of whom are young, poor, Afro-Brazilian women. The clinic staff do not talk about race openly – a trait still typical of many Brazilians (Sheriff 2001), even in an era in which blackness is more of a public issue and affirmative action policies dictate quotas of university places for black students in some state-funded universities. Instead, they talk about class, youth and irresponsibility. They say young women have too many children, too early and without enough thought for how they will support them. This is sometimes explained as a natural result of their youthful biology, but is also seen as a product of their social milieu and their lack of 'culture' (i.e. culturedness or education in the broad sense). However, race lurks below the surface, because their clientele is largely Afro-Brazilian. References to class, social milieu and culture are therefore implicitly racialised.

The clinic staff see their work as the management of the reproductive resources of the nation, which are being threatened by the uncontrolled sexuality of young (black) women, particularly their assumed tendency to have precocious sex. Their mission is to inculcate the self-control seen to be proper to the good, (neo-)liberal citizen, who regulates her own activity in the interests of her family, her community and the nation. Race is taken for granted in the perception of the problem as something involving young, poor, black women, who have little self-control and are poorly adapted to deal with the 'modern world' which does not provide the kind of moral control they need. This case is a good example of how race, class and sexuality mutually constitute each other. The reference to precocious sexuality stands in as a reference to both lower-class origins and non-whiteness, both linked to a lack of 'culture'.[2] In fact, statistical survey data from 2001–02 indicate that Brazilian women who self-identify as *negra* were not more precocious in their first sexual encounter than other women; indeed, women of all racial categories from Salvador were less precocious than those from Rio or Porto Alegre (in the far south) (Heilborn and Cabral 2008: 175). This suggests that stereotypes about black female sexuality were shaping the attitudes of staff at the clinic towards their clients.

Interestingly, McCallum shows that clinic staff valued race mixture in the past: a history of (presumably fairly 'uncontrolled') sexual encounters between white, indigenous and African people had laid the basis for a mixed nation in which racial distinction was not a problem, because most people shared in mixedness. Clinic staff identified with this past mixture as forming part of their personal histories. But the same lack of 'control' by young black women in the present was seen as a threat to the future of the nation. *Mestiçagem*, in other words, was seen as a good basis for national identity, but not to be left in the hands of poor, young, black women and their irresponsible black partners, all driven by their youthful hormonal urges and their selfish desires.

Recent campaigns that target sexual health in Colombia reveal clear parallels. Race entered tacitly and covertly into the practice and discourse of functionaries who delivered state programmes of sexual and reproductive health education to university students and high school students in a working-class neighbourhood in Bogotá (Viveros Vigoya 2006; Viveros Vigoya and Gil Hernández 2006). In the context of a Colombia officially defined in the 1991 constitution as multicultural and pluri-ethnic, functionaries denied the salience of race, as indeed one might have expected them to do before the constitutional reform: they were keen to emphasise that all their clients were treated equally. However, the staff dealt with a racially diverse clientele and tended to talk about this diversity in terms of regional and cultural differences. In Colombia, region and race are quite strongly associated, such that, for example, reference to the Pacific coast is almost inevitably a reference to blackness. Using tropes of region and culture, staff could refer to indigenous students, seen as culturally distinct in their 'timidity' and their reluctance to use condoms; and also to blacks, referred to in terms of their promiscuity and, in relation to black men, their machismo. The key problem was, as in the Salvador clinic, lack of control – symbolised in the inadequate use of condoms. Although this was a general problem associated with rural–urban migrants, *desplazados* (people forcibly displaced to the cities by waves of rural violence) and lower-class city-dwellers, it was clear that indigenous and black people were labelled as having specific problematic traits.

Viveros and Gil (2006) also examined a national PR campaign designed by a sexual health NGO, using television, radio and billboard advertisements to promote the use of condoms by encouraging women to carry them. The advertisements used images of indigenous, black, mixed and white women and the NGO workers explicitly said they were aiming at inclusiveness, which, in the context of a newly recognised multiculturalism, meant representing diversity, but with the overarching aim of transcending that diversity in the interests of a common female identity (one which also ignored real class inequalities among women). However, in Bogotá reactions to the image of a young black woman, shown as urban and modern, were mixed: some people made connections to HIV, on the assumption that black people were more likely to be affected by this condition; others felt little identification with the woman, because she was black and 'not from here'; others commented that it was not effective to use a black woman as men would not like her. In short, despite the inclusive intent of the campaign designers, people tended to reaffirm racial difference, and indeed racial-sexual stereotypes, when confronted with a black model (Viveros Vigoya and Gil Hernández 2006: 97–102).

The campaign was based on the slogan 'The woman carries the condoms' and, of course, one of its unintended messages was to relieve men of the responsibility of regulating sexual activity, thus reinforcing the image of them as sexually free – which is how (white) men appear in the ideology of *mestizaje*. In this context, it is interesting that, when confronted with an image of a *black* woman in control of her own sexuality – and thus contesting the dictates of *mestizaje* according to which her sexuality is available to white and *mestizo* men – at least some people responded by invoking images of sexual promiscuity and availability, as evinced in ideas about the preponderance of HIV among black people. The racial-sexual order of *mestizaje* was thus reaffirmed, in the face of an implicit challenge to it.

The implicit racialisation of sexual health issues can also be seen in the handling of HIV/AIDS in Brazil, where, in the last few years, a discourse has emerged linking Afrodescendants to HIV/AIDS, despite the absence of epidemiological data which might confirm a statistical propensity of this category of the population to suffer from the condition.[3] Fry, Monteiro et al. (2007) interpret this phenomenon as part of the increasingly politicised character of racial identity in Brazil, where, since the mid-1990s, racial inequality has become the subject of open public debate and, from 2001, a series of reforms has sought to address racial inequality by instituting controversial affirmative action policies in some universities (Htun 2004). In the case of discourses about HIV, the racialisation is not explicit – in contrast to South Africa, where it is very overt – and campaigns are directed at 'groups at risk'. But there is a significant tendency on the part of state agencies and NGOs to racialise these groups by targeting black groups for HIV awareness campaigns, using images of black people in advertisements and making statements about the growing number of AIDS cases among the black population. The Minister of Health, at the launch of a 2005 campaign aimed at Afro-Brazilians, said the aim was to 'call attention to the link between racism, poverty and the growing number of AIDS cases in this segment of the Brazilian population' (Fry, Monteiro et al. 2007: 498). This may be a laudable aim in some ways as it draws attention to the operation of racism and poverty, but it also makes HIV/AIDS seem like a 'black problem', related to the supposed tendency of black people to have lots of (unprotected) sexual encounters.

A similar process of racialisation in the governance of sexual reproduction emerges in interactions around sexual health between indigenous communities, NGOs and the state in Ecuador (Radcliffe 2008). Rather than indigenousness being referred to implicitly, it is an overt concern in recent multiculturalist regimes: indigenous women are recognised as a specific minority category with specific needs. However, there is a curious process by which indigenous women are, in fact, marginalised. On the one hand, NGO and state programmes of education and development that focus on reproductive health take gender as an explicit concern, but tend to assume a normative category of (*mestizo*) 'woman', with indigenous women figuring as a vulnerable minority on the sidelines. On the other hand, ethno-development health programmes and the state's National Office for Indigenous Peoples' Health, which focus on indigenous and Afro-Ecuadorian communities, tend to privilege the need to adapt to 'traditional' cultural practices, respecting ethnic rights and identities, while questions of gender take a back seat. One example of this double marginalisation is in Ecuador's 2006 draft law on health. One article addresses sexual and reproductive health, with no mention of racial or ethnic diversity; another article deals with indigenous and Afro-Ecuadorian communities, but simply states the importance of respecting 'traditional practices' of pregnancy and birthing (Radcliffe 2008: 114).

The same problem emerges within the indigenous federations and organisations that also attempt to address issue of sexual health:

> Indigenous women are expected by federations to have children who can maintain ethnic populations. Indigenous women's sexuality is not an explicit cornerstone of multicultural governance, but in the context of neoliberal devolution of governance to ethnic (male) authorities, it can become the battleground for community-based struggles over citizenship. (ibid.: 122–3)

Radcliffe concludes that indigenous women are represented simply as reproducers of ethnic citizens:[4]

> Under [the ideological regime of] mestizaje, indigenous women were positioned literally and metaphorically as sexually available to whiter and more powerful men. In terms of nation-building, indigenous women as a group were represented as outside citizenship as they did not match criteria for inclusion on grounds of literacy, ethnic identity, gender and location. Under multicultural governance, indigenous women's rights to political citizenship are shaped by ongoing contests over sexual and reproductive patterns, in which the ethnic rights biopolitics addresses indigenous women as literally and metaphorically available for ethnic group maintenance. (ibid.: 132–3)

A key conclusion that can be drawn from this and the previous case studies is that the multiculturalist context which has gained strength in Latin America since the 1990s has not undermined the sexualised images attached to racialised categories. While the public endorsement and institutionalisation of cultural diversity can have important positive consequences for anti-racism and the promotion of egalitarian ideas in civic society, multicultural-ism, as has often been noted, may also provide fertile ground in which stereotypical images of racial and ethnic categories can flourish.[5]

More broadly, these examples indicate that in the governance of cultural (read, ethnic and racial) diversity, race continues to have significant sexual dimensions. Radcliffe contrasts regimes of *mestizaje* with regimes of multicultural governance, but there are important continuities. With mixture as a central idea in the formation of the nation, it is reasonably easy to see how sexuality forms a key aspect of racial governance: *mestizaje* places sexual-racial relations at the centre of concepts of the nation and its social order. With multicultural regimes, the role of sexuality may seem less obvious: the image here is of separate 'cultural' groups who reproduce themselves sexually, but do not necessarily mix. I believe there is, in fact, a lot of continuity between Latin American *mestizaje* and Latin American multiculturalism. As Hale (2002: 491) says for Guatemala, multiculturalism 'is the *mestizaje* discourse for the new millennium' – and not just because it takes over as the discursive template for imagining the nation, but also because ideas of mixture do not by any means disappear. Instead, they are rearticulated. Just as, prior to official multiculturalism, there was a constant emphasis in many Latin American nations on the diversity that constituted the very possibility of mixture and that was continuously reproduced, as mixture endlessly generated many different types of *mestizos*, so under multiculturalism the centrality of mixture to the nation persists. This can be seen clearly in the relegation of difference to the margins of the nation: multi-culturalism consists in recognising separate spaces for indigenous and black minorities, while the majority of the population remains mixed. Colombia's 2005 census, for example, does precisely this, asking people to categorise themselves as indigenous, black or 'none of the above'.[6] In Guatemala and Brazil, one of the ways in which mainstream critics attack indigenous movements is to say that, in reality, everyone – even those who claim to be 'indigenous' or 'black' – is mixed and that assertions of cultural or racial separateness are an illusion (Warren 1998; Warren 2001). Being mixed remains the normative identity.

In terms of the persistence of images of sexual mixture, the thing that stands out from the examples discussed above is the contrast (discussed in Chapter 5) between images of black and indigenous sexualities. From the perspective of the regulation of sexual health, black people, and women in particular, are seen as sexually precocious and promiscuous: while blackness may be given a distinct cultural place in the multicultural nation, black people continue to be seen as sexually outgoing, as contributors to the national process of *mestizaje* by virtue of going beyond the sexual boundaries of their category. This may be a cause for concern in maternity clinics and health education programmes, but it also clearly part of the longstanding perception of black men and women as participating in racial-sexual mixture. In contrast, if we can generalise on the basis of the Colombian and Ecuadorean examples, indigenous people are more likely to be seen as introverted sexually, as reproducing themselves as a unit. This fits with the more ambiguous sexual imagery surrounding indigenous men and women (see Chapter 5), in which they often figure as less sexually active and less involved in processes of mixture – or involved principally via the figure of the *chola*, who has long been seen as very much involved, but who is already (imagined as) mixed.

In sum, then, under multiculturalism the governance of race shows important continuities with pre-multiculturalist regimes in the sense that mixture, and its associated images of racial-sexual interaction, are still of key importance and the sexuality of black and indigenous peoples continues to be an area of concern. The examples above also show that in multiculturalist regimes, racial difference is acknowledged (there is racial diversity), but hierarchy is denied (everyone has equal rights to sexual health); at the same time, however, racial hierarchy is reinstated through the negative stereotyping of black sexuality and assumptions about indigenous women as ethnic reproducers. This has obvious parallels with the way in which, in ideologies and practices of *mestizaje*, difference is acknowledged (blackness, indigenousness and whiteness are constantly reiterated), but hierarchy is denied (mixture undoes hierarchy and creates a racial democracy); while, at the same time, racial hierarchy is constantly reproduced, in part through the practices of *mestizaje* itself.

Race, Sex and Social Movements

One the key points Radcliffe makes is that multicultural governance, while it may pay attention to sexual and reproductive health, ignores gender politics. The regulation of indigenous sexuality is effectively handed over to indigenous authorities, given the imperative of 'respecting' traditional custom and practice. But, within the indigenous communities and their leadership, there is a politics of gender and sexuality that many indigenous women experience as constrictive. Radcliffe found that many indigenous women tended to play down gender issues and privilege ethnic identity and rights; yet in private they also commented freely on the sexism and the patriarchal and sometimes violent behaviour of indigenous men. Activism and leadership on the part of women meant going out and travelling alone or with other men in ways that were often interpreted within their communities as linked to sexual licence and prostitution. Husbands and male relatives often became jealous and even violent; female relatives might also be critical. One female leader recounted how her second husband had beaten her and refused to feed her children when she was away on indigenous federation business. Another told how her uncle had beaten her, her godmother had criticised her and her community had called her a prostitute (Radcliffe 2008: 126). Indigenous women also had to face male opposition to the use of contraceptives: as a result, they often relied on abortions (illegal in Ecuador) to end unwanted pregnancies. Botched abortions frequently landed indigenous women in hospital.

The problem of the persistence of sexism within black social movements has also been widely noted, especially for the US, where a number of authors have explored the idea that the assertion of black identity and rights was often bound up, for black men, with an assertion of black masculinity. Indeed, the emergence of black feminism, while it took issue with the tendency of feminism to assume a white female subject and not address issues of race (see Chapter 2), was also inspired by the tendency of race-based social movements to assume a male (and heterosexual) racialised subject and not address issues of gender and sexuality (Collins 2000; hooks 1981; Lao-Montes 2007b; Stephens 2005; Wallace 1979; Wright 2004).

For Latin America, Curiel's research with three black women's organisations in Honduras, the Dominican Republic and Brazil documented the strong tensions that existed between them and the wider black movements in those countries, because of the 'androcentrism and machismo of Afrodescendant men, who in most countries dominate the leadership, manage the resources and information and [who] still have difficulty in understanding that racism, even though it affects both men and women, has differential effects' (Curiel 2008: 474). Indeed, according to the Red de Mujeres Afrolatinoamericanas y Afrocaribeñas (Network of Afro-Latin American and Afro-Caribbean Women), formed in 1992, 'the movement of Afrodescendant women becomes visible and emerges at the end of the 1970s, questioning racism within feminism and sexism within the black movement'.[7] Interestingly, Curiel contends that the black women's organisations that she worked with, although they differed in the degree to which they adopted an explicit feminist stance – with one organisation, for example, focusing on poverty alleviation projects – all tended towards a culturalist position in which a key focus was the promotion and celebration of African-derived cultural expressions such as dance, religious rituals and cooking. In this, women's roles as dancers with 'hyper-sexualised bodies, always directing their eroticism towards men' or as providers of food were generally taken for granted by the women (ibid.: 469). Thus, even black women activists could reproduce (racialised) sexual stereotypes within movements directed at vindicating ethnic and racial identities and rights.

For Brazil, the black feminist Luiza Bairros has commented that 'the black movement, one of the few spaces that is available for the full expression of black people, is also the scene for the exercise of a sexism that could not manifest itself in other spheres of social life, especially in those dominated by (male) whites' (Bairros 2000: 146, n. 7). Although Bairros does not elaborate, it seems she is evoking the idea, expressed by some US black feminists, that black men may see in the black social movement the opportunity to express a sense of male dominance that they feel is curtailed in other areas: that is, the movement becomes a vehicle for black *masculinity*.

The story of the indigenous Bolivian president Evo Morales is suggestive with respect to the link between power and masculinism. Although Morales appointed indigenous women to key ministerial posts, he also wishes 'to challenge the stereotype of the asexual and submissive Indian man', which he does by 'embracing the *mestizo-creole* model of gendered relationships' (Canessa 2008: 54). Not only do jokes and gossip abound about Morales' possible sexual relationships with white women, but he himself makes jokes and remarks that cast him as sexually attractive to non-indigenous women and a virile sexual conqueror. Shortly before his election, he responded to an interviewer's question about how he might get on with white businessmen in the country's predominantly non-indigenous eastern provinces by asserting that most of the (white) beauty queen candidates from that region had said they liked him – a revealing non sequitur (ibid.: 55). He also invited two Miss Bolivias to his presidential inauguration. This is in a country where beauty queens are always tall, white women, often from the eastern provinces. In short, Morales projects an image of himself as sexually virile – especially with non-indigenous women – in order to sustain an aura of political strength.

The masculinist bias of black and indigenous social movements is also revealed in the way they deal with the question of homosexuality and non-heterosexualities. For black social movements in general, this issue is denied, rejected or downplayed.

This has frequently been the case in the US (Collins 2000: 167; Nagel 2003: 121–5; Ross 1998), although the situation is complicated as some black leaders, such as Al Sharpton (in 2005) and Barak Obama (in 2008), have recently explicitly addressed the issue of black homophobia.[8] For Latin America, we have seen in Chapter 5 that blackness and gayness are often seen as contradictory characteristics. This emerges again among black political activists. One Colombian transgendered MTF (male-to-female) person from Cali recounted that she felt least rejection from whites, more from blacks in general and most from black political activists: overall, she had to contend with 'a sexist and homophobic ideology underlying the practices of members of black organizations' (Urrea Giraldo et al. 2008: 302–3). There are also high levels of homophobia among Afro-Brazilian activists. In the mid-1990s, the historian Luiz Mott suggested that the Zumbi, a famous runaway slave figure who serves as an icon for the Brazilian black movement, might have been homosexual and unleashed a torrent of negative reaction from black movement leaders, who saw being gay as a betrayal of the condition of blackness (Díaz 2006: 295). Curiel also observes that, although there were substantial numbers of lesbians in the black women's organisations with which she worked in Brazil and the Dominican Republic, sexual diversity was barely touched on in the discussions and activities of these groups. Indeed, lesbophobia was noticeable, especially in the Honduran organisation (2008: 477–8).

The attitudes towards homosexuality within indigenous social movements is complex, partly because, for a number of indigenous societies, some observers have reported tolerance towards homosexuality and cross-dressing and the presence of what anthropologists have called 'berdache' (ambiguous male-female gender figures, also known as two-spirit people in US and Canadian Native American circles).[9] A similar situation exists in North America, yet in 1979, the Native American scholar Beatriz Medicine (1997: 152–3) wrote that 'Many Native American women in leadership positions have maintained that male homosexuality is a result of contact with Europeans and, mostly, have held such sexual "perverts" with disdain. In general, ridicule by fellow tribespersons has been the rule.' She added that 'the male dominance and "macho-like" expressions of males in Indian militant and reform movements have placed these individuals [homosexuals] – especially the males – in a triple bind'. Commenting on GAI (Gay American Indians), a voluntary association formed in 1975 in San Francisco by two native Americans, she noted that they were concerned with

> dispelling the 'image of Indian as macho militant' (Katz 1976: 502), which has been so prevalent in the Indian protest movements. Sexism is rampant in such movements as the American Indian Movement (AIM), where the militant men often say they are fostering Indian unity by having girlfriends in each tribe and fathering as many children as possible. The intolerance towards homosexuals has been equally enormous.[10]

GAI members were often ridiculed and taunted when they attended Bay Area political meetings. Lang notes that the growth of Native American self-awareness from the 1970s has in some ways strengthened the status of *winkte* figures (the Lakota term for two-spirit people), often with the argument that native American homophobia, rather than homosexuality, has been the result of contact with Europeans. Still, even in the 1990s, 'a negative attitude to all kinds of homosexual behaviour is widespread in the Indian communities, both on and off the reservation' (Lang 1998: 312).

For Latin America, data are sparse. Stephen reports conflicting accounts of *muxe* (the name given to the third gender role taken by Zapotec men, which she distinguishes from 'homosexual' or 'gay' identities imported from elsewhere in Mexico and the US). Generally, men who adopt the *muxe* role are tolerated, although men who are thought to be homosexual, but who do not take on the *muxe* role, may be spoken of pejoratively; on the other hand, she cites Howard Campell, who 'reports having heard disparaging remarks about *muxe* from political activists in Juchitán' (Stephen 2002: 44).[11] Looking at left-wing politics in Latin America, rather than ethnic politics in particular, Green and Babb (2002: 15) refer to the Zapatista Liberation Front, which has a clearly indigenist as well as left-wing agenda, and state that its leader, Comandante Marcos, 'has at least made gestures of inclusion in his references to lesbians and gays in some of his declarations, but his pronouncements unfortunately remain the exception to the rule'. Colombianist colleagues of mine report that issues of sexual diversity figure low on the agendas of the indigenous social movements that they know: it is just not an issue that is seen as important.[12]

In sum, masculinism and power are strongly linked: in order to project a credible political presence, black and indigenous male leaders often feel the need to present an image of themselves as fully and potently masculine – which may translate into being a conqueror of white women and/or exercising complete control over their 'own' women. Women leaders may also want to deploy an image of themselves, and indeed their male counterparts, as heterosexual – or at least downplay lesbianism and gayness. As we saw in Chapter 4, nationalist ideologies, while they deploy images of women as key figures in the reproduction and represen-tation of the nation, generally place men – properly, 'masculine' men – as the real authorities and leaders of the nation. Minority social movements that contest the way the nation is configured and represented may reproduce that nationalist masculinism in their own work. This also acts to reinforce nationalist ideologies of *mestizaje* insofar as these depend on certain notions of sexuality to have their effect. Ethnic and racial social movements do contest ideologies of *mestizaje* by affirming a resilient presence for blackness and indigenousness and challenging the position of black and indigenous women as fodder for sexual predation by white males or as willing partners in whitening strategies. But to the extent that they also reproduce ideas of male dominance and female subordination, and of male control over female sexuality – especially if it is a racialised control in which black men control black women and indigenous men control indigenous women – then they are also reproducing some of the fundamental tenets of *mestizaje*, in which men control female sexuality for the purposes of protecting or promoting their own status. One of the key lessons that emerges from a grasp of how race and sex articulate or intersect is that contesting racial inequality also means contesting gender inequality (and heterosexism): the two (or three) dimensions of oppression are linked and mutually constitute each other; they cannot be dismantled independently of one another.

Latinos in the US

If social movements are contesting ideologies of *mestizaje* in some ways – even if they are reaffirming the underlying sex-gender politics in other ways – then another challenge to dominant ideas about mixture and nationhood comes from the experiences of Latin Americans who migrate to the US, whether to stay, circulate or return. In the 2000 US census, Latinos made up 12.5 per cent of the population and the subject area of Latino studies in the US (not to mention elsewhere) is a vast one.[13] What interests us here is how race and sex articulate around the category. Even here, there is potentially a large field of study if one includes all the dynamics of sexuality and gender that operate among Latinos. As Flores (2000: 210) says,

> If the early 1970s articulation of Latino Studies was guided by a rallying cry of cultural nationalism – boisterous and contestatory but also often parochial and unreflexive – ... [t]heorizing about gender and sexuality has done the most to dissolve the sexist and heterosexist conception of Latino group unity and inclusion, and to complicate the meanings of Latino claims and affirmation.

Latino Studies has been queered by feminist, gay and lesbian scholarship (J. M. Rodríguez 2003), giving rise to a host of discussions and expressions of identity and culture.[14] This, of course, parallels what I have just been discussing for Latin America itself, where assertions of ethnic and racial identity by social movements have been complicated by feminist and gay/lesbian agendas. In thinking about sexuality among Latinos, there is also an interest in the sexual practices of Latino groups (e.g. González-López 2005), which is often linked to sexual health issues concerning HIV/AIDS (e.g. Alonso and Koreck 1999; Asencio 2002).

In keeping with the interests of this book, I shall focus on the way in which the racialised and sexualised category 'Latino/a' is deployed in processes of governance and contestation. The question to address is how sexuality is deployed to construct and govern the racialised category of Latino (which implies the corollary question of how race gets deployed to construct the sexualised category of Latino).

I shall explore two themes: first, images of Latino sexuality, particularly the Latino macho and the Latina temptress, which have been deployed in imagining Latinos as a sexual-racial category; second, the idea that Latinos are racially varied and above all mixed: some may be 'white' and 'black' in US terms, but most Latinos are racially mixed and do not fit easily into US racial classifications – even those who are 'white' and 'black' may still be classified, and classify themselves, as Hispanic or Latino. This is primarily a matter of race, but sex is included insofar as racial mixture is a sexual process and the fact of Latino mixedness speaks to the taboos and hysteria that have surrounded interracial sex in the US. Latin American *mestizaje* thus enters the US domain.

Macho Latino

There are many possible avenues in which this question could be explored, but a starting point must be the sexualised images of Latino men and women. The key images here are those of the macho Latino male and the seductive Latina woman, stereotypes reproduced as part of a process of 'hegemonic tropicalising' (Aparicio and Chávez-Silverman 1997: 8; see also Ramírez Berg 2002; Rodríguez 1997b). The usual counterpart to the macho (and machismo) is said to be the María (and *marianismo*), that is, the submissive, self-sacrificing virgin/mother figure (Asencio 2002: 17–19; Stevens 1973), but it is also clear that the 'Madonna' image exists alongside the 'whore' image and I shall focus on the latter as the more overtly sexualised image. It is also an image that emerges in recent concerns over young Latinas and their birth rates, which are relatively high.[15]

For Latin America, 'both popular and scholarly literature maintain a tacit view that machismo is ubiquitous if not universal', a trait that gives the region a bad reputation as 'without doubt machismo is the most common equivalent for sexism throughout the world today' (Gutmann 2003: 18). However, the terms 'macho' and 'machismo', as applied to the Mexican male, have quite brief histories, appearing in Mexico as a way to talk about 'typical' Mexican men from about 1940 and in English in the US shortly after. While a certain virile masculinity was certainly part of the consolidation of Mexican national identity from an earlier date (as we saw in Chapter 4), the figure of the *macho mexicano* is quite recent (Gutmann 1996: 224–6). In the US, 'the term *machismo* has a rather explicitly racist history ... [and] has been associated with negative character traits not among men in general but specifically among Mexican, Mexican American and Latin American men' (ibid.: 227).

The Mexicans Gutmann worked with were well aware that US people viewed Mexican men through this stereotype and he adds that the image serves the US as a way to displace onto Mexicans the problems of sexism and gender inequality that exist at home (ibid.: 235). Gutmann shows that the image of the macho male is a complex one, with multiple and shifting meanings. Many of the men he talked with rejected the label: the macho was a womanising, hard-drinking, irresponsible wife-beater – sexual conquest and domestic violence were his defining traits – and in some ways he was seen as a rather traditional, rural figure, not suited to the modern urban lives these men saw themselves as leading, even if their working-class status tallied with the image of the macho as plebeian. Yet being macho remained an option for men, who might let their 'heads be controlled by their bodies' (ibid.: 236). It thus also remained a reality for women.

If in Mexico, the image of the macho is complex, contested and negotiated, among Latinos in the US, it is not surprising that the same is true. Often, re-readings of being macho attempt to highlight positive characteristics, which require men to be dedicated to and defend their families, be brave, work hard, be respectful, and so on (Mirandé 1997; Torres et al. 2002). In a more subversive mode, Girman (2004: ch. 6) recounts his own and other gay men's experiences with Latino 'macho' men who have sex with other men (and not always in an active, penetrating role), but routinely deny this and refuse to talk about it. Almaguer (2007) reiterates that the Latino macho figure is an important site of desire for some gay Chicano men. Clearly the role of macho admits of a good deal of flexibility.

In a collection of essays by creative writers on the theme of Latino manhood, Omar Castañeda, writes: 'Machismo is complex and multifaceted and, too often in Anglo-American interpretations, reduced to self-aggrandising male bravado that flirts with physical harm to be sexual, like some rutting for the right to pass on genes' (Castañeda 1996: 37). Like the other contributors to the collection, Castañeda seeks to undermine the label as an ethnic-racial stereotype, but does not discard the idea completely: he sees machismo as characteristic of immature Latino men, a trait that can be grown out of; other contributors attribute the role to their fathers or even, tacitly, to themselves. Gilb, for example, starts his essay: 'I've been accused of suffering from involuntary macho spasms most of my life. Usually not to my face. Very few got the huevos [balls] for that!' And he ends thus:

> Here's a list: I like women. I like women better than men. I think some people deserve to get their asses kicked. I don't go to bullfights ... I don't drink beer very often, and I love baseball and basketball and don't care for football much. You don't like that, screw you. I love my family. I love walking the streets, or up a mountain, or a desert trail, alone. I eat beef. And serrano chillies. (Gilb 1996)

If Latinos are stereotyped as machos by Anglo-Americans (and possibly others too), then Latinos (and Latinas) may complicate that image and balk at it as an ethnic-racial epithet, while not rejecting it out of hand. Mexican Americans in the 1930s and 1940s developed the *pachuco* style as a working-class, ethnic, youth subculture, associated stereotypically by others with gangs, violence and sexual promiscuity, but also, among the men, projecting a certain self-image of tough masculinity, as do later developments of this subcultural style, labelled *cholo* or *chuco* (Cummings 2003; Madrid 2003).[16] Since the 1980s, Latino men have nuanced the macho image a great deal, but, as Gutmann argues for men in Mexico City, it remains as a (now much more flexible) option. It may be enshrined, for example, in the link, constructed in Chicano poetry of the 1960s and 1970s and Chicano rap of later decades, between Latino cultural nationalism – *la raza* – and ideals of the Latino heteronormative and patriarchal family – *la familia* (R. T. Rodríguez 2003). It is clear from the way Latino feminist and queer studies have addressed Latino identity in general that sexism and homophobia were perceived as a problem in expressions of that identity (see also Román 1997).

The image of the Latino macho has had repercussions in the area of sexual health. It has been argued that this image has contributed to problems in dealing with the escalating HIV infection rate in Latino communities (a problem they share with African Americans). Alonso and Koreck (1999: 277) allege that Latinos have been trapped in Anglo-American discursive constructions 'of an "other" sexuality beyond "the bounds of decency", of an out-of-control concupiscence as lush and torrid as the tropical jungles which are our origin sites in the Anglo imagination'. In this, Latino sexuality was always construed as heterosexual and opposed to the image of the Anglo homosexual. Silence about Latino men who have sex with men, both in the Anglo community and among Latinos, fearful of the stigma of homosexuality and bisexuality, led to a blindness to the problem of HIV and AIDS. Latino AIDS activists criticised Latino leaders for their refusal to confront the issue. This problem was driven in part by practices in which Latino men might have sex with other men, without thinking of themselves as homosexuals and without talking about it – what is sometimes called having sex 'on the down low' (González 2007; see also Muñoz-Laboy 2004).

Governance of sexual health in the multicultural US has been caught in the classic social policy dilemma of having to take notice of 'culture' in designing effective policies, while avoiding the trap of using 'culture' as a scapegoat in ways that easily become racist. Asencio (2002) addresses this issue, arguing that policy-makers need detailed knowledge of Puerto Rican youths' ideas about sex and gender in order to make effective interventions into sexual health, but also arguing that it is ineffective and racist to blame 'Puerto Rican culture' for a host of sexual health problems, such as high levels of HIV infection and above-average teen pregnancy rates. Asencio deals with this problem – essentially the same debate as the one surrounding the so-called 'culture of poverty' in previous years – by emphasising that 'culture' is an ongoing process, subject to constant change and negotiation, rather than a homogeneous set of norms that control the behaviour of people locked within its boundaries. Still, the balance between culture as thing and culture as process is a tricky one to strike. The public sphere in the US is full of 'culturally sensitive' guides to Latino families, published by university extension and community outreach departments, aimed at social workers and policy-makers who deal with Latino communities. Such guides are useful, of course, but they always run the risk – despite constant acknowl-edgements of diversity – of essentialising Latino culture into a set of traits shared by all, often based on family unity, loyalty to the family, collectivism and familism, and so on.[17]

In sum: the image of the Latino macho is still current in the US and among Latinos in the US, even if it has been extensively nuanced through self-reflection and critique. It still serves as a racist stereotype – one that may compromise sexual health campaigns that make assumptions about Latino sexual behaviour. However, the racism of the stereotype is complicated by the fact that Latinos and Latinas do not necessarily reject the image, especially when it works to connect Latino cultural nationalism to a secure Latino family life, supported by a tough, masculine male.

Latina Seductress

Images of seductive Latina sexuality have followed a similar path to those of the Latin macho. The image of the Latina seductress has been and is still routinely reproduced (Chávez-Silverman 1997; Cortés 1997: 128–31; Rodríguez 1997a: 2–3). The promotional posters used for the 2003 Latin Grammy music awards showed a scantily clad young woman in a sensual pose with a drum between her legs, above the slogan 'Feel the Latino' (Torres-Saillant 2007: 370). In relation to Shakira, the Latina singer of Colombian origin, the 'disproportionate amount of media attention dedicated to Shakira's sexuality highlights the well-entrenched acceptance of *marianismo* (or the "Madonna/whore" complex) that informs the way Shakira is framed within the transnational media' (Cepeda 2003: 222). However, Shakira herself has 'embraced the notion that her dancing ability is somehow part and parcel of a uniquely Latin(o) American genetic inheritance. In interviews, she has remarked that her ability to move her body is "… something that is in my DNA," and that "no one told me how to move my hips", reinforcing the popular belief in an inherent link between Latina corporality and hypersexuality' (ibid.: 221, references deleted).

Like Latino men – and similar to the way we saw that Latin American black men and women relate to images of themselves as sexually superior – there are indications that Latina women do not reject the racialised image of themselves as sexy. As we shall see below when discussing Latinas' racialised body image, Latinas may work on their bodily 'capital' to approach an aesthetic norm dominated by whiteness (Hunter 2005), but they may also be striving after something more akin to a (whitened) Hispanicity or *latinidad*, characterised by sexiness (Candelario 2007). While there are some pressures towards a whitened look – for example, from *Latina* women's magazine – and Shakira dyed her hair blonde after migrating to the US, other iconic figures such as Selena and Jennifer Lopez embody and celebrate a specifically Latina bodily aesthetic, summed up in the film title *Real Women Have Curves* (Figueroa 2003).[18] Some Latina scholars argue that stars such as Jennifer Lopez endorse a Latina body image in which 'the big rear end acts both as an identification site for Latinas to reclaim their beauty and a "compensatory fantasy" for a whole community' (Frances Negrón-Muntaner, cited in Cepeda 2003: 222). On a rather different note, some Chicana lesbian writers and artists mark their work with Mexican popular Catholic images, such as La Virgen de Guadalupe, and other icons, such as La Malinche (normally the emblem of heterosexual *mestizaje*), to create a space for Chicana lesbian desire that is 'both damaged and erotically empowered by culturally specific sexual/religious meanings' (Yarbro-Bejarano 1995: 183).

The image of the sexy Latina woman is certainly present in the public realm, but it must be put into context. It is very distant, for example, from the lives of working-class Mexican migrants for whom pressures of work may be such that finding the time just to have sex with their partners may be something of a luxury (González-López 2005). There are, of course, other ways for Latinas to carve out an ethnic identity via gendered and sexualised images and practices. For example, the *quinceañera* celebration (by which 15-year-old girls ritually mark their transition to womanhood) are very common among Latinas and, according to Davalos, who worked with Mexican Americans in Chicago, it is an 'event that leads girls to discover and experience themselves as women, Mexicans, Catholics, and adults' (1996: 114). In addition, the practice of motherhood, of having and raising a *familia* – whether or not Latinas conform to some stereotyped image of self-sacrificing *marianismo* in the process – is an important means of asserting an ethnic identity.

Given the prevalence of service work among working-class Latinas – domestic service, for example – a key image is also that of servant. The figure of the maid, of course, can be sexualised as well, but there may be complex processes at work here. Joseph and Rubin report on the work of Pratt on Filipina domestic workers in Vancouver. These women are seen by employers as hard domestic workers and loving with the children, but not necessarily adequately trained to oversee the children's intellectual development. Recruiting agents in the Philippines advised women not to send pictures that make them seem attractive, in case it gave the impression of them as seductresses (Pratt 1999). Within the Filipino community, the nannies are sexualised as promiscuous, intent on stealing husbands from Filipina wives, yet they are also masculinised as the main breadwinners for their families back home; at the same time, they are often denied the right to have their families with them. 'Employers both want and don't want their nanny to replace them as substitute mothers, employers both want and don't want another woman in the house'; it is the condition of being both 'martyrs and whores' that produces Filipina domestics as low cost labour (Pratt, cited in Joseph and Rubin 2007: 443). In short, there are complex sets of images of Filipina domestics, both among employers and among Filipinos/as. It is easy to see how the same analysis could be applied to Latina domestics.

Overall, however, the material above does suggest that links between sexiness and female *latinidad* are far from being rejected by Latinas, just as machismo still has a shifting and contested place in Latino constructions of masculinity. Both images are deeply rooted in ideologies of *mestizaje*, which evoke the idea of the conquering, sexually rampant man and the sexually available and tempting dark-skinned woman. This leads us to a consideration of what happens to the idea of racial mixture in the US context.

Mestizaje in the US

Latinos have long posed problems for US racial categories. When the US acquired Mexico's northern frontier territories in 1848, there was uncertainty about how to deal with Mexicans in racial terms. Initially, they were all given full citizenship rights, but soon individual states (California, Arizona, Texas, New Mexico) introduced formal discrimination against Mexicans of African descent and denied full citizenship to those considered Indian. During the era of legally enforced 'Jim Crow' segregation (1896–1954), dark-skinned Mexicans and Mexican Americans were subject to discrimination alongside African Americans. Sometimes all Mexicans were classed as non-white for particular purposes. Mexicans and Mexican Americans deemed to be of different 'races' could contravene anti-miscegenation laws if they wanted to marry each other, a matter that was still causing legal wrangles as late as 1942 (Menchaca 2007).

More recently, racialised difference still has the power to divide Latinos. Census data from 1990 indicate that, while endogamy was strong among Latinos in general, white Latinos tended to assimilate via marriage with (mostly white) non-Latinos more than did non-white Latinos (Qian and Cobas 2004). Non-white Latinos had higher rates of endogamy than white Latinos and this was more marked for the US-born than the foreign-born, suggesting that life in the US made racial barriers seem more relevant in marital choice. Other evidence suggests that darker-looking Latinos have poorer life-chances than their whiter-looking compatriots in relation to education and income. For the 1990s, more indigenous-looking Mexican Americans tended to be less educated than whiter ones, due to discrimination (although phenotype had a much lesser effect in California than Texas and for English speakers compared to Spanish speakers) (Murguía and Telles 1996). The darkest Mexican Americans also had lower incomes than others of the same category, again due to discrimination (Telles and Murguía 1990), although other evidence suggests the effect of phenotype varies according to the national origin of Latinos (Espino and Franz 2002).

Lighter skin tone affects Mexican American women's education and income chances (although less so than for African American women): light skin and a whiter phenotype acts as 'social capital' which women can use in strategies of upward mobility (Hunter 2002); they could accumulate more capital by bleaching their skin, straightening their hair and using cosmetic surgery (see also Hunter 2005). Survey data show that darker Latinos who report having faced racial discrimination are unlikely to self-identify as white, despite a 'general Latino preference for whiteness' (Golash-Boza and Darity 2008: 929). Various studies of indigenous immigrants from Mexico indicate that they face discrimination not only from white Americans, but also from *mestizo* Mexicans and Mexican Americans (Fox and Rivera-Salgado 2004; Kearney 2000; Stephen 2007).

If this evidence shows that the US black–white binary tends to divide Latinos into lighter and darker categories, other studies indicate that Latinos also resist the black–white binary, or the white–native American binary, and assert the importance of a mixed-race identity. Rodríguez (1994) shows that Puerto Ricans coming to the US mainland ran into racial classifications that were more forceful than those experienced on the island. Darker-skinned Puerto Ricans were sometimes shocked to discover they were 'black', but lighter-skinned people might also be alarmed that they were now officially 'white' and thus considered racially separate from close relatives (and, prior to desegregation, perhaps not allowed to eat with them in a restaurant). But Rodríguez then presents case studies of three individuals, showing that self-identifications are complex and multiple: a person may identify mainly as black, recognising that he is classed as such by most people on the mainland, but also retain a strong Latino identity. Afro-Latinos thus constitute a specific category: they are not simply African American, although they share blackness with that identity, but they are not straightforwardly Latino insofar as they may suffer discrimination from other Latinos (Dzidzienyo and Oboler 2005; Lao-Montes 2007a). Indigenous Latinos also have specific identities: they do not necessarily identify simply as Latinos, insofar as other Latinos may discriminate against them as *indios* and they retain or even reaffirm a sense of identity as Zapotec or Mixtec; yet they are clearly separate from native Americans too (Fox and Rivera-Salgado 2004; Kearney 2000; Stephen 2007).

Latinos tend to resist the black–white and white–native American binary schema when it comes to self-identification in the US census. In the 1980 and 1990 censuses, people were first asked to identify as Latino or non-Latino and then, in a separate question, tick a box that identified their race. In both censuses, over 40 per cent of Latinos ticked the box marked 'some other race' (i.e. simplifying somewhat, other than white, black, native American, Asian or Pacific Islander). Many respondents, following the instruction to 'write in race' accompanying this option, wrote a national identification such as 'Dominican' (Rodríguez 2000: 130). In the 2000 census, people were allowed to tick more than one of the race categories, in recognition of the possibility of multiple racial identities, but the basic pattern was repeated, with over 42 per cent of Latinos ticking the 'other' option, compared to only 0.2 per cent of the non-Latino population. Over 6 per cent of Latinos also ticked two or more race boxes, compared to 2 per cent of non-Latinos. In contrast, only 2 per cent of Latinos ticked the 'black or African American' box and 1 per cent the 'native American' box, while nearly 48 per cent identified themselves as white (Grieco and Cassidy 2001: 10).

Dominicans in the US also evince complex reactions in terms of racial identifications (Candelario 2007). On the one hand, Dominicans, whether in their home country or in the US, tend to distance themselves from blackness: they show a strong antipathy towards Haitians and often identify themselves as *indios* rather than *mulatos, morenos* or other terms indicating black ancestry. In line with Hunter (2005), Candelario shows that Dominican women in the US spend a lot of time and money in beauty salons, cultivating a non-black body aesthetic, especially with their hair. On the other hand, she argues that Dominicans are not involved in a simple flight from blackness towards wholehearted identification with Anglo-American culture. Instead, they embrace Hispanicity as a kind of middle ground that allows them to negotiate their historical relationship to Haiti, on one side, and their experience of US imperialism, on the other, keeping the former at a considerable distance, but not capitulating to the latter. In fact, Dominicans often admit to having a bit of 'black behind the ears' and, in Washington, where there is a large and successful black middle class, she found a stronger tendency among Dominicans to identify as black.

This loyalty of Latinos to a Latin identity, one that is not simply black, white or indigenous – even if the racial difference within Latin identity fractures more deeply under the pressure of life in the US – has arguably had an increasing impact on US racial schemas. The sheer size of the Latino population, its racial ambiguity and the refusal of many Latinos to adhere to binary categories, has led some to 'question whether bi-polarity should continue unquestioned as the characterisation of race relations in the USA' (Skidmore 1993: 380), although Latinos are not the only factor at work in this respect.[19] The Latino presence has also led to what some call the 'browning' of the US. This, however, is often more than a simple observation of empirical reality: for some commentators it is a political and cultural goal. Richard Rodriguez (2002) argues that brown is the 'last discovery of America'. Not only is the US becoming browner – which is a good thing, in his view, as it undermines the classic black–white binary – but in reality it has been brown all along, even if this has traditionally been denied. As Torres-Saillant (2007: 367) says, approvingly, 'he [Rodriguez] envisions a time when the United States will dare to speak the truth about its brownness, the history of cross-racial copulation'. In this view, race mixture and interracial sex are a kind of truth, the unmasking of which will have a liberatory effect: 'I write of brown as complete freedom of substance and narration. I extol impurity'; and 'Brown marks a reunion of peoples, an end to ancient wanderings. Rival cultures and creeds conspire with Spring to create children of a beauty, perhaps a harmony, previously unknown' (Rodriguez 2002: xi, xiii).

Earlier than Rodriguez, the Chicana writer and activist Gloria Anzaldúa famously argued for the importance of the 'new *mestiza*', a borderland figure who could break down racial (and sexist) barriers and find new ways forward by virtue of her ambiguous positioning, which allowed her to move between and combine categories and identities (Anzaldúa 1987). Although different – and belonging to a different era – the views of Vasconcelos on the *raza cósmica* and its place in a better deracialised future share some ground with Anzaldúa in the positive, mould-breaking role given to Latin American *mestizaje* (Rodriguez also mentions Vasconcelos in his work). Likewise, in a presidential address to the Organization of American Historians, Nash (1995) revealed 'the hidden history of *mestizo* America' (actually North America). Nash disapproved of multiculturalism and multiracialism, which have led to 'a definitional absolutism that has unwittingly defeated egalitarian and humanitarian goals by smothering inequalities of class and fuelling interethnic and interracial tensions that give more powerful groups opportunities to manipulate these divisions' (ibid.: 961). What was needed was a 'pan-ethnic, pan-racial, antiracist sensibility'; in his view, 'only through hybridity – not only in physical race crossing but in our minds as a shared pride in and identity with hybridity – can our nation break the "stranglehold that racialist hermeneutics has over cultural identity"' (ibid.: 962, citing Klor de Alva). He saw *mestizaje* (he used the Spanish word) as the enemy of 'racial absolutism' (ibid.: 960) and stated that 'racial blending is undermining the master idea that race is an irreducible marker among diverse peoples' (ibid.: 961).

In short, with increasing frequency, 'what has long been referred to as the "Latin American model" of race relations is being proposed as the potential solution to racial division, the underlying message being that Latina/os, in all their racial diversity, have managed to avoid racial discord' (Jiménez Román 2007: 326). Such a proposition depends on romantic notions of *mestizaje* and associated ideas of Latin American racial democracy. Pérez-Torres (2006: 20–1) argues that Rodriguez fails to get to grips with the relationships of power that infuse brown bodies. Anzaldúa is a more ambivalent figure: recognising that there are overly utopian elements in her views on *mestizaje*, he states that 'there is much in Anzaldúa's vision, however, that serves to inspire and motivate those who seek an empowered and empowering understanding of Chicana mestizaje' (ibid.: 27–8). For Pérez-Torres (2006: xiv), *mestizaje* is ultimately ambiguous: 'it allows for the forging of new multivalent identities *and* it embeds identity in already constraining social relations'. I argue that, because *mestizaje* always contains within it, indeed depends on and reproduces racial difference – usually in a hierarchical ordering – it can never be set up as a simple antidote to racial difference and hierarchy (Wade 2004). Broader notions of hybridity and what Gilroy calls diasporic processes, which produce 'creolised, syncretised, hybridised and chronically impure cultural forms' (2000: 129), may have a subversive and liberatory effect, undermining essentialist and exclusive identities, but this is by no means always the case and various theorists have recognised that hybridity itself has different effects and meanings, some of which reproduce essentialist difference in much the same way as *mestizaje* does: mixture itself does not necessarily undo hierarchy and unequal power relations, or unravel the differences with which mixture starts (Wade 2005a).

If we go back to Latinos in the US, it is clear that, while their presence and their adherence to a set of identities that do not fit into a simple racial binary may unsettle and indeed transform the binary, it is frankly utopian to expect to discover in Latino identity an antidote to racial difference and hierarchy. As we have seen, Latinos in general tend to avoid identifying as blacks or native Americans. Rodriguez may see 'brown' as inclusive of 'black' and say: 'I cannot imagine myself a writer, I cannot imagine myself writing these words, without the example of African slaves stealing the English language, learning to read against the law, then transforming the English language into the American tongue, transforming me, rescuing me, with a coruscating nonchalance' (2002: 31). But most Latinos seem able and willing to keep blackness at arm's length, even if they sometimes admit to having some 'behind the ears'. And, as we have seen, blackness and indigenousness, as manifest in phenotype, can differentiate the Latino population in terms of life-chances, marriage choices and body aesthetics. Lao-Montes (2007b) contends that academia has not helped here, with African diaspora studies and Latino studies tending to carve out separate territories of research in ways that marginalise Afro-Latinos.

I seem to have strayed far from issues of sex, but these are always implicit, because the 'brown' person is, by definition, the product of interracial sex. The challenge that brownness sets for the US is precisely the fact that US racial ideology has been premised on the assumption that brown people belong to the black (or native American) category; it is an ideology that considers 'a white woman capable of giving birth to a black child but denies that a black woman can give birth to a white child' (Fields 1982: 149). The currency of this ideology is seen in the recent popularity of the term 'people of colour' to refer to all 'non-whites' – even Latinos who appear white.[20] But it is an ideology that appears to be shifting only slowly. The admission of multiracial self-identification into the census, the growth of a movement defending the validity of mixed-race identities (Root 1996; Williams 2005) and the increase in interracial marriages from about 2 per cent of the total in 1970 to about 7 per cent in 2000 (Rosenfeld and Kim 2005) all indicate that interracial sex is not the taboo it once was, that the governance of race through sexual control is changing. The Latino presence and associated notions of *mestizaje* may have played a role in this development, but we need to be very cautious in celebrating *mestizaje* as a result: as we have seen, *mestizaje* and mixture in general by no means erase racial hierarchy. The lesson for the US from Latin America is that an increase in interracial sex and mixing is no guarantee that racial hierarchy and racism are on the way out: they can just change their form.

Conclusion

This chapter has covered a varied terrain, from sexual health clinics and ethnic-racial social movements in Latin America to images of sexuality and *mestizaje* among Latinos in the US. The common theme, however, has been *mestizaje* itself as a prime site for the articulation of race and sex. Multicultural regimes have apparently challenged ideologies of *mestizaje*, but as we have seen, they show strong continuities with such ideologies, balancing notions of racial equality with the reproduction of racism, both expressed through ideas about sexuality. The challenges to *mestizo* homogeneity and claims to full citizenship for ethnically and racially diverse citizens, which have been pursued by ethnic-racial social movements, also seem often to reproduce a link between masculinism and power that has to be explicitly challenged by feminist, gay and lesbian activists. Even then, feminist organisations may end up reiterating stereotypes of black female sexuality. In the US, sexualised images of Latinos, which are rooted in ideologies of *mestizaje* and are deployed in the US as part of racist constructions of Latino communities, are nuanced but not rejected by many Latino men and women. Finally, *mestizaje* itself is challenged by Latinos' experiences of living through US racial hierarchies and classification schemas, but in a strong sense these only work on and intensify the racialised divisions and hierarchies that *mestizaje* already contains. This is why the potential *mestizaje* has for reshaping US racial sensibilities, while not to be ignored, must be treated with the greatest caution.

A final comment about emotional ambivalence. This is not a theme I want to discuss at length in this chapter, as I think the situation is very similar to that described in Chapter 5 for black, indigenous and mixed people. It is easy to detect ambivalence in Morales' challenge to white hegemony in Bolivia alongside his apparent interest in being seen with white beauty queens. For Latinos, the Anglo-American hegemony that dominates US value systems is at once an object of desire (e.g. in relation to female body aesthetics) and an object of resentment (because it discriminates against Latinos). Ambivalence is therefore evident in the reaction of Latinos to dominant images of themselves as sexualised, racialised others: on the one hand, they are wary of stereotypes that limit and trivialise them; on the other, they use them to assert some sense of ethnic particularity and indeed value (since the stereotypes themselves are ambivalent, evoking both disapproval and envious desire).

7
CONCLUSION

In a fundamental sense it is true that race and sex articulate together so tightly and with such power because in hierarchical systems that deploy notions of genealogy – as do racialised hierarchies – there will be an intense concern with controlling what gets passed on to whom through genealogical links, with the links formed through sexual reproduction figuring large in such calculations. By no means all concern with genealogy is racialised, and genealogical links can be formed in ways other than by sexual reproduction, added to which there are different views worldwide on the kinds of links sexual reproduction creates and their social significance, but the links between genealogy and power are a key feature of the articulation of race and sex. This is seen in the operation of ideologies of honour, in which white men controlled the sexuality of white women in order to regulate the control of property, inheritance and power in Latin American colonial and postcolonial societies.

But race and sex articulate in the theoretical sense outlined in Chapter 2. They form a new functional entity that is more than the sum of its parts; they are an intersection, not in the sense of two vectors crossing at a single point, but rather in the sense of a new space created by two sets of dynamics operating together, a space in which new phenomena can emerge and develop. As at the intersection of two (or more) roads, a complex community can establish itself, so where race and sex intersect, multiple effects can ensue. But images of articulated entities and complex intersection, while useful, risk implying a certain fixity: race and sex are also discursive processes and the ideological elements deployed in them can be reconfigured in new and sometimes unpredictable ways.

One must not assume that, because race and sex have articulated in a particular way at one time, they cannot rearticulate in other ways; nor that only one articulation can exist at any a given time. The articulation of race and sex in ideas about honour has proved to be enduring, but it has also varied. In the nineteenth century, for example, race and sex became articulated to a discourse of nation that lent the term new discursive powers and potential: for example, ideological elements of race and sex could be reconfigured to create a discourse of cross-class and cross-racial democratic fraternity, based on control of women's sexuality and moral conduct. In the context of late twentieth-century ethnic movements, notions that are arguably linked to honour reappear in ideas of ethnic or racial pride and the expectation that black and indigenous women – but not so much men – should remain within certain ethno-sexual boundaries. The material analysed in this book reveals these changing articulations of race and sex.

In Chapter 3, I showed how sex and race articulated in the process of direct domination of subordinate populations, but also in the construction of a moral order. Controlling white women's sexuality was a means for white men to monopolise power and resources, but it was also a moral statement about how virtuous people lived – a statement that had great power among subordinate classes too. The Inquisition's concern with extirpating idolatry and its targeting of indigenous and black populations (alongside crypto-Jews and Muslims) was clearly an expression of power and dominance, but rather than a direct concern with controlling genealogical transmissions of wealth and control, it articulated race and sex together in a moral mission of transformation and regeneration.

The building of new nations on an international stage became the main context in which to understand the intersections of race and sex, as I showed in Chapter 4. The role of honour remained central, but the concept of the nation as a space for properly masculine men to assert their dominance, and for properly feminine women to do their bit for the reproduction of the nation, was also vital. This was not just about a white elite monopolising control for themselves, but about elite men (and women) building a nation in ways they understood to be valuable, ways that included appropriate sexual behaviour as a key domain. I also argued that images of the new nations as liberal democracies could be constructed by reference to racial equality – often the supposed equality of men in their dominant masculinity – while white men could express their racial dominance through their access to non-white women's sexuality, relatively unhindered by law or moral judgement.

This theme was further developed in Chapter 5, by showing how the simultaneous coexistence of racism and elements of racial democracy operated in large part through the articulation of race and sex: images of mixture seemed to indicate the blurring of racial boundaries, the uncertainty of racial classifications and the possibilities of upwards mobility for black and indigenous people; yet the very same processes of mixture forcefully restated racial hierarchies. *Mestizaje* is precisely the ground on which this coexistence works. In Chapter 6, I looked at challenges to *mestizaje* coming from different angles – black and indigenous social movements, official multiculturalism, encounters with US racial hierarchies – and argued that these challenges have unsettled *mestizaje*, but that they also reproduce it in other ways, particularly through a reaffirmation of the link between masculinism and power, and, in the case of the US, through a worrying tendency to reaffirm *mestizaje* as the answer to racial divisions.

Throughout this book, it has also been my argument that race and sex articulate with each other at a psychological level. This is not unique to racialised hierarchies; it emerges from basic gendered and sexualised processes of self formation in relation to others, in which the other (and, indeed, the self) is constructed as an ambivalent figure – hated and desired, loved and feared, resented and admired – usually in gendered ways and with the potential for a powerful sexual charge, due to the fact that affective relations with self and other are formed as part of the emergence of sexuality itself. In racialised social orders, the other can easily be a racial other – especially because racial difference and gender/sex difference harness a realm of imagined embodied difference that is both visible and superficial, and 'natural' and internal. This helps us to understand why racial others often carry such powerful sexual meanings and why anxiety and desire are so closely intertwined. That rather varied sexual meanings attach to blackness and indigenousness and to men and women results from the fact that psychological processes are not divorced from the social world, but rather are deeply socialised dynamics, shaped by history and social relations.

Transforming *Mestizaje*

There is still some way to go in re-signifying and transforming ideologies and practices of *mestizaje* and race-sex articulations in ways that might lead to greater democracy. There can be no doubt that black and indigenous social movements have been, and will continue to be, vital in this respect; but so too are feminist and queer critiques (I use the word queer here to encompass lesbian, gay, bisexual and transgender perspectives). As this book demonstrates, race and sex operate together in processes of oppression and so must be addressed together in projects of transformation. Struggling against racial inequality on its own is not enough, as racial inequality is sustained by gender and sexual dynamics.

Some object that supporting movements that affirm racial, ethnic, gender and sexuality differences and rights is inherently divisive and distracts attention from class inequalities that cross-cut these differences. This is a potentially long and multifaceted debate – one that is preoccupying many Brazilians following the adoption in that country of affirmative action policies favouring Afrodescendants (and also the poorer classes) at a time when the US, which pioneered such policies, has been dismantling them (Fry, Maggie et al. 2007). My view is that these movements can be divisive, but this is a price that has to be paid in the interests of shifting and transforming an articulation of race and sex that is made of sediments built up over several centuries and still being actively reproduced and added to – as in the continued global commodification of black sexuality and indigenous authenticity that can be observed in tourism, for example. Also, there is the possibility, which needs to be developed, that all these diverse movements can and sometimes do address issues of class inequality and social justice more widely. For example, domestic violence or HIV infection cannot be addressed adequately without considering poverty. Above all, it is naive to expect that racial hierarchies will be dismantled through processes of mixture (Latin America as a whole tells us that), or by addressing social inequality in a race-blind way (Cuba tells us that), or through unencumbered capitalist development (the US and some European countries tell us that).

There remains, however, the tricky question of how to formulate projects of social transformation in ways that effectively address the articulation of multiple dimensions of difference. Is it a question of creating specific movements that cater to each and every intersection of differences? Is it a question of insisting that gender-based projects are race-aware and that race-based projects are gender-aware, among other forms of awareness such as sexual orientation, class, age, etc.? Is it possible or even desirable to break the apparent potential for endless multiplication and fragmentation here? As a grass-roots activist, a policy-maker or an academic, how does one decide what kind of project to create and/or support? Any general answer to such a question must necessarily be pitched at a very abstract level and, at that level, my hunch is that we have to operate on a principle of reflexive movement between the two poles of liberal ideology that generate these dilemmas – sameness and difference. We cannot proscribe difference, nor can we prescribe its form. As Young (1990: 5) puts it, 'normative reflection arises from hearing a cry of suffering or distress, or feeling distress oneself'. Such reflections may or may not give rise in unpredictable ways to transformative projects. But I think, in principle, they should be supported if they are demonstrably directed against oppression (which Young defines in terms of exploitation, marginalisation, powerlessness, cultural imperialism and systematic violence), acknowledging that measuring oppression in this way demands normative judgements. However, such support should always be tempered with a view to commonality, commensality, conviviality – in a word, sameness

(Gilroy 2004). What can be shared with other groups? What dialogues can be sustained? What common interests and goals might create coalitions, albeit temporary and partial? The key terms – sameness and difference – are in one sense fundamentally irreconcilable, but this does not mean that they cannot be held in a productive, as opposed to destructive, tension: the process of moving reflexively between them can never end, but one term should always be viewed from the perspective of the other. This, of course, is not a prescription for a particular type of movement or policy; it is a very general stance that can be adopted towards transformative projects in general.

Latin America and its Internal Variety

A final issue I want to address is the way I have deployed the category of Latin America in this book. I have been trying to draw out common threads, all part of the broad weave of *mestizaje*, which is part of the history of Latin American countries. But it is clear that there is a good deal of internal variation in how *mestizaje* has operated and in how racial dynamics work in different countries. Comparative research has tended to focus on placing the US alongside Latin America as a whole or particular countries within it, often Brazil. There were some early attempts to do comparative work within Latin America (e.g. Hoetink 1973) and some scholars drew broad distinctions between Indo-America and Afro-America (e.g. Harris 1974). Some overview treatments also have a comparative aspect to them (Andrews 2004; Graham 1990) and the theme is currently being advanced by some scholars (e.g. Sawyer et al. 2004). But it is still an under-developed area. This is probably linked to problems with 'Latin America' as a category of knowledge production, with its roots in postcolonial area studies programmes driven by US and other metropolitan concerns and linked to a basic logic of geopolitical control (Coronil 1996; Mignolo 2000). Be that as it may, it is clear that *mestizaje* as it operates in Bolivia is different from its workings in Brazil or Colombia. Racial orders have emerged in the region in different ways. In Brazil and Cuba, slavery remained an important institution until the end of the nineteenth century. In Colombia and Venezuela, it was much less important by the time it was abolished mid-century. In Cuba, black people played a major role in independence struggles, which gave them certain claims for inclusion in the new republic (claims that were, however, marginalised), while in Brazil their role was small. In the Andes and most of Central America and Mexico, blackness has had a very different history and *mestizaje* and racial orders revolve around the figures of white, indigenous, *cholo*, *mestizo*, and so on. I believe that there is enough in common in these various racial orders and *mestizajes* to warrant the general treatment I have given in this book. A goal for further research is to develop a systematic comparative view of *mestizaje* in the region.

A Self-Reflexive Coda: Power and Representation

What happens when one writes about race and sex in Latin America from the standpoint of a white, British, middle-class male (my own position)? There are general ethical and political issues at stake here, connected to the production and circulation of knowledge in an unequal world system. In stark terms, these are debates about who has the 'right' to speak about, or on behalf of, whom. Such issues have been explored at length for Latin America, where the size and strength of the Latin American intellectual scene, and the presence of many Latin American and Latino scholars in the metropolitan centres of knowledge production (mainly the US and Europe), has led to powerful postcolonialist challenges to any metropolitan pretension to superiority or dominance in the intellectual field. It has also meant challenges to assumptions, rooted in metropolitan perspectives, about how to organise knowledge in the first place – for example, into categories such as 'Latin American Studies', or more subtly into categories that reflect a division into a knowing, seeing self and a known, observed other (Beverley 1999; Beverley et al. 1995; Coronil 1996; Mignolo 2000; Restrepo and Escobar 2005; Richard 1997; Said 1985).

By definition, I am caught up in these debates as a metropolitan scholar writing about a place called 'Latin America' and reproducing its existence as an object of knowledge practices – the more so insofar as part of my argument is that Latin America has specific characteristics in relation to the way race and sex articulate through *mestizaje*. I have recognised above the tendency to over-generalisation in this argument, but this is something of an afterword. It is difficult for me to avoid the implications of my positioning, rooted as it is in the political economy of the British university system and my life as an academic, but one can adopt certain strategies. First, I have tried to incorporate Latin American scholarship on race and sex in Latin America: I admit that the references cited in this book nevertheless remains biased towards North American and European scholarship (although some of this is written by Latino scholars). Second, I have looked at Latinos in the US, as well as briefly at patterns of sex migration, partly with the intention of deconstructing the idea of 'Latin America' as a stand-alone region and category of knowledge. Third, as a more general strategy, I have tried to publish as much as I can in Spanish and in Latin America, as an important way of building bridges.

A closely related question interrogates the extent to which writing about race and sex from my particular perspective, or one like it, inevitably tends to reproduce a (neo-)colonial objectification of racialised, sexualised objects of knowledge – for example, black and indigenous women. This is linked to the issue – a version of the problem already broached in relation to 'Latin America' – of to what extent anthropologists end up exoticising, or more generally othering, the people they study (Clifford and Marcus 1986; Fabian 1983; Trouillot 1991). In simple terms, given the historical and current realities that I document in this book, isn't it a bit suspect for a white European man to be writing about black and indigenous Latin American women? This is a difficult matter, because the suspicion works by locating me in the same category as the white men whose behaviour I am describing – a move that is arguably essentialist in the underlying assumption that all white European men will think and act in the same way.

It is easy enough to claim that, as an academic, I am different, even 'objective': but why should I be exempt from these postcolonial suspicions? When I was doing fieldwork in Colombia, I had two quite long-term relationships with black women (Wade 1993c) and I found that, sometimes, these romantic attachments were judged locally by others through the lenses of dynamics I describe in this book: I was identified as a white man who could use his status and resources to get access to black (or other subordinate) women in informal (i.e. non-marital) sexual relationships.[1] And my partners were sometimes seen as black women attempting to use their feminine charms to access resources and whiteness. Although my partners and I certainly saw things differently, we found that to some extent we, like the mixed couples that Viveros talked to in Bogotá, were 'obliged to position' ourselves in relation to sexual stereotypes (Viveros Vigoya 2008: 272).

These are uncomfortable suspicions and are raised more easily in relation to the category of a white, European, male author than in the case of, say, a black, Latin American, female author. But, of course, these questions of who speaks about or for whom are pervasive and affect all authorship, not only that of metropolitan males. In the end, I believe these suspicions do not stick very well to this book, for a number of reasons. First, I have been exploring race and sexuality across the spectrum – white, black, indigenous, mixed, heterosexual, homosexual, male and female – rather than focusing only on black and indigenous women. One of the things that underlies the material presented here is that it is impossible to conceptualise race-sex articulations in an unrelational way: black sexuality only means something in relation to white, mixed and indigenous sexualities. Whiteness is at issue in this book as much as blackness or indigenousness. Indeed, I think that *mestizaje* – because it can invoke ideologies and practices of whitening and the privileged position of the whitened body – predisposes us to interrogate whiteness in the ways that whiteness studies have done in other areas (Frankenberg 1993; Kolchin 2002; Nayak 2007). It predisposes us to ask, what is whiteness and how does one acquire it? Second, where possible I have tried to present views of race-sex articulations from the perspective of subordinate actors

– although, especially in the historical period, there are fewer sources for this perspective. Speaking on behalf of 'the subaltern' is, of course, an enterprise replete with difficulties (Beverley 1999; Spivak 1988), as the attempt to do so can end in precisely the representational objectifications that were the problem in the first place. But better some attempt at this, I believe, than none at all. One can never escape one's positioning in a differentiated and unequal world. As Skeggs (2004: 118) says – in a different context – in relation to class positioning: 'To deny the existence of class, or to deny that one is middle-class, is to abdicate responsibility for the relationships in which one is repeatedly reproducing power.' But one can recognise one's positioning and adopt some strategies that work against its grain.

NOTES

1 Introduction: Defining Race and Sex

1. I hesitate to use the word 'races' or 'racial identities' for the parents' origins here, because, at least until the seventeenth century, the Spanish word *raza* – which first appears sporadically in the thirteenth century and becomes slightly more common by the sixteenth century – does not appear frequently in colonial sources, although reference may quite easily be found to what we would now call racial terms, such as *negro* (black), *indio* (indigenous person), *mulato* (the offspring of a black and a white parent), *mestizo*, and so on. Even in the late eighteenth century in Mexico, terms such as *calidad* (quality) were used to refer to these 'racial' origins (McCaa 1984).

2. Much of the work on the interrelation between race and sex is in history and cultural/literary studies, although some of the work is in interdisciplinary areas such as race studies and gender studies (Alexander 2005; Bhabha 1994; Boggs 2000; Fanon 1986 [1952]; Ferguson 2007; Gilman 1985, 1993; Hendricks and Parker 1994; Hodes 1999; JanMohamed 1990; McClintock 1995; Mosse 1985; Parker et al. 1992b; Smith 1998; Somerville 2000; Stoler 1995, 2002; Wiegman 1995; Young 1995; Zack 1997), with some work in philosophy too (Butler 1993; Fuss 1994). The mainstream social sciences have had less impact in this area, but have also contributed important material (Collins 2000; Harden 1997; Lutz and Collins 1997; Manderson and Jolly 1997b; Nagel 2003; Povinelli 1997, 2006; Ragoné and Twine 2000; Smith 1996; Williams 1996). A lot of this work has focused on the US, where the taboos and hysteria surrounding interracial sex, or 'miscegenation' as it became known from 1863, created a special context. On Latin America, Verena Martinez-Alier's pioneering study, *Marriage, Colour and Class in Nineteenth-century Cuba* (Martinez-Alier [Stolcke] 1989 [1974]), set an influential agenda concerned with how racialised status systems were mediated through patriarchal gender relations, later developed by such scholars as Carol Smith (1996) for Guatemala. More recently (but see Roger Bastide's early [1961] foray) scholars have addressed directly the relationship between race and sex: for example, Vera Kutzinski (1993) on the cult of the erotic *mulata* in Cuba, Nadine Fernandez (1996) on racialised desire and racially

252 RACE AND SEX IN LATIN AMERICA

mixed relationships in Cuba, Kamala Kempadoo (1999b, 2004) and Denise Brennan (2004) on sex work and sex tourism in the Caribbean, Jean Rahier (1998, 1999, 2003) on race, beauty pageants and black women in Ecuador, Peter Fry (1982, 2002) on homosexuality, race and beauty in Brazil, Donna Goldstein (1999, 2003), Amelia Simpson (1993) on the sexual and racial aspects of the Brazilian TV presenter Xuxa and – highlighting the fact that the majority of this literature focuses on the 'black–white' matrix of relations – Diane Nelson (1998, 1999) on gender and desire in Guatemalan discourses of *mestizaje*, Mary Weismantel (2001) on the racial and sexual imaginary of the Andean zone of Peru and Fiol-Matta (2002) on racial and sexual discourses in the work of the queer Chilean writer Gabriela Mistral. Within Latin America, too, there is burgeoning interest in this theme (Díaz 2006; Moutinho 2004, 2006; Moutinho et al. 2006; Viveros Vigoya 2002a, 2002b). From an historical angle, a growing literature is emerging, often focused on sexuality (and gender), but with substantial reference to race: for example, Richard Trexler's (1995) pioneering book on (homo)sexuality in indigenous American cultures before and during the conquest, Luiz Mott's (1985) work on homosexuality in colonial Brazil, Pete Sigal's (2003b) collection on colonial homosexuality in Iberian–indigenous power relations, Ramón Gutiérrez's (1991) book on colonial New Mexico, the special issue he edited of the *Journal of the History of Sexuality*, 16(3), 2007, Sueann Caulfield's (1997, 2003) research on Brazil, Laura Briggs (2002) and Eileen Suárez Findlay (1998) on Puerto Rico, James Green (1999, 2006) on homosexuality in Brazil and Peter Beattie's (2001) on the army and masculinity in Brazil. Many other historical works on gender and sexuality mention race or race mixture, without this being a central theme (e.g. Johnson and Lipsett-Rivera 1998a; Rosemblatt 2000; Twinam 1999); an influential collection on sexuality in the region (Balderston and Guy 1997) has only a couple of discussions of race (by James Green and Sueann Caulfield) and Caulfield's (2001) review of historical work on gender mentions race only a handful of times; a more recent collection on gender and sexuality (French and Bliss 2006) has only one chapter that really analyses race and sexuality (by James Green), while others mention it more in passing (e.g. Lara Putnam and Alejandra Bronfman). Many texts addressing the issue of *mestizaje* inevitably touch on the intersection of race and gender – and, by implication, sex – without making sex and race the focus of their analysis (Mörner 1967; Stepan 1991).

3. Thus, for example, in the late 1700s, the German medic Johann Friedrich Blumenbach divided the human species into five races: the

Negroid, or black race; the Caucasian race or white race; the American or red race; the Mongolian or yellow race; and the Malayan or brown race (which included the Oceanic and Australasian peoples). In a similar manner, the US Bureau of the Census uses a racial classification based on five categories: Black or African American; White; American Indian or Alaska Native; Asian; Native Hawaiian or Other Pacific Islander. A version of these categories also appears in recent genetics – for example, in the DNA ancestry tests offered by DNAPrint, which offers to 'determine with confidence to which of the major bio-geographical ancestry groups, Sub-Saharan African, European, East Asian or Native American, a person belongs, as well as the relative percentages in cases of admixed peoples' (www. dnaprint.com/welcome/productsandservices/anestrybydna/, accessed 18 December 2008).

4. So, for example, eighteenth-century Western thinking saw human nature as relatively plastic compared to the scientific view of human nature as rather fixed that dominated for most of the twentieth century, until its last decades, when genomics and biotechnology combined to unsettle more deterministic ideas of nature, which, in any case, had arguably never held full sway in lay circles (Wade 2002).

5. All references to the *OED* are taken from its online edition at http:// dictionary.oed.com/ (accessed January 2008).

6. The term 'queer theory' was coined by Teresa de Lauretis (1991) to describe current attempts to theorise diverse sexualities, especially gay and lesbian, and to analyse and challenge heteronormativity and heterosexism, usually in the West. De Lauretis (1994a) later cautioned that the term had 'quickly become a conceptually vacuous creature of the publishing industry'. It is now often taken to be an approach that challenges many kinds of normative identity categories, although still usually in relation to sexuality and gender (see also Butler 1993; Warner 1999; Weed and Schor 1997).

7. Stanton (1995: 18) states that 'Catherine A. McKinnon privileged sexuality instead of gender, as the "social process which creates, organizes, expresses, and directs desire, creating the social beings we know as women and men".'

8. Nagel (2003: 8), for example, defines sexuality as relating to 'sexual' practices and attitudes, without defining what sexual means. Stanton (1995: 4) says that sexuality is an 'unstable category' and, doubtless as a result, does not define it. Parker et al. (1992a) also use the term without definition. Di Leonardo and Lancaster (1997: 1) define sexuality in relation to 'gendered, sexual bodies'.

9. Sigal (2003a: 9) at first goes in circles, defining sexual desire in terms of their relation to sexual acts. But he admits that 'The line between

what is sexual and what is not sexual is by no means obvious', and ends by defining the sexual in relation to a series of specific acts which he argues are universally assigned sexual meanings, viz. vaginal intercourse, sodomy and possibly also oral sex, sex acts between women and rape. There is still an evident circularity here (which acts between women are sex acts?) that seems impossible to avoid.

2   Explaining the Articulation of Race and Sex

1. Stoler (1995: 124) notes that 'From Montaigne to Mayhew and Balzac ... imperial images of the colonized native American, African, and Asian as eroticized savage or barbarian saturated the discourses of class'. More specifically, various authors (e.g. Clark and Nagel 2000; Godbeer 1999; Nagel 2003: 78–83; Robe 1972: 50–1; Spear 1999) show that native North American men and women were sexualised and others (Boesten 2008; De la Cadena 2000: ch. 4; Lewis 2003: ch. 5; McClintock 1995: 25–6; Nelson 1999: ch. 6; Silverblatt 2004: 161–86; Weismantel 2001) indicate that the same was true for native South American women, although sometimes this is more true of women who are perceived as slightly distanced from indigenousness, who may be labelled *cholas*. There is some evidence on this issue for native South American men, even though indigenous men are often seen as feminised or asexual (Canessa 2008; Nelson 1999: 218).
2. See also hooks (1981) and Wallace (1979).
3. Stuart Hall has developed the concept of articulation (see Grossberg 1986).
4. This view of rape, as being more about power than sex, was made popular especially by Susan Brownmiller (1975) and Angela Davis (1981). Empirical research with rapists has offered some support for this view (Groth 1979).
5. Such constructions of Otherness can be traced across a variety of contexts, from the idea of the Wild Man, which dates back to ancient times, to ideas about the healing magic of Amazonian indigenous peoples (Dudley and Novak 1972; Taussig 1987).
6. The 'postural schema' (or corporeal schema) is a term used in phenomenology (e.g. by Merleau-Ponty) to mean the lived experience of bodily spatiality or the embodied way in which the subject is articulated in the world.
7. Doane notes that Freud argued that 'civilization is born at the expense of sexuality' (1991: 211). That is, civilisation is achieved through the repression of sexuality: 'Civilization behaves toward sexuality as a people or a stratum of its population does which has

subjected another one to its exploitation' (Freud, cited by Gates 1991: 466).

8. Fanon has a third explanation, which is that the white man realises he has treated the black man badly and sees the resulting black aggression as justified; he then unconsciously legitimates this aggression by masochistically turning it on himself, scaring himself with fantasies about black men's sexual prowess or indulging in plays of racialised subordination and dominance: 'There are men who go to "houses" in order to be beaten by Negroes; passive homosexuals who insist on black partners' (Fanon 1986 [1952]: 177).

9. Various scholars critique Fanon's gender and sexual politics (Campbell 2000: ch. 7; Doane 1991: 209–48; Fuss 1994; Hall 1996; Young 1996); while Bhabha (1986) tries to add ambivalence to Fanon's account.

10. Moore (1994: 42–8) argues that, in grasping processes of self formation, Lacanian approaches provide a more cross-culturally open framework than some other psychoanalytic approaches derived from Freud, Melanie Klein and object-relations theory.

11. On Lacanian ideas of desire, see Butler (1987: ch. 4), Van Zyl (1998), Campbell (2000: chs 3 and 4) and Moore (2007: 50–5). See also De Lauretis (1994a, 1994b). On the Lacanian distinction between 'other' and 'Other', see Fuss (1994: 21).

12. Benjamin (1998: 79) states: 'The ego is not really independent and self-constituting, but is actually made up of the objects it assimilates; the ego cannot leave the other to be an independent outside entity, separate from itself, because it is always incorporating the other, or demanding that the other be like the self ... the self is constituted by the identifications with the other that it deploys in an on-going way, in particular to deny the loss and uncontrollability that otherness necessarily brings ... [and] it is reciprocally constituted in relation to the other, depending on the other's recognition, which it cannot have without being negated, acted on by the other.' See also Benjamin (1988).

13. Key figures in this literature are Hélène Cixous, Luce Irigaray, Julia Kristeva, Juliet Mitchell, Jessica Benjamin, Judith Butler, Teresa de Lauretis, Eve Sedgwick, Elizabeth Grosz and Nancy Chodorow (see e.g. Benjamin 1998; Butler 1990, 1993; Chodorow 1978; De Lauretis 1994b; Grosz 1994; Lacan et al. 1982; Mitchell 1974). For overviews, see Campbell (2000), Dean and Lane (2001) and Minsky (1996).

14. As Moore (2007: 124) says: 'The earliest representations of significant others are caught up with forms of gender difference that have no realisable expression outside their relations with other forms of

difference, such as race, class and ethnicity.' Seshadri-Crooks (2000: 6–7) has a different Lacanian argument in which sexual difference is built on lack and the failure of Oneness, while race – which is not analogous to sexual difference, but must be read in relation to it – is the opposite: 'The signifier Whiteness tries to fill the constitutive lack of the sexed subject. It promises a totality, an overcoming of difference itself.'

15. Compare Toni Morrison, who has a similar thesis about how the African American population of the US acted as a set of 'surrogate selves' which could be used, at least in the writerly imagination, 'for meditation on problems of human freedom, its lure and elusiveness' and 'for meditations on terror – the terror of European outcasts, their dread of failure, powerlessness, Nature without limits ... evil, sin greed' (1993: 37–8).

16. Van Zyl (1998) has a simpler explanation, based on Freud and presented in a critique of Bhabha, whom she chastises for generalising Freud's very specific ideas about sexual fetishism (which were about the obsession of a specific individual with a specific item, generated by the way the Oedipal dynamics of family relationships worked themselves out in a given case) to the much broader case of the colonial stereotype. I think Bhabha's overall point, that there is a parallel between the way sexual and racial othering function, can still stand and is in fact complemented by Van Zyl. She argues that, in Freudian theories of the Oedipus complex, a male child is taught that he must identify with the male and desire the female, while the female child is taught the opposite. Very simply, the desirable is socially defined as the gendered other – a category defined centrally by appearance. Difference is thus desirable, but also threatening, because it menaces identification, which must occur with a category defined as the same. By extension: 'The colonial preoccupation with bodily difference and the complex play of desiring and phobic relations manifest in colonial writing can both ... be explained in terms of an account of Freud's Oedipus' (1998: 97). This is substantially the same argument as Bhabha, albeit phrased in a rather different way: processes of sexual self formation parallel processes of colonial othering.

3   Race and Sex in Colonial Latin America

1. Goody has been criticised for the overly broad concept of Eurasian societies and for positing mechanical connections between technology, inheritance and kinship, but his outline of the basic complex of interrelated elements is helpful for sketching the Iberian case.

2. The terms 'sexual' and 'sexuality' did not exist at the time and 'sex' was used in the context of making categorical distinctions between men and women. Judging from Spanish colonial usage, a range of terms was used to refer to sexual acts, statuses and feelings, such as *honor* (honour, as in 'he took my honour'), *virtud* (virtue), *verguenza* (shame and, by extension, 'shameful' sexual acts; *las verguenzas,* or *as vergonhas* in Portuguese, meant the female genitalia), *vida conyugal* (married [sex] life), *concubinato* (concubinage), *estupro* (rape, or sexual access to a virgin achieved through deception), *lujuria* (lust), *fuego libidinoso* (libidinous fire), *acto carnal* (carnal act), *sodomia* (anal sex, also called the *pecado nefando*, the nefarious sin; the term was also used to describe sex between two women). See, for example, Lavrin (1989a).

3. Mott notes that the belief that Italy was the capital of sodomy 'permeated the Iberian imaginary' (2003: 173).

4. Napolitano (2004) and Bellini (1989) discuss how the Portuguese Inquisition in Pernambuco, Brazil, dealt with cases of female 'sodomy' from 1591 until 1640, when the act was deemed no longer to come within Inquisitorial jurisdiction. It then remained more or less officially invisible until the nineteenth century in Brazil (Napolitano 2008 [2004]). Napolitano and Bellini both argue that there was doubt about whether women could really commit sodomy (and above all 'perfect sodomy', which involved ejaculating semen into the anal cavity and thus wasting it for reproductive purposes) and that sexual acts between women were often seen as adolescent experimentation which, above all, did not threaten a virgin's honour: for these reasons, it was not deemed a matter of great concern. See also Tortorici (2007) and Vainfas (1989: 274–84).

5. Trexler has been criticised for over-generalising about native American homosexual practices on the basis of spotty evidence, which is sometimes taken out of context, and for oversimplifying the relationship between power and sex, reducing all homosexual practices to ones of domination: 'Trexler seems more bent on establishing the "inherent" connection between intercourse and rape than on examining the evidence' (Nesvig 2001: 699). Yet the idea of extending gender hierarchy to understanding male–male relations and of linking sex to power is undeniably a powerful one.

6. Berdache is a European term, in use from the sixteenth century, derived from the Arabic term for a boy prostitute. It has been used generically to refer to many different native American practices in which a person of one anatomical sex (usually, but not always male) assumes the gender roles of the opposite sex. Many native Americans reject the word as pejorative, preferring the term 'two-spirit people'.

Some argue that berdaches are actually an intermediate third sex/
gender (Herdt 1994). For a discussion, see the essays collected in
Sigal (2003c).

7. Some African feminists have argued that African societies had a
matriarchal structure (Amadiume 1997).

8. Block (1999) has an interesting comparison between sexual abuse
of black and white servants in nineteenth-century North America,
which indicates the lack of recourse to legal protection for black
female slaves.

9. Bellini (1989: 22–9) shows that the 30 or so women accused of
sodomy in north-east Brazil in the late sixteenth century were a
mixture of white and mixed-race, with three black slaves mentioned.
There was no obvious pattern of racial-sexual dominance and she
speculates that relationships between mistresses and female slaves
could have been a means for the latter to gain some recognition and
even power.

10. Horswell challenges Trexler's characterisation of berdaches as
'sexual subordinates subjugated by a gender politics' (Horswell
2003: 58).

11. Sigal, however, has a more nuanced view than Trexler of the
articulation of gender, power and sexuality.

12. See the review by Rodríguez (1994).

13. Roughly, present-day Argentina and Uruguay.

14. For a Spanish-language version of Schmidel's *Viage al Río de La
Plata y Paraguay* see www.gutenberg.org/etext/20401 (accessed 18
December 2008).

15. Data from North American also suggest a variety of relationships:
Spear (1999) reports on late seventeenth-century Louisiana where
French and Canadian men commonly lived in concubinage with
indigenous women, sometimes in settings where the women were
servants or even slaves, but often in isolated backwoods settings
and even in indigenous villages. Godbeer (1999) describes relations
between English men and indigenous women in the Carolinas
frontier zone between 1600 and 1780s, which included casual
sex, rape, 'Indian marriage', stable relationships and, occasionally,
Christian marriage.

16. A term used locally to refer to a mixed-race person born to an
indigenous woman, usually of slave status (indigenous people
continued to be enslaved in this region during the colonial period).

17. For colonial Mexico City, Cope (1994: 106–24) documents cases
of non-whites becoming successful.

18. Anyone wishing to marry had to submit to an investigation to
establish that no impediments existed to the marriage.

19. There are many sources on colonial resistance. For a general treatment, see Lockhart and Schwartz (1983). On revolts and uprisings, see Reis (1993), Stern (1987), Cope (1994: 125–60). On slave flight and rebel communities, see Price (1979). On Andean nativism, see Silverblatt (1994). On African-based religious groups and practices, see Harding (2000), Friedemann and Arocha (1986).
20. See notes 4 and 9, above.
21. For colonial Mexico, Tortorici analyses a case that shows 'the conflicts between the sexual, the mystical, and the spiritual but also how often these spheres worked together and reinforced one another' (2007: 368–9). For a different context – Anglo-Saxon England – Lees argues against 'the assumption that medieval religious desire is necessarily distinct from an erotics of pleasure and/or pain' (1997: 17). Achinstein, also for an English context, notes that 'Spiritual longing and sexual longing often intersect in discourses of devotion' (2002: 415).
22. Secular clergy are distinct from regular clergy who belong to a specific religious order, such as the Franciscans.

4   Making Nations through Race and Sex

1. Most areas of Spanish America gained independence between the 1810s and the 1830s. Cuba became independent in 1898 and Puerto Rico in 1897 (although it came under US control from 1898). Brazil became independent of Portugal in 1822, but declared itself an empire and remained a monarchy until 1889.
2. For details, see Wade (2002), Stocking (1982), Stepan (1982) and Anderson (2006).
3. See Wade (1993a), Wright (1990), Knight (1990), Lomnitz-Adler (1992), Kutzinski (1993), De la Fuente (2001), Skidmore (1974). See also Gould (1998) on Nicaragua, De la Cadena (2000) on Peru and Sanjinés (2004) on Bolivia. For general discussions, see Miller (2004), Martínez-Echazábal (1998), Rahier (2003), Klor de Alva (1995).
4. As much of my discussion refers to the context of the nation and processes of nation-building, it is relevant to note that Puerto Rico was only a nation-*state* very briefly (1897–98). However, it has many of the characteristics of a nation in terms of building an identity.
5. Kuznesof (1991) also argues for nineteenth-century Brazil that, although illegitimacy rates were very high, especially among the non-white population, legal marriage was still a valued form.
6. Cf. Gill (1994: 24), who documents how Bolivian *cholas*, who distanced themselves from rural Aymara women, yet did not conform

to the etiquette of the white *señoras*, defended their honour with frequent complaints about alleged slander.

7. In Chihuahua, in the context of frontier wars against the Apache, plebeian *mestizo* colonists were awarded land in exchange for their military efforts. They also gained a sense of egalitarian brotherhood with the local elite, based on ethnic identity as non-indigenous and on masculine honour and the defence of 'their' women, despite the persistence of social hierarchies among men (Alonso 1995).

8. In addition to the works by Caulfield and Findlay cited in the main text, see Guy (1991; 2000), Putnam (2002), Bliss (2001), French (1992), Briggs (2002), Drinot (2006).

9. See also Howes (2001), who argues that *Bom Crioulo* is rather ambiguous in its treatment of homosexuality.

10. Cf. Gill's analysis of how the Bolivian army constructs a sense of national masculinity for indigenous and *mestizo* men (Gill 1997).

11. Salessi (1995) traces the medicalisation of homosexuality in Argentina for this period; see also Green (1999: ch. 3).

12. Green (2006: 189) argues, however, that Brazilian medics resisted the complete imposition of European definitions of homosexuality and continued to give some importance to the distinction between active and passive homosexuality, a distinction that is still significant today (Kulick 1998).

13. Although Bejel pays little attention to race in his study of homosexuality and a Cuban national identity built on homophobia and masculinity, he comments that imperialist American views of Cubans effeminised them and that 'Americanisation' also implied 'whitening and virilising the island's population' (2001: 12). Like Irwin, he contends that disavowed homoeroticism is a ghostly presence in Cuban nationalism.

14. Cf. Stoler (2002: ch. 7) who finds that few Javanese servants recalled sexual predation by their employers (at least in the context of an interview).

15. For general overviews, see Manuel (1988: ch. 2) and Manuel et al. (1995). On *danza*, see Quintero Rivera (1996); on *danzón* and *son*, see Moore (1997); on tango, see Collier et al. (1995), Savigliano (1995); on *maxixe* and samba, see Vianna (1999); on *cumbia* and *porro*, see Wade (2000); on *merengue*, see Austerlitz (1995); on Afro-Pervian music, see Feldman (2006). On black cultural forms more generally, but in a similar dynamic, see Fox (2006).

16. See Mendoza (2000), Romero (2001), Turino (1993). It is notable that Manuel's survey of popular music of the non-Western world does not include a single Andean country in its chapter on Latin America and the Caribbean (Manuel 1988). See Clark and Nagel (2000)

for North American appropriations of images of native American manhood and sexual virility, although not through popular music.

17. Actually, Taylor argues that the young men took the dance first to Paris, where 'the dance of the Argentine brothels became the immediate rage of the continent – and subsequently, with the European stamp of approval to assuage American inferiority complexes, became acceptable in the land of its birth' (1976: 283).

18. José Gers, in the Colombian weekly magazine *Sábado*, 3 June 1944, p. 13. See Wade (2000: 128).

19. See Jackson (1979, 1988), Lewis (1983, 1987), Prescott (2000), Arnedo-Gomez (2006), Kutzinski (1993), Ortiz (2007).

20. Moore traces this for Cuba in the 1920s–1940s (1997: 143); I describe it for Colombia in the 1940s (2000: 118).

5 The Political Economy of Race and Sex in Contemporary Latin America

1. For an overview of these debates, see Wade (1997), Andrews (2004). See also Hale (2006), De la Cadena (2000), Wade (1993a), Sheriff (2001), Telles (2004), De la Fuente (2001).

2. De la Cadena (2000: 147, 202) shows that, for a time in the Peruvian Andes, there was a local intellectual current that did glorify the tough masculine *cholo*, but this seems to have been limited to a particular time and place.

3. In an earlier seminar presentation of this work (Manchester, 9–10 December 2006; see www.socialsciences.manchester.ac.uk/disciplines/socialanthropology/research/race/, accessed 18 December 2008), Boesten noted that indigenous women's testimonies about men who raped them (whether soldiers or Shining Path members) often tended to identify them as 'foreign' and as 'tall, blond and green-eyed' (even if the man also spoke Quechua). In effect, these men were being identified as *pishtacos*.

4. In fact, it is not always clear from Goldstein's examples that women actually had a sexual relationship at all with their *coroas* – e.g. the relationship between Glória and her *coroa*, for whom she was a domestic servant (Goldstein 2003: 127).

5. See also Congolino (2008: 330), who shows that black men may accept the image of themselves as sexual 'machines'; and Pinho (2005) on the Brazilian figure of the *brau*, a young black male who capitalises on the hypersexualised image of the black man as part of the re-Africanisation of Salvador in north-east Brazil.

6. By 2000, overall endogamy rates in the US had fallen to 93 per cent (Rosenfeld and Kim 2005).

7. See www.statistics.gov.uk/cci/nugget.asp?id=1090 (accessed 18 December 2008). Ethnic background in these data is defined as White, Mixed, Asian, Black, Chinese or Other.
8. Although see Fiol-Matta (2002), discussed in Chapter 4, and also Ellis (2002).
9. This is in contrast to the US, where there is a large literature on black lesbians (Boggs 2000). See also the bibliography listed at www.library.ucsb.edu/subjects/blackfeminism/ah_lesbian.html (accessed 18 December 2008).
10. See also Ellis's book on homoeroticism in Latin American autobiography (Ellis 2002).
11. Heilborn and Cabral (2008: 189) also found that Brazilian survey respondents who self-identified as black held less tolerant attitudes to homosexuality compared to others, although this was partly explained by less education, which were strongly associated with such intolerance and more common among blacks. See also Congolino (2008: 331).
12. A black woman, Vanessa Alexandra Mendoza, also won the title of Miss Colombia in 2001.
13. See Giacomini (2006), who analysed the 'professional *mulata*' programmes administered by the Brazilian Serviço Nacional de Aprendizagem Comercial (National Service for Training in Commerce) to train women to act as the typical *mulata* in shows. She found that the women oscillated between a positive representation of the *mulata* as professional dancer and an image of her as prostitute. See also Arrizón (2006: 117), who contends that 'the body of the mulata becomes an assertion that can be imagined beyond her erotic camouflage and within the liberatory discourses of women of color that emerged in the early 1980s'.
14. A good deal of the international sex trade nowadays also involves women from Eastern Europe and Russia.
15. The term was coined by US soldiers stationed in Southeast Asia (O'Connell Davidson and Sanchez Taylor 1999: 45): its military origins attest to the power relations that inhere in sex tourism.
16. Sanchís (2005) states that 'An estimated 50,000 women from the Dominican Republic and 75,000 women from Brazil are currently working in the sex industry abroad, mainly in Europe. However, the proportion of those prostitutes that are victims of trafficking is unclear ... Interpol ... calculates that each year 35,000 women are "exported" for sex work from Colombia.' It is also unclear exactly what 'trafficking' means and whether the emphasis on 'coercion' hides migrant women's agency and motives (Agustín 2007).

17. The origins of these women have been reported by an online sociologist, using 2003 census data (http://wonkapistas.blogspot.com/2005/06/ms-sobre-matrimonios-mixtos-en-espaa.html, accessed 15 July 2008). Relative to their numbers in the country, the women who most often marry Spanish men are, in rank order: Russians, Brazilians, Mexicans, Colombians, Czechs, Cubans and Nigerians. However, marriages with foreign women are outnumbered by those between Spanish women and foreign men, mainly Latin Americans (http://weblogs.madrimasd.org/migraciones/archive/2007/02/01/58489.aspx, accessed 15 July 2008). For Italy, where 'mixed marriages' are also on the rise, Rosina (2007) notes that many of the foreign spouses come from Eastern Europe for Italian men, but North Africa for Italian women. Rosina also observes that Brazilian and Cuban (but also Russian) wives are over-represented compared to their numerical presence in the country, which she links partly to tourism to these countries in search of a 'soul mate'. In contrast, 'There is a very significant number of women living in Italy of Peruvian or Ecuadorian origin, but this has led to few mixed marriages with Italian men.'

18. On nostalgia and modernity, see Robertson (1990).

19. Using statistical data from a large sample of Brazilians between 18 and 24 years old, Heilborn and Cabral (2008) show that those identifying as *negros* and *pardos* differed only slightly from each other or from *brancos* in terms of sexual precocity, number of sexual partners and variety of sexual practices. Black women tended to declare fewer partners, while blacks in general tended to be slightly more restrictive about admitting to variety of sexual practice, suggesting an attempt to distance themselves from sexual stereotypes about blackness.

6   Race, Sex and the Politics of Identity and Citizenship

1. Afrodescendant is the English version of the Portuguese *afrodescendente*, a term coined in 1996 by Sueli Carneiro, a black Brazilian feminist (Arocha 1998: 354), which gained currency with the 2001 Durban conference on racism and which is increasingly used in the black movement and by international NGOs and multilateral agencies, such as the World Bank and the United Nations.

2. Streicker (1995) notes how, in Cartagena, Colombia, sexual behaviour perceived as improper is coded as 'black' and lower class.

3. There is a long history of the racialisation of certain diseases, such as sickle-cell anaemia (Duster 2003; Tapper 1999; Wailoo 2003).

Laguardia (2006) argues that this trend continues in Brazil in relation to sickle-cell anaemia.

4. There are some parallels here with Povinelli (1997), who argues that, in order to be recognised as legitimate claimants of land rights, Australian Aborigines are forced to conform to heterosexist definitions of descent and genealogical connection that figure the community as a (hetero)sexually-bounded unit.

5. For a discussion of multiculturalism in general, see Modood (2007: ch. 5) and Taylor (1992). See also Povinelli (2002) for a critique of liberal multiculturalism in relation to Australia, but with broader applicability.

6. I am simplifying slightly as the category of Rom is also available for selection and there are a number of distinct categories which are subsumed under Afrodescendant (Wade 2009 (in press)). See also www.dane.gov.co/files/censo2005/cuestionario.pdf (accessed 18 December 2008).

7. Memoria del Tercer Encuentro de la Red de Mujeres Afrolatino-americanas, Afrocaribeñas y de la Diáspora, Managua, 14–17 July 2006, p. 7 (www.mujeresafro.org/files/publicacion/1176924104_Memoria%20III.pdf, accessed 13 August 2008).

8. Many surveys also suggest that homophobia is more pronounced among African Americans than whites, although again the situation is complicated by the fact that, paradoxically, support for gay civil rights is higher among African Americans than among whites, possibly due to African American support for civil rights in general (Negy and Eisenman 2005).

9. Murray collects anthropological data on homosexuality for indigenous societies in Amazonia (Murray 1995a) and along the western coast of South America (Murray 1995b). Chiñas (1995) comments on Isthmus Zapotecs in Oaxaca, Mexico, as does Stephen (2002). Williams (1986: 144–7), although focusing mostly on North America, also comments on Mayans in the Mexican Yucatan peninsular. See also Reding (2000: 17–23) for an overview of indigenous Mexico.

10. The citation from Katz goes on to say that this image is one held by 'gay white people' (1976: 502).

11. Campbell (1995: 238) also says he found 'considerable disdain among many "straight" Zapotec men towards *muxe*'.

12. The anthropologist Joanne Rappaport (personal communication) says that the matter is not discussed in CRIC (Consejo Regional Indígena del Cauca) or much in the Nasa communities she knows, although homosexual relationships may occur there and are tolerated. Pablo Jaramillo, a doctoral student, Manchester University (personal

communication), reports that, among the Wayuu (Guajiro), he observed cases of recognised female and male homosexual couples. One leader proposed a project on homosexuality, but this was not well received by other leaders, who considered homosexuality to be a private, family affair, not a political one. Sarah Radcliffe (personal communication) recounted an incident at a 2001 conference at Princeton University on indigenous movements, development and democracy in Latin America, when a Bolivian indigenous man said that the indigenous movement had never dealt with homosexuality. His comment met with 'an awkward silence'. Fernando Urrea (personal communication) reports that Nasa and Kamsá women leaders in south-west Colombia tended to see homosexuality as a Western trait, but also seemed tolerant of it in general.

13. The term Latino/a is not a clearly defined one but is usually taken to include Latin Americans residing in the US and their descendants to the extent that these people retain some kind of link to parental Latino 'culture' (e.g. through language) and/or self-identify as Latino or Hispanic (e.g. in the US census). The term thus includes the category of Chicano/a, which usually refers to children of Mexican migrants. For general treatments of Latinos, see Flores and Rosaldo (2007), Darder and Torres (1998). Stanford University has a useful website of resources on Chicano/Latino studies: www-sul.stanford. edu/depts/ssrg/adams/shortcu/chic.html (accessed 18 December 2008).

14. See, for example, the variety of topics covered – and the influence of queer studies – in the conference on Race, Sex, Power: New Movements in Black and Latina/o Sexualities held at the University of Illinois at Chicago, 11–12 April 2008 (see http://condor.depaul. edu/~rsp2008/, accessed 18 December 2008). See also Arrizón (2006) and Pérez-Torres (2006).

15. See, for example, 'A Look at Latinos', a publication of the National Campaign to Prevent Teen and Unplanned Pregnancy, which labels Latinos as the main problem in combating teen pregnancies (itself seen unequivocally as undesirable) and says that '53% of Latina teens get pregnant at least once before age 20 – nearly twice the national average' (www.thenationalcampaign.org/espanol/PDF/ latino_overview.pdf, accessed 18 December 2008).

16. Madrid (2003: 37) contends that the *pachuco* has been portrayed in various ways but that he escapes 'emasculating classifications'.

17. See, for example, 'Working with Latino Parents/Families' (www. cyfernet.org/parent/latinofam.html, accessed 18 December 2008); 'A Guide to Better Understanding of Latino Family Culture' (www. ianrpubs.unl.edu/epublic/pages/publicationD.jsp?publicationId=53,

accessed 18 December 2008); 'Fact Sheet On Latino Youth: Families' (http://bixbycenter.ucsf.edu/publications/files/Latino.fam. pdf, accessed 18 December 2008); 'Understanding Latino Families, Implications for Family Education' (http://extension.usu.edu/files/ publications/publication/FR_Family_2005-02.pdf, accessed 18 December 2008).

18. The film *Real Women Have Curves* (directed by Patricia Cardoso, 2002) was based on the play of the same name by Mexican American playwright Josefina Lopez.

19. The growth of the mixed-race or multiracial movement – people of mixed ancestry who want to be recognised as distinct in terms of official reckoning of race – has also played an important role (Root 1992, 1996; Spickard 2001). Williams (2005: 56) notes that much of the drive for state recognition of mixed-race identities was from parents – typically black men with white women – rather than mixed-race individuals.

20. A very European-looking Colombian professor in a US university told me how, to his amazement, he discovered from his department's secretary that, for the purposes of the university's ethnic head-counting procedures, he was classified as 'a person of colour' because of his Latin American origins.

7 Conclusion

1. These relationships have also been judged by other Western academics as 'unethical'. Goode (2002: 532) interprets my actions as purely instrumental research tactics, which was not the case.

REFERENCES CITED

Achinstein, Sharon (2002) Romance of the spirit: female sexuality and religious desire in early modern England, *English Literary History (ELH)* 69(2): 413–38.

Agustín, Laura María (2007) *Sex at the margins: migration, labour markets and the rescue industry* (London: Zed Books).

Alexander, M. Jacqui (2005) *Pedagogies of crossing: meditations on feminism, sexual politics, memory, and the sacred* (Durham, NC: Duke University Press).

Allen, Jafari Sinclaire (2007) Means of desire's production: male sex labor in Cuba, *Identities* 14(1): 183–202.

Almaguer, Tomás (2007) Looking for papi: longing and desire among Chicano gay men. In *A companion to Latina/o Studies*, Juan Flores and Renato Rosaldo (eds), pp. 138–50 (Oxford: Blackwell).

Alonso, Ana María (1994) The politics of space, time and substance: state formation, nationalism, and ethnicity, *Annual Review of Anthropology* 23: 379–405.

—— (1995) *Thread of blood: colonialism, revolution, and gender on Mexico's northern frontier* (Tucson, AZ: University of Arizona Press).

Alonso, Ana Maria and Teresa Koreck (1999) Silences: 'Hispanics,' AIDS, and sexual practices. In *Culture, society and sexuality: a reader*, Richard Parker and Peter Aggleton (eds), pp. 267–83 (New York: Routledge).

Alvarado, Juan A. (1998) Estereotipos y prejuicios raciales en tres barrios habaneros, *América Negra* 15: 89–115.

Amadiume, Ifi (1987) *Male daughters, female husbands: gender and sex in an African society* (London: Zed Books).

—— (1997) *Re-inventing Africa: matriarchy, religion and culture* (London: Zed Books).

Amos, Valerie and Pratibha Parmar (1984) Challenging imperial feminism, *Feminist Review* 17: 3–19.

Anderson, Kay (2006) *Race and the crisis of humanism* (London: Routledge).

Andrews, George Reid (2004) *Afro-Latin America, 1800–2000* (Oxford: Oxford University Press).

Anzaldúa, Gloria (1987) *Borderlands/la frontera: the new mestiza* (San Francisco: Aunt Lute Books).

Aparicio, Frances R. and Susana Chávez-Silverman (1997) Introduction. In *Tropicalizations: transcultural representations of latinidad*, Frances R. Aparicio and Susana Chávez-Silverman (eds), pp. 1–17 (Hanover, NH: University of New England Press).

Appelbaum, Nancy P., Anne S. Macpherson and Karin A. Rosemblatt (eds) (2003) *Race and nation in modern Latin America* (Chapel Hill, NC: University of North Carolina Press).

Arnedo-Gomez, Miguel (2006) *Writing rumba: the Afrocubanista movement in poetry* (Charlottesville, VA: University of Virginia Press).

Arocha, Jaime (1998) La inclusión de la afrocolombianos: meta inalcanzable? In *Los afrocolombianos*, Adriana Maya (ed.), pp. 339–98. La geografía humana de Colombia, Vol. 6 (Bogotá: Instituto Colombiano de Cultura Hispánica).

Arrizón, Alicia (2006) *Queering mestizaje: transculturation and performance* (Ann Arbor, MI: University of Michigan Press).

Asencio, Marysol (2002) *Sex and sexuality among New York's Puerto Rican youth* (Boulder, CO: Lynne Rienner).

Assies, Willem, Gemma van der Haar and André Hoekema (eds) (2000) *The challenge of diversity: indigenous peoples and reform of the state in Latin America* (Amsterdam: Thela-Thesis).

Austerlitz, Paul (1995) *Merengue: Dominican music and Dominican identity* (Philadelphia: Temple University Press).

Bairros, Luiza (2000) Nuestros feminismos revistados, *Política y Cultura* 14: 141–49.

Balderston, Daniel and Donna J. Guy (eds) (1997) *Sex and sexuality in Latin America* (New York: New York University Press).

Balibar, Etienne (1991) Racism and nationalism. In *Race, nation and class: ambiguous identities*, Etienne Balibar and Immanuel Wallerstein (eds), pp. 37–67 (London: Verso).

Banton, Michael (1987) *Racial theories* (Cambridge: Cambridge University Press).

Bastide, Roger (1961) Dusky Venus, black Apollo, *Race* 3: 10–19.

Baumeister, Andrea (2000) *Liberalism and the 'politics of difference'* (Edinburgh: Edinburgh University Press).

Beattie, Peter (1997) Conflicting penile codes: modern masculinity and sodomy in the Brazilian military, 1860–1916. In *Sex and sexuality in Latin America*, Daniel Balderston and Donna J. Guy (eds), pp. 65–85 (Albuquerque, NM: University of New Mexico Press).

—— (2001) *Tribute of blood: army, honor, race and nation in Brazil, 1864–1945* (Durham, NC: Duke University Press).

—— (2003) Measures of manhood: honor, enlisted army service, and slavery's decline in Brazil, 1850–90. In *Changing men and masculinities in Latin America*, Matthew C. Gutmann (ed.), pp. 233–55 (Durham, NC: Duke University Press).

Bederman, Gail (1995) *Manliness and civilization: a cultural history of gender and race in the United States, 1880–1917* (Chicago, IL: University of Chicago Press).

Behar, Ruth (1989) Sexual witchcraft, colonialism and womens' powers: views from the Mexican Inquisition. In *Sexuality and marriage in colonial Latin America*, Asunción Lavrin (ed.), pp. 178–206 (Lincoln, NB: University of Nebraska Press).

Bejel, Emilio (2001) *Gay Cuban nation* (Chicago, IL: University of Chicago Press).

Bellini, Ligia (1989) *A coisa obscura: mulher, sodomia e inquisicão no Brasil colonial* (Sa o Paulo: Editora Brasiliense).

Benjamin, Jessica (1984) Master and slave: the fantasy of erotic domination. In *Desire: the politics of sexuality*, Ann Snitow, Christine Stansell and Sharon Thompson (eds), pp. 292–311 (London: Virago).

—— (1988) *The bonds of love: psychoanalysis, feminism, and the problem of domination* (New York: Pantheon).

—— (1998) *Shadow of the other: intersubjectivity and gender in psychoanalysis* (New York: Routledge).

Bertold, Andreas (1998) Oedipus in (South) Africa?: psychoanalysis and the politics of difference, *American Imago* 55(1): 101–34.

Beverley, John (1999) *Subalternity and representation: arguments in cultural theory* (Durham, NC: Duke University Press).

Beverley, John, José Oviedo and Michael Aronna (eds) (1995) *The Postmodernism Debate in Latin America* (Durham, NC: Duke University Press).

Bhabha, Homi (1986) Foreword: Remembering Fanon. In *Black skin, white masks*, pp. vii–xxvi (London: Pluto Press).

—— (1994) *The location of culture* (London: Routledge).

Bhana, Deevia, Robert Morrell, Jeff Hearn and Relebohile Moletsane (2007) Power and identity: an introduction to sexualities in Southern Africa, *Sexualities* 10(2): 131–9.

Bliss, Katherine Elaine (2001) *Compromised positions: prostitution, public health, and gender politics in Revolutionary Mexico City* (University Park, PN: Pennsylvania State University Press).

Block, Sharon (1999) Lines of color, sex and service: comparative sexual coercion in early America. In *Sex, love, and race: crossing boundaries in North American history*, Martha Hodes (ed.), pp. 141–63 (New York: New York University Press).

Boesten, Jelke (2008) Narrativas de sexo, violencia y disponibilidad: raza, género y jerarquías de la violación en Perú. In *Raza, etnicidad y sexualidades: ciudadanía y multiculturalismo en América Latina*,

Peter Wade, Fernando Urrea Giraldo and Mara Viveros Vigoya (eds), pp. 199–220 (Bogotá: Instituto CES, Facultad de Ciencias Humanas, Universidad Nacional de Colombia).

Boggs, Nicholas (2000) Queer black studies: an annotated bibliography, 1994–1999, *Callaloo* 23(1): 479–94.

Borja Gómez, Jaime Humberto (1996) El control sobre la sexualidad: negros e indios (1550–1650). In *Inquisición, muerte y sexualidad en el Nuevo Reino de Granada*, Jaime Humberto Borja Gómez (ed.), pp. 171–98 (Bogotá: Editorial Ariel).

—— (2001) Tendencias y herencias de la sexualidad: de la Cristiandad medieval a la colonial. Paper presented at Otros cuerpos, otras sexualidades. Ciclo Rosa Von Praunheim, 27 June 2001, Bogota. Available at www.sexologia.com/articulos/religion/tendenciasyherencias.htm, accessed 31 March 2008.

Boyer, Richard (1998) Honor among plebeians: *mala sangre* and social reputation. In *The faces of honor: sex, shame, and violence in colonial Latin America*, Lyman L. Johnson and Sonya Lipsett-Rivera (eds), pp. 152–78 (Albuquerque, NM: University of New Mexico Press).

Brennan, Denise (2004) *What's love got to do with it? Transnational desires and sex tourism in the Dominican Republic* (Durham, NC: Duke University Press).

Briggs, Laura (2002) *Reproducing empire: race, sex, science, and U.S. imperialism in Puerto Rico* (Berkeley, CA: University of California Press).

Brownmiller, Susan (1975) *Against our will: men, women, and rape* (London: Secker & Warburg).

Bush, Barbara (2000) 'Sable venus', 'she devil', or 'drudge'? British slavery and the 'fabulous fiction' of black women's identities, c. 1650–1838, *Women's History Review* 9(4): 761–89.

Butler, Judith (1987) *Subjects of desire: Hegelian reflections in twentieth-century France* (New York: Columbia University Press).

Butler, Judith P. (1990) *Gender trouble: feminism and the subversion of identity* (London: Routledge).

—— (1993) *Bodies that matter: on the discursive limits of 'sex'* (London: Routledge).

Campbell, Howard (1995) *Zapotec renaissance: ethnic politics and cultural revivalism in Southern Mexico* (Albuquerque, NM: University of New Mexico Press).

Campbell, Jan (2000) *Arguing with the phallus: feminist, queer and postcolonial theory: a psychoanalytic contribution* (London: Zed Books).

Candelario, Ginetta E. B. (2007) *Black behind the ears: Dominican racial identity from museums to beauty shops* (Durham, NC: Duke University Press).

Canessa, Andrew (2008) Sex and the citizen: Barbies and beauty queens in the age of Evo Morales, *Journal of Latin American Cultural Studies* 17(1): 41–64.

Casaus Arzú, Marta (1992) *Guatemala: linaje y racismo* (San José, Costa Rica: FLACSO).

Castañeda, Omar S. (1996) Guatemalan macho oratory. In *Muy macho: Latino men confront their manhood*, Ray González (ed.), pp. 35–50 (New York: Anchor Books/Doubleday).

Caulfield, Sueann (1997) The birth of Mangue: race, nation and the politics of prostitution in Rio de Janeiro, 1850–1942. In *Sex and sexuality in Latin America*, Daniel Balderston and Donna J. Guy (eds), pp. 86–100 (New York: New York University Press).

—— (2000) *In defense of honor: sexual morality, modernity, and nation in early-twentieth-century Brazil* (Durham, NC: Duke University Press).

—— (2001) The history of gender in the historiography of Latin America, *Hispanic American Historical Review* 81(3–4): 451–90.

—— (2003a) Interracial courtship in the Rio de Janeiro courts, 1918–1940. In *Race and nation in modern Latin America*, Nancy P. Appelbaum, Anne S. Macpherson and Karin A. Rosemblatt (eds), pp. 163–86 (Chapel Hill, NC: University of North Carolina Press).

Caulfield, Sueann, Sarah C. Chambers and Lara Putnam (eds) (2005) *Honor, status, and law in modern Latin America* (Durham, NC: Duke University Press).

Cepeda, Maria Elena (2003) Shakira as the idealized, transnational citizen: a case study of Colombianidad in transition, *Latino Studies* 1(2): 211.

Chambers, Sarah C. (1999) *From subjects to citizens: honor, gender, and politics in Arequipa, Peru, 1780–1854* (University Park, PA: Pennsylvania State University Press).

Chasteen, John Charles (2004) *National rhythms, African roots: the deep history of Latin American popular dance* (Albuquerque, NM: University of New Mexico Press).

Chávez-Silverman, Susana (1997) Tropicolada: inside the U.S. Latino/a gender b(l)ender. In *Tropicalizations: transcultural representations of latinidad*, Frances R. Aparicio and Susana Chávez-Silverman (eds), pp. 101–18 (Hanover, NH: University of New England Press).

Chiñas, Beverly N. (1995) Isthmus Zapotec attitudes toward sex and gender anomalies. In *Latin American male homosexualities*, Stephen

O. Murray (ed.), pp. 293–302 (Albuquerque, NM: University of New Mexico Press).

Chodorow, Nancy (1978) *The reproduction of mothering* (Berkeley, CA: University of California Press).

Clark, David Anthony Tyeeme and Joane Nagel (2000) White men, red masks: appropriations of 'Indian' manhood in imagined Wests, 1876–1934. In *Across the Great Divide: cultures of manhood in the American West*, Matthew Basso, Laura McCall and Dee Garceau (eds), pp. 109–30 (New York: Routledge).

Clifford, James (2001) Indigenous articulations, *Contemporary Pacific* 13(2): 468–90.

Clifford, James and George E. Marcus (eds) (1986) *Writing culture: the poetics and politics of ethnography* (Berkeley, CA: University of California Press).

Cock, Jacklyn (1980) *Maids and madams: a study in the politics of exploitation* (Johannesburg: Raven Press).

Collier, Simon (1995) The tango is born: 1880s–1920s. In *¡Tango! The dance, the song, the story*, Simon Collier, Artemis Cooper, María Susana Azzi and Richard Martin (eds), pp. 18–66 (London: Thames & Hudson).

Collier, Simon, Artemis Cooper, María Susana Azzi and Richard Martin (1995) *¡Tango! The dance, the song, the story* (London: Thames & Hudson).

Collins, Patricia Hill (2000) *Black feminist thought: knowledge, consciousness and the politics of empowerment* (New York: Routledge).

Congolino, Mary Lilia (2008) ¿Hombres negros potentes, mujeres negras candentes? Sexualidades y estereotipos raciales: la experiencia de jóvenes universitarios en Cali, Colombia. In *Raza, etnicidad y sexualidades: ciudadanía y multiculturalismo en América Latina*, Peter Wade, Fernando Urrea Giraldo and Mara Viveros Vigoya (eds), pp. 317–41 (Bogotá: Instituto CES, Facultad de Ciencias Humanas, Universidad Nacional de Colombia).

Cope, R. Douglas (1994) *The limits of racial domination: plebeian society in colonial Mexico City, 1660–1720* (Madison, WI: University of Wisconsin Press).

Cornwall, Andrea (ed.) (2005) *Readings in gender in Africa* (Bloomington, IN: Indiana University Press).

Coronil, Fernando (1996) Beyond occidentalism: toward nonimperial geohistorical categories, *Cultural Anthropology* 11(1): 51–87.

Cortés, Carlos E. (1997) Chicanas in film: history of an image. In *Latin looks: images of Latinas and Latinos in the U.S. media*, Clara E. Rodríguez (ed.), pp. 121–41 (Boulder, CO: Westview Press).

Cottrol, Robert J. (2001) The long lingering shadow: law, liberalism, and cultures of racial hierarchy and identity in the Americas, *Tulane Law Review* 76: 11–80.

Craig, Maxine Leeds (2006) Race, beauty and the tangled knot of a guilty pleasure, *Feminist Theory* 7(2): 159–77.

Crenshaw, Kimberlé (1991) Mapping the margins: intersectionality, identity politics, and violence against women of color, *Stanford Law Review* 43(6): 1241–99.

Cummings, Laura L. (2003) Cloth-wrapped people, trouble, and power: pachuco culture in the greater Southwest, *Journal of the Southwest* 45(3): 329(20).

Curiel, Ochy (2008) Superando la interseccionalidad de categorías por la construcción de un proyecto político feminista radical. Reflexiones en torno a las estrategias políticas de las mujeres afrodescendientes. In *Raza, etnicidad y sexualidades: ciudadanía y multiculturalismo en América Latina*, Peter Wade, Fernando Urrea Giraldo and Mara Viveros Vigoya (eds), pp. 461–84 (Bogotá: Instituto CES, Facultad de Ciencias Humanas, Universidad Nacional de Colombia).

Darder, Antonia and Rodolfo Torres (eds) (1998) *The Latino Studies reader* (Oxford: Blackwell).

Davalos, Karen Mary (1996) 'La quinceañera': making gender and ethnic identities, *Frontiers: A Journal of Women Studies* 16(2/3): 101–27.

Davis, Angela (1981) *Women, race and class* (New York: Random House).

De la Cadena, Marisol (2000) *Indigenous mestizos: the politics of race and culture in Cuzco, 1919–1991* (Durham, NC: Duke University Press).

De la Fuente, Alejandro (2001) *A nation for all: race, inequality, and politics in twentieth century Cuba* (Chapel Hill, NC: University of North Carolina Press).

De Lauretis, Teresa (1991) Queer theory: lesbian and gay sexualities. An introduction, *differences: A Journal of Feminist Cultural Studies* 3(2): iii–xviii.

—— (1994a) Habit changes (response to article by Elizabeth Grosz in this issue). (More Gender Trouble: Feminism Meets Queer Theory.) *Differences: A Journal of Feminist Cultural Studies* 6 (2–3): 296–314. Accessed January 2008. Available from http://find.galegroup.com/itx/infomark.do?&contentSet=IAC-Documents&type=retrieve&tabID=T002&prodId=EAIM&docId=A17250614&source=gale&srcprod=EAIM&userGroupName=jrycal5&version=1.0.

—— (1994b) *The practice of love: lesbian sexuality and perverse desire* (Bloomington, IN: Indiana University Press).

De Moya, E. Antonio and Rafael García (1999) Three decades of male sex work in Santo Domingo. In *Men who sell sex: international perspectives on male prostitution and HIV/AIDS*, Peter Aggleton (ed.), pp. 127–40 (Philadelphia, PA: Temple University Press).

Dean, Tim and Christopher Lane (eds) (2001) *Homosexuality and psychoanalysis* (Chicago, IL: University of Chicago Press).

Deleuze, Gilles (1994) Desire and pleasure. Translation by Melissa McMahon of 'Désir et plaisir', *Magazine littéraire* 325, October 1994, pp. 59–65. Accessed 28 January 2008. Available from http://slash.autonomedia.org/article.pl?sid=02/11/18/1910227.

Deleuze, Gilles and Félix Guattari (1975) Psychoanalysis and ethnology, *SubStance* 4(11–12): 170–97.

—— (1983) *Anti-Oedipus: capitalism and schizophrenia*, trans. Robert Hurley, Mark Seem and Helen R. Lane (Minneapolis, MN: University of Minnesota Press).

Di Leonardo, Micaela (1997) White lies, black myths: rape, race, and the black 'underclass'. In *The gender/sexuality reader: culture, history, political economy*, Roger N. Lancaster and Micaela Di Leonardo (eds), pp. 53–68 (London: Routledge).

Di Leonardo, Micaela and Roger N. Lancaster (1997) Introduction: embodied meanings, carnal practices. In *The gender/sexuality reader: culture, history, political economy*, Roger N. Lancaster and Micaela Di Leonardo (eds), pp. 1–10 (London: Routledge).

Díaz, María Elvira (2006) Jerarquías y resistencias: raza, género y clase en universos homosexuales. In *De mujeres, hombres y otras ficciones: género y sexualidad en América Latina*, Mara Viveros, Claudia Rivera and Manuel Rodríguez (eds), pp. 283–304 (Bogotá: Facultad de Ciencias Humanas, Universidad Nacional de Colombia; Tercer Mundo Editores).

Doane, Mary Ann (1991) *Femmes fatales: feminism, film theory, psychoanalysis* (New York: Routledge).

Drinot, Paulo (2006) Moralidad, moda y sexualidad: el contexto moral de la creación del barrio rojo de Lima. In *Mujeres, familia y sociedad en la historia de América Latina, siglos XVIII–XXI*, Scarlett O'Phelan Godoy and Margarita Zegarra Flórez (eds), pp. 333–54 (Lima: CENDOC-Mujer, Pontificia Universidad Católica del Perú, Instituto Riva-Agüero, Instituto Francés de Estudios Andinos).

Du Bois, W. E. B. (1897) Strivings of the Negro people, *Atlantic Monthly* 80: 194–98.

Dudley, Edward and Maximillian E. Novak (eds) (1972) *The wild man within: an image in Western thought from the Renaissance to Romanticism* (Pittsburgh, PA: University of Pittsburgh Press).

Duster, Troy (2003) *Backdoor to eugenics* (London: Routledge).

Dzidzienyo, Anani and Suzanne Oboler (eds) (2005) *Neither enemies nor friends: Latinos, Blacks, Afro-Latinos* (New York: Palgrave Macmillan).

Edmonds, Alexander (2007) Triumphant miscegenation: reflections on beauty and race in Brazil, *Journal of Intercultural Studies* 28(1): 83–97.

Ellis, Robert Richmond (1998) The inscription of masculinity and whiteness in the autobiography of Mario Vargas Llosa, *Bulletin of Latin American Research* 17(2): 223–36.

—— (2002) *They dream not of angels but of men: homoeroticism, gender, and race in Latin American autobiography* (Gainesville, FL: University Press of Florida).

Espino, Rodolfo and Michael M. Franz (2002) Latino phenotypic discrimination revisited: the impact of skin color on occupational status, *Social Science Quarterly* 83(2): 612–23.

Fabian, Johannes (1983) *Time and the other: how anthropology makes its object* (New York: Columbia University Press).

Fanon, Frantz (1986 [1952]) *Black skin, white masks* (London: Pluto Press).

Fausto-Sterling, Anne (1985) *Myths of gender: biological theories about women and men* (New York: Basic Books).

—— (2000) *Sexing the body: gender politics and the construction of sexuality* (New York: Basic Books).

Feldman, Heidi Carolyn (2006) *Black rhythms of Peru: reviving African musical heritage in the Black Pacific* (Middletown, CT: Wesleyan University Press).

Ferguson, Roderick A. (2003) *Aberrations in black: toward a queer of color critique* (Minneapolis, MN: University of Minnesota Press).

—— (2007) The relevance of race for the study of sexuality. In *A companion to lesbian, gay, bisexual, transgender, and queer studies*, George E. Haggerty and Molly McGarry (eds), pp. 109–23 (Malden, MA: Blackwell).

Fernandez, Nadine T. (1996) The color of love: young interracial couples in Cuba, *Latin American Perspectives* 23(1): 99–117.

—— (1999) Back to the future: women, race and tourism in Cuba. In *Sun, sex and gold: tourism and sex work in the Caribbean*, Kamala Kempadoo (ed.), pp. 81–9 (Lanham, MD: Rowman & Littlefield).

Ferreira, Marcelo (2005) E se o gringo for negão?: 'raça', gênero e sexualidade no Rio de Janeiro – a experiência dos turistas negros norte-americanos. MA thesis, Universidade do Estado do Rio de Janeiro.

Fields, Barbara J. (1982) Ideology and race in American history. In *Region, race, and reconstruction: essays in honor of C. Vann Woodward*,

J. Morgan Kousser and James M. McPherson (eds), pp. 143–77 (Oxford: Oxford University Press).

Figueroa, María P. (2003) Resisting 'beauty' and *Real women have curves*. In *Velvet barrios: popular culture and Chicana/o sexualities*, Alicia Gaspar de Alba (ed.), pp. 265–82 (New York: Palgrave Macmillan).

Findlay, Eileen J. Suárez (1998) *Imposing decency: the politics of sexuality and race in Puerto Rico, 1870–1920* (Durham, NC: Duke University Press).

Fiol-Matta, Licia (2000) Race woman: reproducing the nation in Gabriela Mistral, *GLQ: A Journal of Lesbian and Gay Studies* 6(4): 491–527.

—— (2002) *A queer mother for the nation: the state and Gabriela Mistral* (Minneapolis, MN: University of Minnesota Press).

Flores, Juan (2000) *From bomba to hip-hop: Puerto Rican culture and Latino identity* (New York: Columbia University Press).

Flores, Juan and Renato Rosaldo (eds) (2007) *A companion to Latina/o Studies* (Oxford: Blackwell).

Foner, Laura and Eugene Genovese (eds) (1969) *Slavery in the New World: a reader in comparative history* (Englewood Cliffs, NJ: Prentice-Hall).

Fontaine, Pierre-Michel (1981) Transnational relations and racial mobilization: emerging black movements in Brazil. In *Ethnic identities in a transnational world*, John F. Stack (ed.), pp. 141–62 (Westport, CT: Greenwood Press).

Ford, Eleanor (2004) *The Internet bride*. In MA in Visual Anthropology Final Project Film. Pp. 29 mins (Manchester: Granada Centre for Visual Anthropology, University of Manchester).

Foucault, Michel (1998 [1979]) *The will to knowledge. The history of sexuality: Volume 1*, trans. Robert Hurley (London: Penguin Books).

Fox, Jonathan and Gaspar Rivera-Salgado (eds) (2004) *Indigenous Mexican migrants in the United States* (San Diego, CA: Center for U.S.–Mexican Studies, Center for Comparative Immigration Studies, University of California at San Diego).

Fox, Patricia D. (2006) *Being and blackness in Latin America: uprootedness and improvisation* (Gainesville, FL: University Press of Florida).

Frankenberg, Ruth (1993) *White women, race matters: the social construction of whiteness* (London: Routledge).

French, William E. (1992) Prostitutes and guardian angels: women, work, and the family in Porfirian Mexico, *The Hispanic American Historical Review* 72(4): 529–53.

French, William E. and Katherine Elaine Bliss (eds) (2006) *Gender, sexuality, and power in Latin America since independence* (Lanham, MD: Rowman & Littlefield).

Friedemann, Nina de and Jaime Arocha (1986) *De sol a sol: génesis, transformación y presencia de los negros en Colombia* (Bogotá: Planeta).

Fry, Peter (1982) *Para inglês ver: identidade e política na cultura brasileira* (Rio de Janeiro: Zahar Editores).

—— (1995) Male homosexuality and Afro-Brazilian possession cults. In *Latin American male homosexualities*, Stephen O. Murray (ed.), pp. 193–220 (Albuquerque, NM: University of New Mexico Press).

—— (1995–96) O que a Cinderela Negra tem a dizer sobre a 'politica racial' no Brasil, *Revista USP* 28: 122–35.

—— (2000) Politics, nationality, and the meanings of 'race' in Brazil, *Daedalus* 129(2): 83–118.

—— (2002) Estética e política: relações entre 'raça', publicidade e produção da beleza no Brasil. In *Nu e vestido: dez antropólogos revelam a cultura do corpo carioca*, Mirian Goldenberg (ed.), pp. 303–26 (Rio de Janeiro: Record).

Fry, Peter H., Simone Monteiro, Marcos Chor Maio, Francisco I. Bastos and Ricardo Ventura Santos (2007) AIDS tem cor ou raça? Interpretação de dados e formulação de políticas de saúde no Brasil, *Cadernos de Saúde Pública* 23(3): 497–523.

Fry, Peter, Yvonne Maggie, Simone Monteiro and Ricardo Ventura Santos (eds) (2007) *Divisões perigosas: políticas raciais no Brasil contemporâneo* (Rio de Janeiro: Civilização Brasileira).

Fuss, Diana (1994) Interior colonies: Frantz Fanon and the politics of identification, *Diacritics* 24(2–3): 20–42.

Garrett, David T. (2005) *Shadows of empire: the Indian nobility of Cusco, 1750–1825* (Cambridge: Cambridge University Press).

Gates, Jr., Henry Louis (1991) Critical Fanonism, *Critical Inquiry* 17(3): 457–70.

Giacomini, Sonia Maria (2006) Mulatas profissionais: raça, gênero e ocupação, *Revista Estudos Feministas* 14(1): 85–101.

Giddens, Anthony (1992) *The transformation of intimacy: sexuality, love and eroticism in modern societies* (Cambridge: Polity Press).

Gilb, Dagoberto (1996) Me macho, you Jane. In *Muy macho: Latino men confront their manhood*, Ray González (ed.), pp. 1–16 (New York: Anchor Books/Doubleday).

Gill, Lesley (1994) *Precarious dependencies: gender, class, and domestic service in Bolivia* (New York: Columbia University Press).

—— (1997) Creating citizens, making men: the military and masculinity in Bolivia, *Cultural Anthropology* 12(4): 527–50.

Gilliam, Angela (1998) The Brazilian mulata: images in the global economy, *Race and Class* 40(1): 57–69.

Gilman, Sander L. (1985) *Difference and pathology: stereotypes of sexuality, race, and madness* (Ithaca, NY: Cornell University Press).

—— (1993) *Freud, race, and gender* (Princeton, NJ: Princeton University Press).

Gilroy, Paul (2000) *Between camps: nations, cultures and the allure of race* (London: Penguin Books).

—— (2004) *After empire: melancholia or convivial culture* (London: Routledge).

Girman, Chris (2004) *Mucho macho: seduction, desire, and the homoerotic lives of Latin men* (New York: Harrington Park Press).

Godbeer, Richard (1999) Eroticizing the middle ground: Anglo-Indian sexual relations along the eighteenth-century frontier. In *Sex, love, and race: crossing boundaries in North American history*, Martha Hodes (ed.), pp. 91–111 (New York: New York University Press).

Golash-Boza, Tanya and William Darity (2008) Latino racial choices: the effects of skin colour and discrimination on Latinos' and Latinas' racial self-identifications, *Ethnic and Racial Studies* 31(5): 899–934.

Goldstein, Donna (1999) 'Interracial' sex and racial democracy in Brazil: twin concepts?, *American Anthropologist* 101(3): 563–78.

Goldstein, Donna M. (2003) *Laughter out of place: race, class, violence and sexuality in a Rio shantytown* (Berkeley, CA: University of California Press).

González-López, Gloria (2005) *Erotic journeys: Mexican immigrants and their sex lives* (Berkeley, CA: University of California Press).

González, M. Alfredo (2007) Latinos *on da down low*: the limitations of sexual identity in public health, *Latino Studies* 5(1): 25.

Goode, Erich (2002) Sexual involvement and social research in a fat civil rights organization, *Qualitative Sociology* 25(4): 501–34.

Goody, Jack (1976) *Production and reproduction: a comparative study of the domestic domain* (Cambridge: Cambridge University Press).

Gopinath, Gayatri (2003) Nostalgia, desire, diaspora: South Asian sexualities in motion. In *Uprootings/regroundings: questions of home and migration*, Sara Ahmed, Claudia Castañeda, Anne-Marie Fortier and Mimi Sheller (eds), pp. 137–56 (Oxford: Berg).

Gould, Jeffrey L (1998) *To die in this way: Nicaraguan Indians and the myth of the mestizaje, 1880–1960* (Durham, NC: Duke University Press).

Graham, Richard (ed.) (1990) *The idea of race in Latin America, 1870–1940* (Austin, TX: University of Texas Press).

Green, James N. (1999) *Beyond carnival: male homosexuality in twentieth-century Brazil* (Chicago, IL: University of Chicago Press).

—— (2006) Doctoring the national body: gender, race, eugenics and the 'invert' in urban Brazil, ca. 1920–1945. In *Gender, sexuality, and power in Latin America since independence*, William E. French and Katherine Elaine Bliss (eds), pp. 187–211 (Lanham, MD: Rowman & Littlefield).

Green, James N. and Florence E. Babb (2002) Introduction (special issue: Gender, sexuality, and same-sex desire in Latin America), *Latin American Perspectives* 29(2): 3–23.

Greene, Sandra E. (1996) *Gender, ethnicity and social change on the Upper Slave Coast: a history of the Anlo-Ewe* (Portsmouth, NH and London: Heinemann and James Currey).

Greene, Shane (2007) Introduction: on race, roots/routes, and sovereignty in Latin America's Afro-indigenous multiculturalisms, *Journal of Latin American and Caribbean Anthropology* 12(2): 441–74.

Grieco, Elizabeth M. and Rachel C. Cassidy (2001) *Overview of race and Hispanic origin* (Washington, DC: US Census Bureau), accessed.

Grossberg, Lawrence (1986) On postmodernism and articulation: an interview with Stuart Hall, *Journal of Communication Inquiry* 10: 45–60.

Grosz, Elizabeth (1994) The labors of love. Analyzing perverse desire: an interrogation of Teresa de Lauretis's *The Practice of Love*. (More Gender Trouble: Feminism Meets Queer Theory). *Differences: A Journal of Feminist Cultural Studies* 6 (2–3): 274–96. Accessed January 2008. Available from http://find.galegroup.com/itx/infomark. do?&contentSet=IAC-Documents&type=retrieve&tabID=T002&pro dId=EAIM&docId=A17250612&source=gale&srcprod=EAIM&use rGroupName=jrycal5&version=1.0.

Groth, Nicholas A. (1979) *Men who rape: the psychology of the offender* (New York: Plenum Press).

Gutiérrez, Ramón (1991) *When Jesus came, the corn mothers went away: marriage, sexuality and power in New Mexico, 1500–1846* (Stanford, CA: Stanford University Press).

—— (2007) Women on top: the love magic of the Indian witches of New Mexico, *Journal of the History of Sexuality* 16(3): 373–90.

Gutmann, Matthew C. (1996) *The meanings of macho: being a man in Mexico City* (Berkeley, CA: University of California Press).

—— (2003) Introduction: discarding manly dichotomies in Latin America. In *Changing men and masculinities in Latin America*, Matthew C. Gutmann (ed.), pp. 1–26 (Durham, NC: Duke University Press).

Guy, Donna (1991) *Sex and danger in Buenos Aires: prostitution, family, and nation in Argentina* (Lincoln, NB: University of Nebraska Press).

Guy, Donna J. (2000) *White slavery and mothers alive and dead: the troubled meeting of sex, gender, public health, and progress in Latin America* (Lincoln, NB: University of Nebraska Press).

Hale, Charles R. (1996) *Mestizaje*, hybridity and the cultural politics of difference in post-revolutionary Central America, *Journal of Latin American Anthropology* 2(1): 34–61.

—— (2002) Does multiculturalism menace? Governance, cultural rights and the politics of identity in Guatemala, *Journal of Latin American Studies* 34: 485–524.

—— (2005) Neoliberal multiculturalism: the remaking of cultural rights and racial dominance in Central America, *PoLAR: Political and Legal Anthropology Review* 28(1): 10–28.

—— (2006) *Más que un indio (More than an Indian): racial ambivalence and neoliberal multiculturalism in Guatemala* (Santa Fe, NM: School of American Research Press).

Hall, Jacquelyn Dowd (1984) 'The mind that burns in each body': women, rape, and racial violence. In *Desire: the politics of sexuality*, Ann Snitow, Christine Stansell and Sharon Thompson (eds), pp. 339–60 (London: Virago).

Hall, Stuart (1996) The after-life of Frantz Fanon. Why Fanon? Why now? Why Black Skin, White Masks? In *The fact of blackness: Frantz Fanon and visual representation*, Alan Read (ed.), pp. 12–37 (London: Institute of Contemporary Arts).

Hammonds, Evelynn (1994) Black (w)holes and the geometry of Black female sexuality. (More Gender Trouble: Feminism Meets Queer Theory), *differences: A Journal of Feminist Cultural Studies* 6(2–3): 126–46.

Hanchard, Michael (1994) *Orpheus and Power: the Movimento Negro of Rio de Janeiro and São Paulo, Brazil, 1945–1988* (Princeton, NJ: Princeton University Press).

—— (1999a) Black Cinderella? Race and the public sphere in Brazil. In *Racial politics in contemporary Brazil*, Michael Hanchard (ed.), pp. 59–81 (Durham, NC: Duke University Press).

—— (1999b) Introduction. In *Racial politics in contemporary Brazil*, Michael Hanchard (ed.), pp. 1–29 (Durham, NC: Duke University Press).

Harden, Jacalyn D. (1997) The enterprise of empire: race, class, gender and Japanese national identity. In *The gender/sexuality reader: culture, history, political economy*, Roger N. Lancaster and Micaela Di Leonardo (eds), pp. 487–501 (London: Routledge).

Harding, Rachel E. (2000) *A refuge in thunder: candomblé and alternative spaces of blackness* (Bloomington, IN: Indiana University Press).

Harris, Marvin (1974) *Patterns of race in the Americas* (New York: Norton Library).

Heilborn, Maria Luiza and Cristiane S. Cabral (2008) Sexualidad, género y color entre jóvenes brasileros. In *Raza, etnicidad y sexualidades: ciudadanía y multiculturalismo en América Latina*, Peter Wade, Fernando Urrea Giraldo and Mara Viveros Vigoya (eds), pp. 167–97 (Bogotá: Instituto CES, Facultad de Ciencias Humanas, Universidad Nacional de Colombia).

Helg, Aline (1990) Race in Argentina and Cuba, 1880–1930. In *The idea of race in Latin America, 1870–1940*, Richard Graham (ed.), pp. 37–70 (Austin, TX: University of Texas Press).

—— (1995) *Our rightful share: the Afro-Cuban struggle for equality, 1886–1912* (Chapel Hill, NC: University of North Carolina Press).

Hendricks, Margo and Patricia Parker (eds) (1994) *Women, 'race,' and writing in the early modern period* (London: Routledge).

Herdt, Gilbert (ed.) (1994) *Third sex, third gender: beyond sexual dimorphism in culture and history* (New York: Zone Books).

Hernton, Calvin (1970) *Sex and racism* (London: Paladin).

Herold, Edward, Rafael Garcia and Tony DeMoya (2001) Female tourists and beach boys: romance or sex tourism?, *Annals of Tourism Research* 28(4): 978–97.

Hobson, Janell (2005) *Venus in the dark: blackness and beauty in popular culture* (New York: Routledge).

Hodes, Martha (1993) The sexualization of reconstruction politics: white women and black men in the South after the Civil War, *Journal of the History of Sexuality* 3(3): 402–17.

—— (1997) *White women, black men: illicit sex in the nineteenth-century South* (New Haven, CT: Yale University Press).

—— (ed.) (1999) *Sex, love, and race: crossing boundaries in North American history* (New York: New York University Press).

Hoetink, Harry (1973) *Slavery and race relations* (New York: HarperTorchbooks).

Hooker, Juliet (2005) Indigenous inclusion/black exclusion: race, ethnicity and multicultural citizenship in contemporary Latin America, *Journal of Latin American Studies* 37(2): 285–310.

hooks, bell (1981) *Ain't I a woman? Black women and feminism* (London: Pluto Press).

—— (1991) *Yearning: race, gender and cultural politics* (London: Turnaround).

Horswell, Michael J. (2003) Toward an Andean theory of ritual, same-sex sexuality and third gender subjectivity. In *Infamous desire: male homosexuality in colonial Latin America*, Pete Sigal (ed.), pp. 25–69 (Chicago, IL: University of Chicago Press).

—— (2005) *Decolonizing the sodomite: queer tropes of sexuality in colonial Andean culture* (Austin TX: University of Texas Press).

Howard, Philip A. (1998) *Changing history: Afro-Cuban cabildos and societies of color in the nineteenth century* (Baton Rouge, LA: Louisiana State University Press).

Howes, Robert (2001) Race and transgressive sexuality in Adolfo Caminha's *Bom-Crioulo, Luso-Brazilian Review* 38(1): 41–62.

Htun, Mala (2004) From 'racial democracy' to affirmative action: changing state policy on race in Brazil, *Latin American Research Review* 39(1): 60–89.

Hulme, Peter (1986) *Colonial Encounters: Europe and the Native Caribbean, 1492–1797* (London: Methuen).

Humphrey, John (1987) *Gender and work in the Third World: sexual divisions in Brazilian industry* (London: Tavistock).

Hunt, Lynn (1995) Foucault's subject in *The history of sexuality*. In *Discourses of sexuality: from Aristotle to AIDS*, Domna C. Stanton (ed.), pp. 78–93 (Ann Arbor, MI: University of Michigan Press).

Hunter, Margaret L. (2002) 'If you're light you're alright': light skin color as social capital for women of color, *Gender and Society* 16(2): 175–93.

—— (2005) *Race, gender, and the politics of skin tone* (New York: Routledge).

Hurtado Saa, Teodora (2008) Movilidades, identidades y sexualidades en mujeres afrocolombianas migrantes en Europa: el caso de las 'italianas'. In *Raza, etnicidad y sexualidades: ciudadanía y multiculturalismo en América Latina*, Peter Wade, Fernando Urrea Giraldo and Mara Viveros Vigoya (eds), pp. 34–376 (Bogotá: Instituto CES, Facultad de Ciencias Humanas, Universidad Nacional de Colombia).

Hyam, Ronald (1990) *Empire and sexuality: the British experience* (Manchester: Manchester University Press).

Irwin, Robert McKee (2000) The Famous 41: the scandalous birth of modern Mexican homosexuality, *GLQ: A Journal of Lesbian and Gay Studies* 6(3): 353–76.

—— (2003) *Mexican masculinities* (Minneapolis, MN: University of Minnesota Press).

Jackson, Richard L. (1979) *Black writers in Latin America* (Albuquerque, NM: University of New Mexico Press).

—— (1988) *Black literature and humanism in Latin America* (Athens, GA: University of Georgia Press).

JanMohamed, Abdul R. (1990) Sexuality on/of the racial border: Foucault, Wright and the articulation of 'racialized sexuality'. In *Discourses of sexuality from Aristotle to AIDS*, Domna C. Stanton (ed.), pp. 94–116 (Cambridge, MA: Harvard University Press).

Jeffreys, Sheila (2008) *The industrial vagina: the political economy of the global sex trade* (London: Routledge).

Jiménez Román, Miriam (2007) Looking at that middle ground: racial mixing as panacea? In *A companion to Latina/o Studies*, Juan Flores and Renato Rosaldo (eds), pp. 325–36 (Oxford: Blackwell).

Joekes, Susan (1985) Working for lipstick? Male and female labour in the clothing industry in Morocco. In *Women, work and ideology in the Third World*, Haleh Afshar (ed.), pp. 183–213 (London: Tavistock).

Johnson, Lyman L. (1998) Dangerous words, provocative gestures and violent acts. In *The faces of honor: sex, shame, and violence in colonial Latin America*, Lyman L. Johnson and Sonya Lipsett-Rivera (eds), pp. 127–51 (Albuquerque, NM: University of New Mexico Press).

Johnson, Lyman L. and Sonya Lipsett-Rivera (eds) (1998a) *The faces of honor: sex, shame, and violence in colonial Latin America* (Albuquerque, NM: University of New Mexico Press).

—— (1998b) Introduction. In *The faces of honor: sex, shame, and violence in colonial Latin America*, Lyman L. Johnson and Sonya Lipsett-Rivera (eds), pp. 1–17 (Albuquerque, NM: University of New Mexico Press).

Jordan, Winthrop (1977) *White over black: American attitudes toward the Negro, 1550–1812* (New York: Norton).

Joseph, Miranda and David Rubin (2007) Promising complicities: on the Sex, Race and Globalization Project. In *A companion to lesbian, gay, bisexual, transgender, and queer studies*, George E. Haggerty and Molly McGarry (eds), pp. 430–51 (Malden, MA: Blackwell).

Karras, Ruth Mazo (2005) *Sexuality in medieval Europe: doing unto others* (New York: Routledge).

Katz, Jonathan N. (1976) *Gay American history: lesbians and gay men in the U.S.A., a documentary* (New York: Crowell).

Katzew, Ilona (2004) *Casta painting: images of race in eighteenth-century Mexico* (New Haven, CT: Yale University Press).

Kearney, Michael (2000) Transnational Oaxacan indigenous identity: the case of Mixtecs and Zapotecs, *Identities - Global Studies in Culture and Power* 7(2): 173–95.

Kempadoo, Kamala (1999a) Continuities and change: five centuries of prostitution in the Caribbean. In *Sun, sex and gold: tourism and sex work in the Caribbean*, Kamala Kempadoo (ed.), pp. 3–33 (Lanham, MD: Rowman & Littlefield).

—— (ed.) (1999b) *Sun, sex, and gold: tourism and sex work in the Caribbean* (Lanham, MD: Rowman and Littlefield).

—— (2004) *Sexing the Caribbean: gender, race and sexual labor* (New York: Routledge).

Kevles, Daniel J. (1995) *In the name of eugenics: genetics and the uses of human heredity* (Cambridge, MA: Harvard University Press).

Klor de Alva, J. Jorge (1995) The postcolonization of the (Latin) American experience: a reconsideration of 'colonialism,' 'postcolonialism' and 'mestizajes'. In *After colonialism, imperial histories and postcolonial displacements*, Gyan Prakash (ed.), pp. 241–75 (Princeton, NJ: Princeton University Press).

Knight, Alan (1990) Racism, revolution and indigenismo in Mexico, 1910–1940. In *The idea of race in Latin America*, Richard Graham (ed.), pp. 71–113 (Austin, TX: University of Texas Press).

Kolchin, Peter (2002) Whiteness studies: the new history of race in America, *Journal of American History* 89(1): 154–73.

Kulick, Don (1998) *Travesti: sex, gender, and culture among Brazilian transgendered prostitutes* (Chicago, IL: University of Chicago Press).

Kutzinski, Vera (1993) *Sugar's secrets: race and the erotics of Cuban nationalism* (Charlottesville, VA: University of Virginia Press).

Kuznesof, Elizabeth (1991) Sexual politics, race and bastard-bearing in nineteenth-century Brazil: a question of culture or power? *Journal of Family History* 16(3): 241–60.

Kuznesof, Elizabeth Anne (1993) Sexuality, gender and the family in colonial Brazil, *Luso-Brazilian Review* 30(1): 119–32.

Lacan, Jacques (2001) *Écrits: a selection*, trans. Alan Sheridan (London: Routledge).

Lacan, Jacques, Juliet Mitchell and Jacqueline Rose (eds) (1982) *Feminine sexuality: Jacques Lacan and the école Freudienne* (New York: Pantheon).

Laguardia, Josué (2006) No fio da navalha: anemia falciforme, raça e as implicações no cuidado à saúde, *Revista Estudos Feministas* 14(1): 243–62.

Lang, Sabine (1998) *Men as women, women as men: changing gender in Native American cultures*, trans. John L. Vantine (Austin, TX: University of Texas Press).

Lao-Montes, Agustin (2007a) Afro-Latinidades: bridging blackness and latinidad. In *Technofuturos: critical interventions in Latina/o Studies*, Nancy Raquel Mirabal and Agustin Lao-Montes (eds), pp. 117–40 (Lanham, MD: Rowman & Littlefield).

—— (2007b) Decolonial moves: trans-locating African diaspora spaces, *Cultural Studies* 21(2): 309–38.

Laqueur, Thomas (1990) *Making sex: body and gender from the Greeks to Freud* (Cambridge, MA: Harvard University Press).

Lauderdale Graham, Sandra (1998) Honor among slaves. In *The faces of honor: sex, shame, and violence in colonial Latin America*, Lyman

L. Johnson and Sonya Lipsett-Rivera (eds), pp. 201–28 (Albuquerque, NM: University of New Mexico Press).

Lavrin, Asunción (ed.) (1989a) *Sexuality and marriage in colonial Latin America* (Lincoln, NB: University of Nebraska Press).

—— (1989b) Sexuality in colonial Mexico: a Church dilemma. In *Sexuality and marriage in colonial Latin America*, Asunción Lavrin (ed.), pp. 47–95 (Lincoln, NB: University of Nebraska Press).

Lees, Clare A. (1997) Engendering religious desire: sex, knowledge, and Christian identity in Anglo-Saxon England, *Journal of Medieval and Early Modern Studies* 27(1): 17–46.

Lewis, Laura A. (2003) *Hall of mirrors: power, witchcraft, and caste in colonial Mexico* (Durham, NC: Duke University Press).

Lewis, Marvin A. (1983) *Afro-Hispanic poetry, 1940–1980: from slavery to 'negritud' in South American verse* (Columbia, MO: University of Missouri Press).

—— (1987) *Treading the ebony path: ideology and violence in contemporary Afro-Colombian prose fiction* (Columbia, MO: University of Missouri Press).

Lockhart, James and Stuart Schwartz (1983) *Early Latin America: a history of colonial Spanish America and Brazil* (Cambridge: Cambridge University Press).

Lomnitz-Adler, Claudio (1992) *Exits from the labyrinth: culture and ideology in the Mexican national space* (Berkeley, CA: University of California Press).

López-Vicuña, Ignacio (2004) Approaches to sexuality in Latin America: recent scholarship on gay and lesbian studies, *Latin American Research Review* 39(1): 238–53.

Lovell, Peggy (1994) Race, gender and development in Brazil, *Latin American Research Review* 29(3): 7–35.

Lutz, Catherine A. and Jane L. Collins (1997) The color of sex: postwar photographic histories of race and gender in *National Geographic Magazine*. In *The gender/sexuality reader: culture, history, political economy*, Roger N. Lancaster and Micaela Di Leonardo (eds), pp. 291–306 (London: Routledge).

Madrid, Arturo (2003) In search of the authentic pachuco: an interpretive essay. In *Velvet barrios: popular culture and Chicana/o sexualities*, Alicia Gaspar de Alba (ed.), pp. 17–40 (New York: Palgrave Macmillan).

Mallon, Florencia E. (1996) Constructing *mestizaje* in Latin America: authenticity, marginality and gender in the claiming of ethnic identities, *Journal of Latin American Anthropology* 2(1): 170–81.

Manderson, Leonore and Margaret Jolly (1997a) Introduction: sites of desire/economies of pleasure in Asia and the Pacific. In *Sites of desire/*

economies of pleasure: sexualities in Asia and the Pacific, Leonore Manderson and Margaret Jolly (eds), pp. 1–26 (Chicago, IL: University of Chicago Press).

—— (eds) (1997b) *Sites of desire/economies of pleasure: sexualities in Asia and the Pacific* (Chicago, IL: University of Chicago Press).

Manrique, Nelson (1993) *Vinieron los sarracenos: el universo mental de la conquista de América* (Lima: DESCO).

Manuel, Peter (1988) *Popular musics of the non-Western world: an introductory survey* (Oxford: Oxford University Press).

Manuel, Peter, Kenneth Bilby and Michael Largey (1995) *Caribbean currents: Caribbean music from rumba to reggae* (Philadelphia, PA: Temple University Press).

Martinez-Alier [Stolcke], Verena (1989 [1974]) *Marriage, colour and class in nineteenth-century Cuba: a study of racial attitudes and sexual values in a slave society* (Ann Arbor, MI: University of Michigan Press).

Martínez-Echazábal, Lourdes (1998) Mestizaje and the discourse of national/cultural identity in Latin America, 1845–1959, *Latin American Perspectives* 25(3): 21–42.

Martínez, María Elena (2004) The black blood of New Spain: Limpieza-de-Sangre, racial violence, and gendered power in early colonial Mexico, *William and Mary Quarterly* 61(3): 479–520.

—— (2008) *Genealogical fictions: limpieza de sangre, religion, and gender in colonial Mexico* (Stanford, CA: Stanford University Press).

Marx, Anthony (1998) *Making race and nation: a comparison of South Africa, the United States, and Brazil* (Cambridge: Cambridge University Press).

Mason, Peter (1990) *Deconstructing America: Representations of the other* (London: Routledge).

Matory, J. Lorand (1994) *Sex and the empire that is no more: gender and the politics of metaphor in Oyo Yoruba religion* (Minneapolis, MN: University of Minneapolis Press).

Maya Restrepo, Adriana (2005) *Brujería y reconstrucción de identidades entre los africanos y sus descendientes en la Nueva Granada, siglo XVII* (Bogotá: Ministerio de Cultura).

McCaa, Robert (1984) Calidad, clase and marriage in colonial Mexico: the case of Parral, 1788–90, *Hispanic American Historical Review* 64(3): 477–501.

McCallum, Cecilia (2008) Víctimas egoístas: perspectivas sobre la sexualidad, raza, clase y adolescencia desde un hospital de maternidad en Salvador, Brasil. In *Raza, etnicidad y sexualidades: ciudadanía y multiculturalismo en América Latina*, Peter Wade, Fernando Urrea Giraldo and Mara Viveros Vigoya (eds), pp. 137–66 (Bogotá:

Instituto CES, Facultad de Ciencias Humanas, Universidad Nacional de Colombia).

McClintock, Anne (1993) Family feuds: gender, nationalism and the family, *Feminist Review* 44: 61–80.

—— (1995) *Imperial leather: race, gender and sexuality in the colonial contest* (London: Routledge).

Medicine, Beatriz (Standing Rock Lakota) (1997) Changing Native American roles in an urban context *and* changing Native American sex roles in an urban context. In *Two-spirit people: Native American gender identity, sexuality, and spirituality*, Sue-Ellen Jacobs, Wesley Thomas and Sabine Lang (eds), pp. 145–55 (Urbana, IL: University of Illinois Press).

Mello e Souza, Laura de (2003) *The Devil and the land of the holy cross: witchcraft, slavery and popular religion in colonial Brazil*, trans. Diane Grosklaus Whitty (Austin, TX: University of Texas Press).

Menchaca, Martha (2007) Latinas/os and the mestizo racial heritage of Mexican Americans. In *A companion to Latina/o Studies*, Juan Flores and Renato Rosaldo (eds), pp. 313–24 (Oxford: Blackwell).

Mendoza, Zoila S. (2000) *Shaping society through dance: mestizo ritual performance in the Peruvian Andes* (Chicago, IL: University of Chicago Press).

Mignolo, Walter (2000) *Local histories/global designs: coloniality, subaltern knowledges, and border thinking* (Princeton, NJ: Princeton University Press).

Miller, Marilyn Grace (2004) *Rise and fall of the cosmic race: the cult of mestizaje in Latin America* (Austin, TX: University of Texas Press).

Minsky, Rosalind (ed.) (1996) *Psychoanalysis and gender: an introductory reader* (London: Routledge).

Mintz, Sidney and Richard Price (1992 [1976]) *The birth of Afro-American culture: an anthropological perspective* (Boston, MA: Beacon Press).

Mirandé, Alfredo (1997) *Hombres y machos: masculinity and Latino culture* (Boulder, CO: Westview Press).

Mitchell, Juliet (1974) *Psychoanalysis and feminism* (London: Allen Lane).

Modood, Tariq (2007) *Multiculturalism: a civic idea* (Cambridge: Polity).

Moore, Henrietta (1994) *A passion for difference* (Cambridge: Polity Press).

Moore, Henrietta L. (2007) *The subject of anthropology, gender, symbolism and psychoanalysis* (Cambridge: Polity).

Moore, Robin (1997) *Nationalizing blackness: afrocubanismo and artistic revolution in Havana, 1920–1940* (Pittsburgh, PA: University of Pittsburgh Press).

Mörner, Magnus (1967) *Race mixture in the history of Latin America* (Boston, MA: Little, Brown).

Morrison, Toni (1993) *Playing in the dark: whiteness and the literary imagination* (New York: Vintage Books).

Mosse, George (1985) *Nationalism and sexuality: respectability and abnormal sexuality in modern Europe* (New York: Howard Fertig).

Mott, Luiz (1985) Relações raciais entre homossexuais no Brasil colônial, *Revista Brasileira de História* 5(10): 99–122.

—— (1994) Etno-história da homossexualidade na América Latina Accessed 12 March 2008. Available from http://ich.ufpel.edu.br/ndh/Luiz_Mott_Volume_04.pdf.

—— (2003) Crypto-sodomites in colonial Brazil. In *Infamous desire: male homosexuality in colonial Latin America*, Pete Sigal (ed.), pp. 168–96 (Chicago, IL: University of Chicago Press).

Moutinho, Laura (2004) *Razão, 'cor' e desejo: uma análise comparativa sobre relacionamentos afetivo-sexuais 'inter-raciais' no Brasil e África do Sul* (São Paulo: Editora da UNESP).

—— (2006) Negociando com a adversidade: reflexões sobre 'raça', (homos)sexualidade e desigualdade social no Rio de Janeiro, *Revista Estudos Feministas* 14(1): 103–16.

Moutinho, Laura et al. (2006) Raça, sexualidade e saúde. (Special journal issue), *Revista Estudos Feministas* 14(1).

Muñoz-Laboy, Miguel A. (2004) Beyond 'MSM': sexual desire among bisexually-active Latino men in New York City, *Sexualities* 7(1): 55–80.

Murguía, Edward and Edward E. Telles (1996) Phenotype and schooling among Mexican Americans, *Sociology of Education* 69(4): 276–89.

Murray, Stephen O. (1995a) Machismo, male homosexuality and Latino culture. In *Latin American male homosexualities*, Stephen O. Murray (ed.), pp. 49–70 (Albuquerque, NM: University of New Mexico Press).

—— (1995b) 'Sentimental effusions' of genital contact in Amazonia. In *Latin American male homosexualities*, Stephen O. Murray (ed.), pp. 264–73 (Albuquerque, NM: University of New Mexico Press).

—— (1995c) South American west coast indigenous homosexualities. In *Latin American male homosexualities*, Stephen O. Murray (ed.), pp. 279–92 (Albuquerque, NM: University of New Mexico Press).

Murray, Stephen O. and Will Roscoe (eds) (1998) *Boy-wives and female husbands: studies of African homosexualities* (New York: St. Martin's Press).

Myrdal, Gunnar (1944) *An American dilemma: the Negro problem and modern democracy* (New York: Harper & Row).

Nagel, Joane (2003) *Race, ethnicity, and sexuality: intimate intersections, forbidden frontiers* (Oxford: Oxford University Press).

Napolitano, Minisa Nogueira (2004) A sodomia feminina na primeira visitação do Santo Ofício ao Brasil. *Revista História Hoje* 1 (3). Accessed 18 March 2008. Available from www.anpuh.uepg.br/historia-hoje/vol1n3/sodomia.htm.

—— (2008 [2004]) A construção do lesbianismo na sociedade carioca oitocentista Accessed 1 April 2008. Available from www.abep.nepo.unicamp.br/site_eventos_abep/PDF/ABEP2004_69.pdf.

Nash, Gary (1995) The hidden history of mestizo America, *Journal of American History* 82(3): 941–64.

Nash, Jennifer C. (2008) Re-thinking intersectionality, *Feminist Review* 89(1): 1–15.

Nayak, Anoop (2007) Critical whiteness studies, *Sociology Compass* 1(2): 737-55.

Nazzari, Muriel (1989) An urgent need to conceal: the system of honor and shame in colonial Brazil. In *The faces of honor: sex, shame, and violence in colonial Latin America*, Lyman L. Johnson and Sonya Lipsett-Rivera (eds), pp. 103–26 (Albuquerque, NM: University of New Mexico Press).

—— (1991) *Disappearance of the dowry: women, families and social change in São Paulo, 1600–1900* (Stanford, CA: Stanford University Press).

—— (1996) Concubinage in colonial Brazil: the inequalities of race, class, and gender, *Journal of Family History* 21(2): 107–24.

Nederveen Pieterse, Jan (1992) *White on black: images of Africa and blacks in Western popular culture* (New Haven, CT: Yale University Press).

Negy, Charles and Russell Eisenman (2005) A comparison of African American and White college students' affective and attitudinal reactions to lesbian, gay, and bisexual individuals: an exploratory study, *Journal of Sex Research* 42(4): 291–9.

Nelson, Diane M. (1998) Perpetual creation and decomposition: bodies, gender, and desire in the assumptions of a Guatemalan discourse of mestizaje, *Journal of Latin American Anthropology* 4(1): 74–111.

—— (1999) *A finger in the wound: body politics in quincentennial Guatemala* (Berkeley, CA: California University Press).

Nesvig, Martin (2001) The complicated terrain of Latin American homosexuality, *Hispanic American Historical Review* 81(3–4): 689–729.

O'Connell Davidson, Julia and Jacqueline Sanchez Taylor (1999) Fantasy islands: exploring the demand for sex tourism. In *Sun, sex and gold: tourism and sex work in the Caribbean*, Kamala Kempadoo (ed.), pp. 37–54 (Lanham, MD: Rowman & Littlefield).

Ortiz, Fernando (1917 [1906]) *Hampa afrocubana: los negros brujos* (Madrid: Editorial America).

Ortiz, Lucía (ed.) (2007) '*Chambacú, la historia la escribes tú*'. Ensayos sobre la cultura afrocolombiana (Madrid, Frankfurt: Iberoamericana, Vervuert).

Pagden, Anthony (1982) *The fall of natural man: the American Indian and the origins of comparative ethnology* (Cambridge: Cambridge University Press).

Parker, Andrew, Mary Russo, Doris Sommer and Patricia Jaeger (1992a) Introduction. In *Nationalisms and sexualities*, Andrew Parker, Mary Russo, Doris Sommer and Patricia Yaeger (eds), pp. 1–18 (London: Routledge).

—— (eds) (1992b) *Nationalisms and sexualities* (London: Routledge).

Parker, Richard G. (1999) *Beneath the equator: cultures of desire, male homosexuality and emerging gay communities in Brazil* (London: Routledge).

Pérez-Torres, Rafael (2006) *Mestizaje: critical uses of race in Chicano culture* (Minneapolis, MN: University of Minnesota Press).

Phillips, Joan L. (1999) Tourist-oriented prostitution in Barbados. In *Sun, sex and gold: tourism and sex work in the Caribbean*, Kamala Kempadoo (ed.), pp. 183–200 (Lanham, MD: Rowman & Littlefield).

Piccini, Amina Maggi (1992) Visão psicanalítica do imaginário dos inquisidores e das bruxas (*Malleus Maleficarum*). In *Inquisição: ensaios sobre mentalidade, heresias e arte. Trabalhos apresentados no I Congresso Internacional–Inquisição, Universidade de São Paulo, maio 1987*, Anita Novinsky and Maria Luiza Tucci Carneiro (eds), pp. 72–93 (Rio de Janeiro, São Paulo: Expressão e Cultura, EDUSP).

Pinho, Osmundo de Araújo (2004) O efeito do sexo: políticas de raça, gênero e miscigenação, *Cadernos Pagu* 23: 89–119.

—— (2005) Etnografias do brau: corpo, masculinidade e raça na reafricanização em Salvador, *Revista Estudos Feministas* 13(1): 127–45.

Piscitelli, Adriana (2002) Exotismo e autenticidade: relatos de viajantes à procura de sexo, *Cadernos Pagu* 19: 195–231.

—— (2004) Entre a praia de Iracema e a União Européia: turismo sexual internacional e migração feminina'. In *Sexualidade e saberes: convenções e fronteiras*, Adriana Piscitelli, Maria Filomena Gregori and Sérgio Carrara (eds), pp. 283–318 (Rio de Janeiro: Garamond).

Poole, Stafford (1999) The politics of limpieza de sangre: Juan de Ovando and his circle in the reign of Philip II, *Americas* 55(3): 359–89.

Povinelli, Elizabeth A. (1997) Sex acts and sovereignty: race and sexuality in the construction of the Australian nation. In *The gender/sexuality reader: culture, history, political economy*, Roger N. Lancaster and Micaela Di Leonardo (eds), pp. 513–28 (London: Routledge).

—— (2002) *The cunning of recognition: indigenous alterities and the making of Australian multiculturalism* (Durham, NC: Duke University Press).

—— (2006) *The empire of love: toward a theory of intimacy, genealogy, and carnality* (Durham, NC: Duke University Press).

Powers, Karen Vieira (2005) *Women in the crucible of conquest: the gendered genesis of Spanish American society, 1500–1600* (Albuquerque, NM: University of New Mexico Press).

Pratt, Geraldine (1999) From registered nurse to registered nanny: discursive geographies of Filipina domestic workers in Vancouver, B.C., *Economic Geography* 75(3): 215–36.

Pravaz, Natasha (2003) Brazilian *mulatice*: performing race, gender, and the nation, *Journal of Latin American Anthropology* 8(1): 116–46.

Prescott, Laurence E. (2000) *Without hatreds or fears: Jorge Artel and the struggle for black literary expression in Colombia* (Detroit, MI: Wayne State University Press).

Price, Richard (ed.) (1979) *Maroon societies: rebel slave communities in the Americas* (Garden City, NY: Anchor Books).

Price, Sally and Richard Price (1999) *Maroon arts: cultural vitality in the African diaspora* (Boston, MA: Beacon Press).

Putnam, Lara (2002) *The company they kept: migrants and the politics of gender in Caribbean Costa Rica, 1870–1960* (Chapel Hill, NC: University of North Carolina Press).

Qian, Zhenchao and José A. Cobas (2004) Latinos' mate selection: national origin, racial, and nativity differences, *Social Science Research* 33(2): 225–47.

Quintero Rivera, Angel (1996) The somatology of manners: class, race and gender in the history of dance etiquette in the Hispanic Caribbean. In *Ethnicity in the Caribbean*, Gert Oostindie (ed.), pp. 152–81 (London: Macmillan).

Radano, Ronald (2000) Hot fantasies: American modernism and the idea of black rhythm. In *Music and the racial imagination*, Ronald Radano and Philip Bohlman (eds), pp. 459–80 (Chicago, IL: University of Chicago Press).

Radcliffe, Sarah (1990) Ethnicity, patriarchy and incorporation into the nation: female migrants as domestic servants in southern Peru, *Environment and Planning D: Society and Space* 8: 379–93.

—— (1999) Embodying national identities: *mestizo* men and white women in Ecuadorian racial-national imaginaries, *Transactions of the Institute of British Geographers* 24(2): 213–25.

—— (2001) Development, the state, and transnational political connections: state and subject formations in Latin America, *Global Networks: A Journal of Transnational Affairs* 1(1): 19–36.

—— (2008) Las mujeres indígenas ecuatorianas bajo la gobernabilidad multicultural y de género. In *Raza, etnicidad y sexualidades: ciudadanía y multiculturalismo en América Latina*, Peter Wade, Fernando Urrea Giraldo and Mara Viveros Vigoya (eds), pp. 105–36 (Bogotá: Instituto CES, Facultad de Ciencias Humanas, Universidad Nacional de Colombia).

Radcliffe, Sarah A. and Sallie Westwood (1996) *Remaking the nation: place, identity and politics in Latin America* (London: Routledge).

Ragoné, Helena and France Winddance Twine (eds) (2000) *Ideologies and technologies of motherhood: race, class, sexuality, nationalism* (London: Routledge).

Rahier, Jean (1998) Blackness, the 'racial'/spatial order, migrations, and Miss Ecuador 1995–1996, *American Anthropologist* 100(2): 421–30.

—— (1999) Body politics in black and white: señoras, mujeres, blanqueamiento and Miss Esmeraldas 1997–1998, Ecuador, *Women and Performance: A Journal of Feminist Theory* 21: 103–19.

—— (2003) Racist stereotypes and the embodiment of blackness: some narratives of female sexuality in Quito, Ecuador. In *Millennial Ecuador: critical essays on cultural transformations and social dynamics*, Norman Whitten (ed.), pp. 296–324 (Iowa City, IA: University of Iowa Press).

Rahier, Jean Muteba (2003) Introduction: mestizaje, mulataje, mestiçagem in Latin American ideologies of national identities, *Journal of Latin American Anthropology* 8(1): 40–50.

Ramírez Berg, Charles (2002) *Latino images in film: stereotypes, subversion, resistance* (Austin, TX: University of Texas Press).

Ramos, Donald (1979) Vila Rica: profile of a colonial Brazilian urban center, *The Americas* 35(4): 495–526.

Rappaport, Joanne (1998) *The politics of memory: native historical interpretation in the Colombian Andes* (Durham, NC: Duke University Press).

Reding, Andrew A. (2000) *Mexico: update on treatment of homosexuals* (Washington, DC: Resource Information Center, Immigration and Naturalization Service, US Department of Justice). www.uscis.gov/files/nativedocuments/QAMEX00.pdf, accesssed 15 August 2008.

Reis, João José (1993) *Slave rebellion in Brazil: the Muslim uprising of 1835 in Bahia* (Baltimore, MD: Johns Hopkins University Press).

Restrepo, Eduardo and Arturo Escobar (2005) 'Other anthropologies and anthropology otherwise': steps to a world anthropologies framework, *Critique of Anthropology* 25(2): 99–129.

Richard, Nelly (1997) Intersectando Latinoamérica con el Latinoamericanismo: saberes académicos, práctica teórica y crítica cultural, *Revista Iberoaméricano* LXIII(180): 345–61.

Robe, Stanley L. (1972) Wild men and Spain's brave new world. In *The wild man within: an image in Western thought from the Renaissance to Romanticism*, Edward Dudley and Maximillian E. Novak (eds), pp. 39–54 (Pittsburgh, PA: University of Pittsburgh Press).

Robertson, Roland (1990) After nostalgia: wilful nostalgia and the phases of globalization. In *Theories of modernity and post-modernity*, Bryan Turner (ed.), pp. 45–61 (London: Sage).

Rodríguez, Clara E. (1994) Challenging racial hegemony: Puerto Ricans in the United States. In *Race*, Steven Gregory and Roger Sanjek (eds), pp. 131–45 (New Brunswick, NJ: Rutgers University Press).

—— (1997a) Introduction. In *Latin looks: images of Latinas and Latinos in the U.S. media*, Clara E. Rodríguez (ed.), pp. 1–12 (Boulder, CO: Westview Press).

—— (ed.) (1997b) *Latin looks: images of Latinas and Latinos in the U.S. media* (Boulder, CO: Westview Press).

—— (2000) *Changing race: Latinos, the census, and the history of ethnicity in the United States* (New York: New York University Press).

Rodríguez, Juana María (2003) *Queer Latinidad: identity practices, discursive spaces* (New York: New York University Press).

Rodriguez, Richard (2002) *Brown: the last discovery of America* (New York: Viking).

Rodríguez, Richard T. (2003) The verse of the godfather: signifying family and nationalism in Chicano rap and hip-hop culture. In *Velvet barrios: popular culture and Chicana/o sexualities*, Alicia Gaspar de Alba (ed.), pp. 107–23 (New York: Palgrave Macmillan).

Rodriguez, Sylvia (1994) Subaltern historiography on the Rio Grande: on Gutierrez's *When Jesus came, the corn mothers went away*, *American Ethnologist* 21(4): 892–99.

Román, David (1997) Tropical fruit. In *Tropicalizations: transcultural representations of latinidad*, Frances R. Aparicio and Susana Chávez-Silverman (eds), pp. 119–35 (Hanover, NH: University of New England Press).

Romero, Raúl (2001) *Debating the past: music, memory, and identity in the Andes* (Oxford: Oxford University Press).

Root, Maria P. P. (ed.) (1992) *Racially mixed people in America* (London: Sage).

—— (ed.) (1996) *The multiracial experience: racial borders as the new frontier* (Thousand Oaks, CA: Sage).

Rosemblatt, Karin A. (2000) *Gendered compromises: political cultures and the state in Chile, 1920–1950* (Chapel Hill, NC: University of North Carolina Press).

Rosenfeld, Michael J. and Byung-Soo Kim (2005) The independence of young adults and the rise of interracial and same-sex unions, *American Sociological Review* 70: 541–62.

Rosina, Alessandro (2007) A growing phenomenon throughout the West Accessed 14 July 2008. Available from www.resetdoc.org/EN/Rosina-marriages.php.

Ross, Marlon B. (1998) In search of black men's masculinities, *Feminist Studies* 24(3): 599–626.

Said, Edward (1985) *Orientalism: Western Concepts of the Orient* (Harmondsworth: Penguin Books).

Salessi, Jorge (1995) *Médicos, maleantes y maricas: higiene, criminología y homosexualidad en la construcción de la nación argentina, Buenos Aires, 1871–1914* (Rosario: B. Viterbo).

Samper, José María (1868) El bambuco Accessed 18 April 2008. Available from www.elabedul.net/Documentos/Temas/Folklor/Bambuco/el_bambuco_samper.php.

—— (1980) Un viaje completo. In *Crónica grande del río de la Magdalena*, Aníbal Noguera Mendoza (ed.), pp. 87–100, Vol. 2 (Bogotá: Sol y Luna).

Sanchís, Norma (2005) Trafficking in women in the Latin American region Accessed 14 July 2008. Available from www.choike.org/nuevo_eng/informes/3641.html.

Sanjinés, Javier (2004) *Mestizaje upside down: aesthetic politics in modern Bolivia* (Pittsburgh, PA: University of Pittsburgh Press).

Sansi-Roca, Roger (2007) *Fetishes and monuments: Afro-Brazilian art and culture in the 20th century* (Oxford: Berghahn Books).

Sansone, Livio (2003) *Blackness without ethnicity: constructing race in Brazil* (Basingstoke: Palgrave Macmillan).

Saunders, A.C. de C.M (1982) *A social history of black slaves and freedmen in Portugal, 1441–1555* (Cambridge: Cambridge University Press).

Savigliano, Marta E. (1995) *Tango and the political economy of passion* (Boulder, CO: Westview Press).

Sawyer, Mark Q. (2005) *Racial politics in post-revolutionary Cuba* (Cambridge: Cambridge University Press).

Sawyer, Mark Q., Yesilernis Peña and James Sidanius (2004) Cuban exceptionalism: group based hierarchy and the dynamics of patriotism in Puerto Rico, the Dominican Republic and Cuba, *The Dubois Review* 1(1): 93–114.

Scheper-Hughes, Nancy (2000) The global traffic in human organs, *Current Anthropology* 41(2): 191–224.

Scott, James (1985) *Weapons of the weak: everyday forms of peasant resistance* (New Haven, CT: Yale University Press).

Sedgwick, Eve Kosofsky (1985) *Between men: English literature and male homosocial desire* (New York: Columbia University Press).

Seed, Patricia (1988) *To love, honor, and obey in colonial Mexico: conflicts over marriage choice, 1574–1821* (Stanford, CA: Stanford University Press).

Seigel, Micol (2009) *Uneven encounters: making race and nation in Brazil and the United States* (Durham, NC: Duke University Press).

Seshadri-Crooks, Kalpana (2000) *Desiring whiteness: a Lacanian analysis of race* (London: Routledge).

Sharp, William (1976) *Slavery on the Spanish frontier: the Colombian Chocó, 1680–1810* (Norman, OK: University of Oklahoma Press).

Sheriff, Robin E. (2001) *Dreaming equality: color, race, and racism in urban Brazil* (New Brunswick, NJ: Rutgers University Press).

Shumway, Jeffrey (2001) 'The purity of my blood cannot put food on my table': changing attitudes towards interracial marriage in 19th-century Buenos Aires, *The Americas* 58(2): 201–20.

Sieder, Rachel (ed.) (2002) *Multiculturalism in Latin America: indigenous rights, diversity and democracy* (Basingstoke: Palgrave Macmillan).

Sigal, Pete (2003a) Gendered power, the hybrid self and homosexual desire in late colonial Yucatan. In *Infamous desire: male homosexuality in colonial Latin America*, Pete Sigal (ed.), pp. 102–33 (Chicago, IL: University of Chicago Press).

—— (2003b) (Homo)sexual desire and masculine power in colonial Latin America: notes towards an integrated analysis. In *Infamous desire: male homosexuality in colonial Latin America*, Pete Sigal (ed.), pp. 1–24 (Chicago, IL: University of Chicago Press).

—— (ed.) (2003c) *Infamous desire: male homosexuality in colonial Latin America* (Chicago, IL: University of Chicago Press).

Silverblatt, Irene (1987) *Moon, sun, and witches: gender ideologies and class in Inca and colonial Peru* (Princeton, NJ: Princeton University Press).

—— (1994) Andean witches and virgins: seventeenth-century nativism and subversive gender ideologies. In *Women, 'race,' and writing in the early modern period*, Margo Hendricks and Patricia Parker (eds), pp. 259–71 (London: Routledge).

—— (2004) *Modern Inquisitions: Peru and the colonial origins of the civilized world* (Durham, NC: Duke University Press).

Simpson, Amelia (1993) *Xuxa: the mega-marketing of gender, race and modernity* (Philadelphia, PA: Temple University Press).

Skeggs, Beverley (2004) *Class, self, culture* (London: Routledge).

Skidmore, Thomas (1974) *Black into white: race and nationality in Brazilian thought* (New York: Oxford University Press).

—— (1993) Bi-racial USA vs. multi-racial Brazil: is the contrast still valid?, *Journal of Latin American Studies* 25(2): 373–86.

Smedley, Audrey (1993) *Race in North America: origin and evolution of a worldview* (Boulder, CO and Oxford: Westview Press).

Smith, Carol A. (1996) Race/class/gender ideology in Guatemala: modern and anti-modern forms. In *Women out of place: the gender of agency and the race of nationality*, Brackette Williams (ed.), pp. 50–78 (New York: Routledge).

—— (1997) The symbolics of blood: mestizaje in the Americas, *Identities: Global Studies in Power and Culture* 3(4): 495–521.

Smith, Merrill D. (ed.) (1998) *Sex and sexuality in early America* (New York: New York University Press).

Socolow, Susan Midgen (2000) *The women of colonial Latin America* (Cambridge: Cambridge University Press).

Somerville, Siobhan B. (2000) *Queering the color line: race and the invention of homosexuality in American culture* (Durham, NC: Duke University Press).

Sommer, Barbara (2003) Cupid on the Amazon: sexual witchcraft and society in late colonial Pará, Brazil, *Colonial Latin American Historical Review* 12(4): 415–46.

Sommer, Doris (1991) *Foundational fictions: the national romances of Latin America* (Berkeley, CA: University of California Press).

Spear, Jennifer M. (1999) 'They need wives': métissage and the regulation of sexuality in French Louisiana, 1699–1730. In *Sex, love, and race: crossing boundaries in North American history*, Martha Hodes (ed.), pp. 35–59 (New York: New York University Press).

Spickard, Paul (2001) The subject is mixed race: the boom in biracial biography. In *Rethinking 'mixed race'*, David Parker and Miri Song (eds) (London: Pluto Press).

Spivak, Gayatri Chakravorty (1988) Can the subaltern speak? In *Marxism and the interpretation of culture*, Cary Nelson and Lawrence Grossberg (eds), pp. 271–315 (Champaign, IL: University of Illinois Press).

Spurling, Geoffrey (1998) Honor, sexuality and the colonial Church: the sins of Dr Gonzalez, Cathedral canon. In *The faces of honor: sex, shame, and violence in colonial Latin America*, Lyman L. Johnson and

Sonya Lipsett-Rivera (eds), pp. 45–67 (Albuquerque, NM: University of New Mexico Press).

Stanton, Domna C. (1995) The subject of sexuality. In *Discourses of sexuality: from Aristotle to AIDS*, Domna C. Stanton (ed.), pp. 1–46 (Ann Arbor, MI: University of Michigan Press).

Stepan, Nancy (1982) *The idea of race in science: Great Britain, 1800–1960* (London: Macmillan in association with St Antony's College, Oxford).

Stepan, Nancy Leys (1986) Race and gender: the role of analogy in science, *Isis* 77(2): 261–77.

—— (1991) *'The hour of eugenics': race, gender and nation in Latin America* (Ithaca, NY: Cornell University Press).

Stephen, Lynn (2002) Sexualities and genders in Zapotec Oaxaca, *Latin American Perspectives* 29(2): 41–59.

—— (2007) *Transborder lives: indigenous Oaxacans in Mexico, California, and Oregon* (Durham, NC: Duke University Press).

Stephens, Michelle Ann (2005) *Black empire: the masculine global imaginary of Caribbean intellectuals in the United States, 1914–1962* (Durham, NC: Duke University Press).

Stern, Steve (1995) *The secret history of gender: women, men, and power in late colonial Mexico* (Chapel Hill, NC: University of North Carolina Press).

Stern, Steve J. (ed.) (1987) *Resistance, rebellion and consciousness in the Andean peasant world, 18th to 20th centuries* (Madison, WI: University of Wisconsin Press).

Stevens, Evelyn P. (1973) Marianismo: the other face of machismo in Latin America. In *Female and male in Latin America*, Ann Pescatello (ed.), pp. 89–101 (Pittsburgh, PA: University of Pittsburgh Press).

Stocking, George (1982) *Race, culture and evolution: essays on the history of anthropology* (Chicago, IL: Chicago University Press).

Stolcke, Verena (1993) Is sex to gender as race is to ethnicity? In *Gendered anthropology*, Teresa Del Valle (ed.) (London: Routledge).

—— (1994) Invaded women: gender, race, and class in the formation of colonial society. In *Women, 'race,' and writing in the early modern period*, Margo Hendricks and Patricia Parker (eds), pp. 272–86 (London: Routledge).

—— (2002) Race and sex, *Current Anthropology* 43: 679–80.

Stoler, Ann Laura (1995) *Race and the education of desire: Foucault's History of Sexuality and the colonial order of things* (Durham, NC: Duke University Press).

—— (2001) Tense and tender ties: the politics of comparison in North American history and (post) colonial studies, *Journal of American History* 88(3): 829–65.

—— (2002) *Carnal knowledge and imperial power: race and the intimate in colonial rule* (Berkeley, CA: University of California Press).

—— (ed.) (2006) *Haunted by empire: geographies of intimacy in North American history* (Durham, NC: Duke University Press).

Streicker, Joel (1995) Policing boundaries: race, class, and gender in Cartagena, Colombia, *American Ethnologist* 22(1): 54–74.

Sweet, James H. (2003) *Recreating Africa: culture, kinship and religion in the African-Portuguese world, 1441–1770* (Chapel Hill, NC: University of North Carolina Press).

Tapper, Melbourne (1999) *In the blood: sickle cell anemia and the politics of race* (Philadelphia, PA: University of Pennsylvania Press).

Taussig, Michael (1980a) *The devil and commodity fetishism in South America* (Chapel Hill, NC: University of North Carolina Press).

—— (1980b) Folk healing and the structure of conquest in South-West Colombia, *Journal of Latin American Folklore* 6(2): 217–78.

—— (1987) *Shamanism, colonialism and the wild man: a study in terror and healing* (Chicago, IL: Chicago University Press).

—— (1993) *Mimesis and alterity: a particular history of the senses* (London: Routledge).

Taylor, Charles (1992) *Multiculturalism and 'the politics of recognition'* (Princeton, NJ: Princeton University Press).

Taylor, Julie M. (1976) Tango: theme of class and nation, *Ethnomusicology* 20(2): 273–91.

Telles, Edward E. (2004) *Race in another America: the significance of skin color in Brazil* (Princeton, NJ: Princeton University Press).

Telles, Edward E. and Edward Murguía (1990) Phenotypic discrimination and income differences among Mexican Americans, *Social Science Quarterly* 71(4): 683–96.

Todorov, Tzvetan (1991) *Les morales de l'histoire* (Paris: Éditions Grasset et Fasquelle).

Torres-Saillant, Silvio (2007) Afro-Latinas/os and the racial wall. In *A companion to Latina/o Studies*, Juan Flores and Renato Rosaldo (eds), pp. 363–75 (Oxford: Blackwell).

Torres, Jose B., V. Scott H. Solberg and Aaron H. Carlstrom (2002) The myth of sameness among Latino men and their machismo, *American Journal of Orthopsychiatry* 72(2): 163–81.

Tortorici, Zeb (2007) Masturbation, salvation, and desire: connecting sexuality and religiosity in colonial Mexico, *Journal of the History of Sexuality* 16(3): 355–72.

Trexler, Richard C. (1995) *Sex and conquest: gendered violence, political order, and the European conquest of the Americas* (Cambridge: Polity).

Trouillot, Michel-Rolph (1991) Anthropology and the savage slot: the poetics and politics of otherness. In *Recapturing anthropology: working in the present*, Richard G. Fox (ed.), pp. 17–44 (Santa Fe, NM: School of American Research Press).

Turino, Thomas (1993) *Moving away from silence: music of the Peruvian altiplano and the experience of urban migration* (Chicago, IL: University of Chicago Press).

Twinam, Ann (1999) *Public lives, private secrets: gender, honor, sexuality and illegitimacy in colonial Spanish America* (Stanford, CA: Stanford University Press).

Tyler, Carole-Anne (1994) Passing: narcissism, identity and difference. (More Gender Trouble: Feminism Meets Queer Theory), *differences: A Journal of Feminist Cultural Studies* 6(2–3): 212–49.

Urrea Giraldo, Fernando, Waldor Botero Arias, Hernán Darío Herrera Arce and José Ignacio Reyes Serna (2006) Afecto y elección de pareja en jóvenes de sectores populares de Cali, *Revista Estudos Feministas* 14(117–148).

Urrea Giraldo, Fernando, José Ignacio Reyes and Waldor Botero (2008) Tensiones en la construcción de identidades de jóvenes negros homosexuales en Cali. In *Raza, etnicidad y sexualidades: ciudadanía y multiculturalismo en América Latina*, Peter Wade, Fernando Urrea Giraldo and Mara Viveros Vigoya (eds), pp. 279–316 (Bogotá: Instituto CES, Facultad de Ciencias Humanas, Universidad Nacional de Colombia).

Vainfas, Ronaldo (1989) *Trópico dos pecados: moral, sexualidade e Inquisição no Brasil* (Rio de Janeiro: Campus).

—— (2008 [1997]) Moralidades brasílicas: deleites sexuais e linguagem erótica na sociedade escravista Accessed 1 April 2008. Available from http://200.156.96.110/artigos/vainfas_moralidades.pdf.

Van Cott, Donna Lee (2000) *The friendly liquidation of the past: the politics of diversity in Latin America* (Pittsburgh, PA: University of Pittsburgh Press).

Van Zyl, Susan (1998) The Other and other others: post-colonialism, psychoanalysis and the South African question *American Imago* 55(1): 77–100.

Vasconcelos, José (1997 [1925]) *The cosmic race: a bilingual edition*, trans. Didier T. Jaén (Baltimore, MD: Johns Hopkins University Press).

Vasvári, Louise O. (1999) *The heterotextual body of the 'mora morilla'* (London: Department of Hispanic Studies, Queen Mary and Westfield College).

Vianna, Hermano (1999) *The mystery of samba: popular music and national identity in Brazil*, trans. John Charles Chasteen (Chapel Hill, NC: University of North Carolina Press).

Viveros Vigoya, Mara (2002a) *De quebradores y cumplidores: sobre hombres, masculinidades y relaciones de género en Colombia* (Bogotá: CES, Universidad Nacional de Colombia, Fundación Ford, Profamilia Colombia).

—— (2002b) Dionysian blacks: sexuality, body, and racial order in Colombia, *Latin American Perspectives* 29(2): 60–77.

—— (2006) Políticas de sexualidad juvenil y diferencias étnico-raciales en Colombia, *Revista Estudos Feministas* 14(1): 149–69.

—— (2008) Más que una cuestión de piel. Determinantes sociales y orientaciones subjetivas en los encuentros y desencuentros heterosexuales entre mujeres y hombres negros y non negros en Bogotá. In *Raza, etnicidad y sexualidades: ciudadanía y multiculturalismo en América Latina*, Peter Wade, Fernando Urrea Giraldo and Mara Viveros Vigoya (eds), pp. 247–78 (Bogotá: Instituto CES, Facultad de Ciencias Humanas, Universidad Nacional de Colombia).

Viveros Vigoya, Mara and Franklin Gil Hernández (2006) De las desigualdades sociales a las diferencias culturales. Género, 'raza' y etnicidad en la Salud Sexual y Reproductiva en Colombia. In *Saberes, culturas y derechos sexuales en Colombia*, Mara Viveros Vigoya (ed.), pp. 87–108 (Bogotá: Centro de Estudios Sociales, Universidad Nacional de Colombia, Tercer Mundo Editores).

Wade, Peter (1993a) *Blackness and race mixture: the dynamics of racial identity in Colombia* (Baltimore, MD: Johns Hopkins University Press).

—— (1993b) 'Race', nature and culture, *Man* 28(1): 1–18.

—— (1993c) Sex and masculinity in fieldwork among Colombian blacks. In *Gendered fields*, Wazir Karim, Diane Bell and Pat Caplan (eds), pp. 199–214 (London: Routledge).

—— (1995) The cultural politics of blackness in Colombia, *American Ethnologist* 22(2): 342–58.

—— (1997) *Race and ethnicity in Latin America* (London: Pluto Press).

—— (1999) Representations of blackness in Colombian popular music. In *Representations of blackness and the performance of identities*, Jean M. Rahier (ed.), pp. 173–91 (Westport, CT: Greenwood Press).

—— (2000) *Music, race and nation: música tropical in Colombia* (Chicago: University of Chicago Press).

—— (2002a) The Colombian Pacific in perspective, *Journal of Latin American Anthropology* 7(2): 2–33.

—— (2002b) *Race, nature and culture: an anthropological perspective* (London: Pluto Press).

—— (2004) Images of Latin American mestizaje and the politics of comparison, *Bulletin of Latin American Research* 23(1): 355–66.

—— (2005a) Hybridity theory and kinship thinking, *Cultural Studies* 19(5): 602–21.

—— (2005b) Rethinking mestizaje: ideology and lived experience, *Journal of Latin American Studies* 37: 1–19.

—— (2006a) Afro-Latin studies: reflections on the field, *Latin American and Caribbean Ethnic Studies* 1(1): 105–24.

—— (2006b) Understanding 'Africa' and 'blackness' in Colombia: music and the politics of culture. In *Afro-Atlantic dialogues: anthropology in the diaspora*, Kevin Yelvington (ed.), pp. 351–78 (Santa Fe, NM: School of American Research Press).

—— (2007a) Race, ethnicity and nation: perspectives from kinship and genetics. In *Race, ethnicity and nation: perspectives from kinship and genetics*, Peter Wade (ed.), pp. 1–31 (Oxford: Berghahn Books).

—— (ed.) (2007b) *Race, ethnicity and nation: perspectives from kinship and genetics* (Oxford: Berghahn Books).

—— (2009 (in press)) Defining blackness in Colombia, *Journal de la Société des Américanistes* 94(2).

Wailoo, Keith (2003) Inventing the heterozygote: molecular biology, racial identity and the narratives of sickle-cell disease, Tay-Sachs and cystic fibrosis. In *Race, nature and the politics of difference*, Donald S. Moore, Jake Kosek and Anand Pandian (eds), pp. 235–53 (Durham, NC: Duke University Press).

Walcot, Peter (1998) Plutarch on sex, *Greece & Rome* 45(2): 166–87.

Waldron, Kathy (1989) The sinners and the bishop in colonial Venezuela: the *visita* of Bishop Mariano Martí, 1771–1784. In *Sexuality and marriage in colonial Latin America*, Asunción Lavrin (ed.), pp. 156–77 (Lincoln, NB: University of Nebraska Press).

Wallace, Michèle (1979) *Black macho and the myth of the superwoman* (London: John Calder).

Warner, Michael (1999) *The trouble with normal: sex, politics, and the ethics of queer life* (Cambridge, MA: Harvard University Press).

Warren, Jonathan W. (2001) *Racial revolutions: antiracism and Indian resurgence in Brazil* (Durham, NC: Duke University Press).

Warren, Kay B. (1998) *Indigenous movements and their critics: Pan-Maya activism in Guatemala* (Princeton, NJ: Princeton University Press).

Weed, Elizabeth (1997) Introduction. In *Feminism meets queer theory*, Elizabeth Weed and Naomi Schor (eds), pp. i–xx (Bloomington, IN: Indiana University Press).

Weed, Elizabeth and Naomi Schor (eds) (1997) *Feminism meets queer theory* (Bloomington, IN: Indiana University Press).

Weinbaum, Alys Eve (2004) *Wayward reproductions: genealogies of race and nation in transatlantic modern thought* (Durham, NC: Duke University Press).

Weismantel, Mary (2001) *Cholas and pishtacos: stories of race and sex in the Andes* (Chicago IL: University of Chicago Press).

White, Hayden (1972) The forms of wildness: archaeology of an idea. In *The wild man within: an image in Western thought from the Renaissance to Romanticism*, Edward Dudley and Maximillian E. Novak (eds), pp. 3–38 (Pittsburgh, PA: University of Pittsburgh Press).

White, Heather Rachelle (2005) Between the devil and the Inquisition: African slaves and the witchcraft trials in Cartagena de Indies, *The North Star: A Journal of African American Religious History* 8(2): 1–15.

Wiegman, Robyn (1995) *American anatomies: theorizing race and gender* (Durham, NC: Duke University Press).

Wiesner-Hanks, Merry E. (1999) *Christianity and sexuality in the early modern world: regulating desire, reforming practice* (London: Routledge).

Williams, Brackette (ed.) (1996) *Women out of place: the gender of agency and the race of nationality* (New York: Routledge).

Williams, Kim M. (2005) Multiracialism and the civil rights future, *Daedalus* 134(1): 53–60.

Williams, Walter L (1986) *The spirit and the flesh: sexual diversity in American Indian culture* (Boston, MA: Beacon Press).

Wood, Stephanie (1998) Sexual violation in the conquest of the Americas. In *Sex and sexuality in early America*, Merrill D. Smith (ed.), pp. 9–34 (New York: New York University Press).

Wright, Michelle M. (2004) *Becoming black: creating identity in the African diaspora* (Durham, NC: Duke University Press).

Wright, Michelle M. and Antje Schuhmann (eds) (2007) *Blackness and sexualities* (Berlin: LIT Verlag).

Wright, Winthrop (1990) *Café con leche: race, class and national image in Venezuela* (Austin, TX: University of Texas Press).

Yarbro-Bejarano, Yvonne (1995) The lesbian body in Latina cultural production. In *¿Entiendes? Queer readings, Hispanic writings*, Emilie L. Bergmann and Paul Julian Smith (eds), pp. 181–97 (Durham, NC: Duke University Press).

Young, Iris Marion (1990) *Justice and the politics of difference* (Princeton, NJ: Princeton University Press).

Young, Lola (1996) Missing persons: fantasising black women in *Black skin, white masks*. In *The fact of blackness: Frantz Fanon and visual representation*, Alan Read (ed.), pp. 102–01 (London: Institute of Contemporary Arts).

Young, Robert (1995) *Colonial desire: hybridity in theory, culture and race* (London: Routledge).

Yuval-Davis, Nira and Floya Anthias (eds) (1989) *Woman-nation-state* (New York: St. Martin's Press).

Yuval-Davis, Nira and Pnina Werbner (eds) (1999) *Women, citizenship and difference* (London: Zed Books).

Zack, Naomi (ed.) (1997) *Race/sex: their sameness, difference and interplay* (New York: Routledge).

Zinn, Maxine Baca and Bonnie Thornton Dill (2005) Theorizing difference from multiracial feminism. In *Gender through the prsim of difference*, Maxine Baca Zinn, Pierrette Hondagneu-Sotelo and Michael A. Messner (eds), pp. 19–25 (New York: Oxford University Press).

INDEX

Printed and bound by CPI Group (UK) Ltd, Croydon, CR0 4YY

09/06/2025

14685871-0003